BRITISH POLITICS TODAY

Fourth edition

Bill Jones
Dennis Kavanagh

Manchester University Press
Manchester and New York

Distributed exclusively in the USA and Canada by St. Martin's Press

Copyright © W. D. A. Jones and D. A. Kavanagh 1991

First edition 1979, reprinted 1980, 1981
Second edition 1983, reprinted 1984, 1985
Third edition 1987, reprinted 1989, 1990

Published by Manchester University Press
Oxford Road, Manchester M13 9PL, UK
and Room 400, 175 Fifth Avenue,
New York, NY 10010, USA

*Distributed exclusively in the USA and Canada
by* St. Martin's Press, Inc.,
175 Fifth Avenue, New York, NY 10010, USA

British Library cataloguing in publication data
Jones, Bill *1946–*
   British politics today – 4th ed. – (Politics today)
   1. Great Britain. Politics
   I. Title II. Kavanagh, Dennis III. Series
   320.941

Library of Congress cataloging in publication data
Jones, Bill, 1946–
   British politics today / Bill Jones. Dennis Kavanagh. – 4th ed.
     p. cm. – (Politics today)
   Includes index.
   ISBN 0-7190-3407-8 (hardback) – ISBN 0-7190-3408-6 (paperback)
   1. Great Britain – Politics and government – 1964–1979. 2. Great
Britain – Politics and government – 1979– I. Kavanagh, Dennis.
II. Title. III. Series: Politics today (Manchester, England)
320.941–dc20 90-13544

ISBN 0 7190 3407 8 *hardback*
      0 7190 3408 6 *paperback*

Typeset in Great Britain
by Williams Graphics, Llanddulas, North Wales

Printed in Great Britain
by Bell & Bain Limited, Glasgow

CONTENTS

CONTENTS

INTRODUCTION

Cynically witty judgements about politics and politicians abound: 'Politics ruin the character' (Bismarck); 'Men who have greatness within them don't go in for politics' (Camus); 'Politics are ... nothing more than a means of rising in the world' (Dr Johnson). And yet without these much pilloried politicians – whose imperfections merely reflect our own – we would be in an infinitely worse situation. Events in Eastern Europe since 1989 have revealed the extent to which even relatively civilised leaders can be corrupted by power and use the strength of the State to impose vicious physical and intellectual tyrannies upon their people. Whatever the shortcomings of the British political system, it is still genuinely answerable, at least once every five years, to the popular will. The best guarantee of our freedom is a population which is well informed politically, watchful of its democratic rights and used to exercising them regularly.

The political education of young people, therefore, is more than just an element in the school curriculum; it helps provide one of the cornerstones of our democracy. The Politics Association – the professional body of politics teachers in the UK – was founded in 1969 to advance this view. Part of its work has entailed a network of national and regional sixth-form conferences and it was from a series of such conferences, organised by the very active Manchester branch of the Politics Association in collaboration with the Extra-Mural Department of Manchester University, that the first edition of this book emerged. It became apparent to the organiser (B.J.) and to one of the principal speakers (D.K.) that the interest in and need for clear, up-to-date and stimulating analyses of politics, which regularly attracted 600 or 700 young people, could also be met by a particular sort of book.

The format and approach are indeed a little unusual and we should say a word about our intentions. The book is designed not as a substitute for the standard texts but as a complement to them. Students will benefit from it most if they combine its use with other wide and informed reading. Nor have we aimed to produce an 'exam crammer' or a set of model answers, but have tried to treat the main issues on each topic succinctly, with the emphasis being analytical and interpretive, rather than factual. The note-style presentation is designed to direct attention immediately to the most important points.

The first edition appeared in 1979. Eleven years on, the book has sold some 50,000 copies and, we hope, made a modest but useful contribution to political education. This fourth edition is as up to date as possible, given the deadlines of authors and publishers, and takes account of events up to the summer of 1990. All chapters have been updated, some completely revised and rewritten and one extra has been added, on the media.

We hope that teachers and students alike will continue to find the book stimulating, interesting and useful.

B.J.
D.K.
Manchester, July 1990

1

BRITAIN SINCE 1945

A knowledge and understanding of a country's history are essential for a student who wishes to understand its politics. Many of a state's political institutions, values and patterns of behaviour are traditional, handed down from the past (e.g. universal suffrage, the Cabinet system, the constitutional monarchy). Even where radical changes are introduced, e.g. the USSR post-1917 − the past is important because it provides the counterpoint to subsequent action.

This chapter briefly reviews some of the more important themes in British politics since 1945. Of course many of the more significant developments and influences occurred long before this date. However, 1945 is a reasonable starting point because:

(*a*) It saw the election of the first majority Labour government, which therefore had the opportunity to carry through its legislative programme. For the next decade or so Britain was regarded as the best example of social democratic planning.

(*b*) It saw the creation of what is often called the post-war political consensus (see below).

(*c*) Britain's international prestige was high. She was one of the victorious powers, indeed the only independent country to be on the winning side from the outset of war in 1939.

(*d*) The party system was at its simplest; two-party domination by Labour and Conservative.

(*e*) Immigration from the Caribbean began, especially into inner-city areas − to be followed later by immigrants from the 'New Commonwealth', e.g. Pakistan and India.

The main developments since 1945

1. International decline. There has been a marked loss of international prestige since 1945 when Britain was one of the 'big three' victorious powers, along with the USA and the USSR. But of course, she was much the weakest of the three in terms of military and economic strength. With the onset of the Cold War in the late 1940s and the growth of East–West tensions between the American and USSR-dominated blocs, Britain was clearly part of the Western alliance and a junior partner of the United States. The loss of prestige has been hastened by relative economic decline. To a large extent the loss is really a readjustment. Britain, as a medium-sized state, could not hope to compete with the superpowers. The loss of influence was clearly illustrated in 1956, when the occupation of the Suez Canal had to be abandoned in the face of American disapproval. Since then Britain has retreated further and further from international responsibilities.

2. The Commonwealth. The post-war process of abandoning the British Empire began with the Labour government's granting of full independence to Burma, India and Pakistan in 1947. The main opponents of this process were right-wing Conservatives. But the retreat from empire was continued by Conservative governments in the 1950s and 1960s. Today more than thirty ex-colonies are members of the Commonwealth, an association of independent states which look to the Queen as their head. The more affluent Western members are the predominantly white states of Britain, Australia, New Zealand and Canada. But the Commonwealth is dominated in terms of membership and concerns by countries from the Third World (Africa and Asia), who are more interested in the problems of poverty, aid to the underdeveloped countries, and trade. The Commonwealth's economic importance to Britain has declined, and there are few issues on which it can speak with one voice. Mrs Thatcher's solitary but fiercely sustained opposition to economic sanctions against South Africa has distanced the British government from the Commonwealth in recent years.

3. Europe. After 1945 moves to the greater economic and political integration of West European states were encouraged by the wish to promote peace and Franco-German co-operation; the belief that economies of scale would lead to an economically more powerful Western Europe; and the expectation that a unified Western Europe would have greater international influence than separate medium-sized states.

Britain, though strenuously courted by other states, determinedly stood aside from the early stages of integration. She refused to join in:

1951 European Coal and Steel Community (France, Italy, West Germany, the Netherlands, Belgium and Luxembourg).

1957 Euratom (for atomic energy), and the European Economic Community of the above six states established by the Treaty of Rome.

Britain was already a member of other groups, such as NATO for defence, and OECD for economic co-operation. Why did she stand aside from the EEC?

(*a*) *A sense of superiority* and national pride, resulting from defiance of Hitler in 1940 and victory in war. This contrasted with the different experiences of the other six countries, which were either defeated or occupied in the war.

(*b*) *Her international status* and links with the USA, the Commonwealth and Europe: the so-called 'three circles'. Why choose to be *merely* a European influence?

(*c*) *A sense of difference.* Britain has had a more secure experience of nationhood. Another difference was that most of the Six had frequently experimented with coalitions and with proportional representation, and had written constitutions and multi-party systems. In France and Italy the largest left-wing parties were Communist and the centre-right parties were Christian Democrat in outlook. One may also add the sense of difference stemming from Britain's insular separation from her neighbours.

But British political leaders in the late 1950s and 1960s became aware of the faster economic growth of the EC states, as well as of the weakening of the Commonwealth ties and the 'special relationship' with the USA. As part of the search for a new role:

1961 Macmillan opened negotiations for British entry -- which failed.

1967 Wilson repeated the bid -- which also failed.

1971 British entry was achieved, and the terms were approved by
      Parliament. But Labour opposed until the:
1975 Referendum – which approved membership by a two-to-one
      'yes' vote.

The impact of the EEC on Britain has been seen in:

(*a*) Political and constitutional matters. It has involved the
introduction of the device of the referendum, the relaxation of
collective Cabinet responsibility (in the 1975 referendum and in
1977 on the form of electoral system for the direct elections), and
the introduction of a large element of a written constitution, with a
consequently greater role for the courts and a limit to parliamentary
sovereignty.

(*b*) The debate, and Britain's decision to enter, reflect an
acknowledgement of her reduced standing in the world, and the
failure of a 'special relationship' with the USA or the Commonwealth to provide a useful role.

Labour was bitterly divided over Europe until the mid-1980s
when it abandoned its withdrawal policy. In 1989 it won a re-
sounding victory in the elections to the European Parliament.
The Conservatives are divided over further integration, with a
pro-European group and another which follows the distinctly
unenthusiastic line spelt out by Mrs Thatcher in her 1988 Bruges
speech. In the 1990s there are pressures for more integration
and unification in the European Community. Conservative
divisions have been expressed over Britain's proposed membership of the European Monetary System (whereby exchange rates
are kept at agreed levels): Mrs Thatcher is more sceptical about
the benefits than most of her party. Labour is in favour of
joining.

There is also pressure for a more enhanced role for the European
Parliament and for convergence of policies. Mrs Thatcher has been
suspicious of these moves. She envisages the European Community
as an association of independent states, acting in concert on only
a limited number of policy areas. Others, like Mr Heseltine, favour
a greater degree of integration.

4. Economic decline. Britain's economic prowess in the nineteenth century stemmed from being the world's first industrial
nation. But since the end of the century her economic strength has

declined in relation to many other countries as these have had their own versions of our industrial revolution. For decades there have been complaints about British slowness to innovate, reluctance to invest, and unwillingness to abandon traditional industries and work practices. As recently as 1960 Britain was the most prosperous country in Europe. But since then she has had higher rates of inflation than the average of OECD states, unemployment has risen faster, and output per head in manufactures has grown more slowly than in any of the twenty-four OECD states. By virtually every indicator of economic performance, post-war Britain has performed badly in relation to her industrial competitors (see Chapter 16).

The growing sense, and evidence, that Britain was falling behind in the 1960s encouraged politicians of all parties to compete in promising to make the economy grow faster. After all, economic growth was the way to provide workers with higher take-home pay and finance desirable programmes of social expenditure on housing, roads, education, pensions and so on. Politicians made promises to expand these programmes on the basis of anticipated rates of economic growth. Invariably their hopes were disappointed and to an extent the parties were discredited in government.

After 1981 the economic growth rate in Britain was faster than that of most other European states. This was largely because the growth rates of the latter slowed down. By 1990, however, Britain was once more at the wrong end of league tables for inflation, trade balance and interest rates.

5. Social change. Yet for all the social dissatisfaction Britain is a more affluent country than in the 1950s and 1960s, and living standards have improved. The spread of television, cars and home ownership is quite impressive. Home ownership spread from 29 to 65 per cent of the population between 1950 and 1987. The biggest change since the war was the return of mass unemployment in the mid-1980s, on a scale comparable to the inter-war years (see Chapter 2).

6. The changing political agenda: the decline of consensus. The closing stages of the wartime coalition gave birth to many of the planks of the *post-war political consensus*. This term refers to the main features of public policy which prevailed until the mid-1970s, regardless of whether Labour or Conservative were in office. It was during the wartime coalition that the Keynesian White Paper on unemployment was produced, the Butler Education Act passed and Beveridge's proposals for the reform of social security were made. The 1945 Labour government took three main measures:

(a) Taking the major industries of coal, gas, electricity, railways, steel and road transport into public ownership. This transformed the balance between the public and private sectors, established a mixed economy, and gave the government more control over the economy.

(b) In 1947 it established a National Health Service, under which treatment was free to all citizens.

(c) In line with the Beveridge recommendations it produced many other measures to consolidate the welfare state.

The Conservative party won the next three elections in the 1950s but accepted much of the 1945 government's legacy. The first serious attempt to undo some of its work, notably in reducing state intervention in the economy, was under the Heath government of 1970. But Edward Heath's government had by 1972 reversed its policies.

The post-war consensus involved a change in the relationship between citizens and the State. During and after the war the view gained ground that economic and social conditions should be improved and that the State could, and indeed had a duty to, do something about it. The policy of managing economic demand so as to sustain full employment involved an active role for the government. The heavy expenditure on the National Health Service, welfare services and education meant much higher levels of taxation. Government became more active in the social and economic field than it had been before the war.

This consensus between the two main parties gradually broke down in the mid-1970s. Governments, both Labour and Conservative, came into conflict with trade unions when the former tried to control the rise in wages, which outpaced the growth of productivity. On the whole, slow economic growth gradually sapped the support for the old policies and encouraged people to look for new ones.

The following section briefly chronicles the decline of the consensus after the election defeat of Labour in 1951 (see also diagram at end of Chapter 4).

The decline of consensus since 1951

Conservatives in government, 1951–64: consensus reinforced. The governments of Churchill, Eden and Macmillan did little to undo their predecessors' achievements but chose to preside over them. The Keynesian policies of the Chancellor, R. A. Butler, were so similar to those of his Labour predecessor, Hugh Gaitskell, that the term 'Butskellism' was jocularly coined to describe them. Macmillan gently nudged his party down the 'middle way', strengthening economic planning with the creation of the National Economic Development Council. Labour, during this period, divided into a left-wing, which called for more nationalisation, and a right-wing 'revisionist' leadership that wished to leave the mixed economy as it stood (see Chapter 4).

Labour in government, 1964–70: consensus sustained. During the 1950s Harold Wilson had been associated with the left, but in government he proved a cautious revisionist, strengthening the emphasis on economic planning and developing the social services. However, Britain's relative economic decline became a major political issue in the late 1960s; in reacting to it, parties tended to move away from consensus towards the fundamentals of their faith.

Conservatives in government, 1970–74: consensus fractured. Edward Heath began with free-market economic measures to reduce government intervention in the economy, but when they raised problems he embarked on a celebrated series of U-turns which swung policy back to full-blooded Keynesianism in an attempt to stimulate economic growth by government borrowing and spending. Labour in opposition shifted sharply to the left under the impact of radicalised trade unions, and in 1973 produced a programme calling for withdrawal from the EEC and national-isation of the twenty-five largest companies.

Labour in government, 1974–79: increasing polarity. Back in power, Labour's leaders sidestepped the 1973 programme and pinned their hopes of beating runaway inflation upon the 'social contract', a deal with the unions whereby they agreed to limit pay demands. But it only alienated an embittered left wing, which elaborated an alternative strategy and used it to attack their colleagues in government. Fissures also open up in the Conservative party. Following Heath's second election defeat in 1974, he was replaced in February 1975 by Margaret Thatcher, whose associates repudiated consensus Keynesianism and developed an approach based upon tight monetary control, an anti-inflation policy which eschewed prices-and-incomes measures but entailed (initially at least) unemployment, and cuts in public spending (see Chapter 16). The Labour Chancellor's partial acceptance of strict monetary control after 1976 further infuriated the left. In the winter of 1978–79 the Social Contract finally collapsed amid a welter of high wage demands, strikes and industrial unrest. Mrs Thatcher's confident assertions caught the mood of a depressed and disillusioned electorate, and she was returned to power in the May 1979 election.

The Conservatives in government after 1979. The consensus on the mixed economy and the welfare state disintegrated and was followed by a polarisation of the centres of control in both parties and by much intra-party dissension. Mrs Thatcher's uncompromising right-wing policies caused bankruptcies, economic contraction, greatly increased unemployment and, initially, continuing inflation. The relevance of Labour's left-wing solutions consequently seemed to increase, and the left made political advances, winning sweeping policy victories at the 1980 and 1981 conferences and changing Labour's constitution to make MPs more accountable to party activists. The beleaguered right wing kept quiet or joined the breakaway Social Democratic party in March 1981 in an attempt to rebuild the centre ground in association with the Liberals. Initially this venture met with great success; it seemed that, among the public at least, the post-war consensus still had much support. However, in spring 1982, with the Conservatives showing barely 20 per cent in opinion polls, the Falklands campaign changed everything once again. The extraordinary risks paid off, and politically Mrs Thatcher was the chief beneficiary, with Conservative support in the polls soaring to nearly 50 per cent.

The afterglow of the Falklands still influenced the June 1983 election, but it was the Alliance, splitting the non-Conservative vote, which delivered Mrs Thatcher a huge majority. Her second ministry was characterised by bitter fights like that over trade-union representation at GCHQ, and the miners' strike, as well as by well-publicised internal disagreements, e.g. over the Westland helicopter company in 1986. But economic growth was steady. The Chancellor, Nigel Lawson, increased public expenditure and prepared a vote-winning package for the 1987 election. By 1990, however, the political tide had turned again, with the economy in trouble and the new 'moderate' Labour party well ahead in the opinion polls.

Further reading

C. J. Bartlett, *A History of Postwar Britain*, Longman, 1977.

D. Childs, *Britain since 1945: A Political History*, Ernest Benn, 1979.

P. Hennessy and A. Seldon (eds.), *Ruling Performance*, Basil Blackwell, 1987.

D. Kavanagh and P. Morris, *Consensus Politics from Attlee to Thatcher*, Basil Blackwell, 1989.

P. J. Madgwick, D. Steeds and L. J. Williams, *Britain since 1945*, Hutchinson, 1982.

K. O. Morgan, *Labour in Power 1945–51*, Oxford University Press, 1985.

Questions

1. Assess the advantages and disadvantages of compromise in politics.

2. Identify the factors which have made for stability and instability in British politics since 1945.

3. Assess the achievements of two post-war prime ministers.

THE SOCIAL AND ECONOMIC CONTEXT OF POLITICS

Traditionally political science has focused on the institutions and processes of government. In recent years, however, the subject has been studied and taught increasingly as a branch of the social sciences, and disciplines like sociology, economics and psychology have been drawn upon where necessary. This development can only be applauded. Our rulers do not make decisions in a vacuum but for a nation of $57 \cdot 1$ million people with a variety of characteristics, e.g. 52 per cent are women, over 18 per cent are pensioners, 5 per cent are coloured. Political processes and decisions, moreover, are very much about conflicts of interest between different groups in society, so it helps to know something about the occupational and class structure and the distribution of resources within it. This chapter provides a brief introduction to this important contextual aspect of politics: the reading suggested at the end will provide more detail and depth for those who want to learn more.

Class and the economy

The way in which social groups are formed is closely connected with the way in which goods and services are produced. The ancient Greeks and the early settlers in the Americas used slave labour: a large group of people became literally the legal property of a smaller, richer class. Until the middle of the eighteenth century the economy of Britain was basically agricultural. The wealth of the nobility and gentry was drawn from land tilled by peasants and serfs whose descendants have lived for centuries in feudal village communities.

Underemployment in the countryside, combined with advances in industrial production, provided the conditions for the industrial revolution. Entrepreneurial factory owners − financed often by the nobility and the professional and merchant classes – employed large numbers of people living close to their place of work in what soon became huge new urban centres.

Writing in the mid-nineteenth century, Karl Marx saw two main antagonistic social classes; the small 'capitalist' property-owning class (to some extent usurping and to some extent collaborating with the traditional aristocracy) and the vast subordinate class of skilled and unskilled workers. Marx perceived that these new social groupings, based upon their economic relationship to the means of production, had created class allegiances which displaced in importance previous loyalties like religion or locality.

At the turn of the century the social structure was more or less pyramidal. The richest 1 per cent of the population owned two-thirds of the wealth. Those comprising the wealthy tip of the pyramid were connected by bonds of education (usually public – i.e. private – school and Oxbridge), marriage, kinship and social contact. This degree of cohesion helped them to occupy key roles in government, business and the Empire. The middle classes – the professional occupations, small businessmen and clerks – were less wealthy but usually owned their own homes and were eligible by education for positions of responsibility. The broad base of the pyramid was made up of skilled and unskilled workers – for the most part with no property, little education and dependent on weekly wages.

Those lucky enough to be at the 'top of the heap' had excellent choices or *life-chances* regarding career, health, and leisure activities. They also enjoyed high prestige or *social status* and were able as a result to exercise political power and influence. Those at the bottom of the pyramid had poor life-chances, no social status and little or no political power. Bilton *et al.* suggest that this situation has not changed much. They argue that society is still basically pyramidal, as the diagram below illustrates.

The diagram is useful for focusing our ideas, but any judgements upon its validity will have to await consideration of important changes which have occurred since the early years of this century.

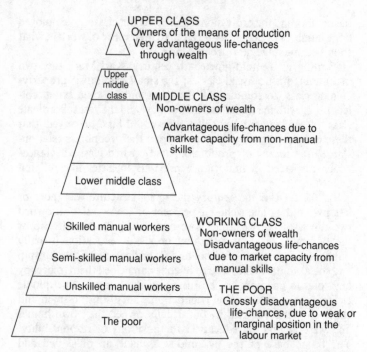

1. The occupational structure has changed considerably, and this had had implications for the class structure. Traditional labour-intensive industries like coal mining and shipbuilding have declined, to be replaced by highly automated light manufacturing and service industries like tourism, leisure and information technology.

There has also been a massive increase in the 'public' as opposed to the 'private' sector, with the civil service growing from some 40,000 at the turn of the century to ⅔ million at present, not to mention the 2 million or so people employed in local government.

The implications for the class structure have been immense. In 1914 80 per cent of the work force were working-class; now less than half our 27½ million work force can be so categorised. The professional and clerical classes have more than doubled, from under 20 per cent at the turn of the century to over 40 per cent now. The occupational pattern is more pear-shaped than pyramidal, with an expanded middle class and a smaller working class. For the first time in a century and a half the working class − by tradition the most politically self-conscious section of society — are out-numbered by members of other social groups. Various new white-collar groups have emerged, commanding a wide range of skills and being paid accordingly. As these new groupings have emerged from the old social structure, their attitudes are hard to characterise and in any case are in a state of flux.

The working classes now live and work under changing conditions, and their attitudes are changing too. At the turn of the century about 10 per cent of the population owned their home; now the figure is over 60 per cent and includes a large proportion of the skilled and unskilled working classes. Since 1979 over 1 million council houses have been sold under the Conservative government's sale-to-tenants scheme. The implications of this new property ownership for working-class political attitudes and behaviour are considerable. Working-class people are now less likely to live in a council house, to be engaged in a traditional industry, be a member of a trade union and live close to their workmates.

It is now much more difficult to generalise about classes in the old way, especially in relation to politics. Studies show that the traditionally crucial division between manual and non-manual workers is no longer so useful for explaining different social attitudes (see Roberts *et al.*). Some political scientists have tried to reformulate social groupings to take account of all these changes. Dunleavy, for example, suggests that it may make more sense to distinguish between 'public-sector' employees, 'private-sector' big business, private-sector small business and groups dependent on state welfare support (see Moran, pp. 28–32).

2. Wealth and income differentials have narrowed — but not much. *Income* is what is regularly earned from work. In 1913–14 male higher professionals earned three and a half times average male earnings, whilst unskilled manual workers earned 67 per cent of the same figure. By 1978 *real* income had increased, of course, several times over, and the gap between the two groups had narrowed. Higher professionals earned 173 per cent of average earnings whilst unskilled manual workers earned 71 per cent (Moran, p. 17). Another measure is provided by Hudson and Williams (p. 23), who show the difference in final income (disposable income adjusted for the effects of indirect taxes) between the bottom fifth and top fifth of earners. This data (shown in Table 1) reveals an increasing income differential in recent years.

Table 1 *Distribution of income, UK, 1976–85 (% share of national total)*

Year	Bottom fifth	Top fifth
1976	7·4	37·9
1985	6·7	40·2

But these figures do not tell the whole story because:

(*a*) They do not indicate the very high salaries earned by top executives ranging from a quarter of a million pounds per year to well over a million. In 1989 the annual reports of twenty-seven of the country's biggest companies revealed rises for top executives of 33 per cent compared with a national average of around 8 per cent.

(*b*) They do not reveal the considerable additional income derived by high earners from expenses, company cars, sick pay and pension schemes, and other fringe benefits.

(*c*) They do not reflect the work conditions of different occupational groups. According to one study in the early 1970s nearly 50 per cent of manual workers had to eat in different canteens and use separate sports centres, where such facilities existed. Ninety-eight per cent of workers had to 'clock in' and 90 per cent suffered a deduction in pay if late, compared with 6 and 4 per cent respectively for senior management. In addition management had longer holidays and most lost no pay for time off to visit the doctor or dentist, whereas less than one-third of manual workers were similarly privileged.

(*d*) They do not reveal the earning profiles of different occupations. The middle classes tend to double their twenties income by their late forties, but manual workers increase their income from their twenties by some 15 per cent to a peak during their thirties. From this point it declines below their original twenties level towards a poorly provided-for retirement.

(e) Taxation seems to have only a marginal impact on the distribution of income. The reason is partly that, despite nominally high tax rates, rich people can minimise their liability by employing skilled accountants.

(f) They do not show the considerable differential which exists between the earnings of men and women. Female manual workers earn, on average, two-thirds of average male manual worker incomes and women non-manuals earn even less compared with male non-manuals.

(g) Substantial differences exist between the low-income earners and the very poor, who are found among the old, the unemployed, immigrants and families with young children. The complacent notion popular in the 1960s that poverty had been abolished has long been exploded. In July 1986 the DHSS admitted that by 1983 some 16 million people were living on or below the official poverty level (compared with 11·3 million in 1979).

The distribution of wealth

As Britain still ranks among the richest 10 per cent of countries in the world, a substantial amount of wealth is owned by individuals in the form of bank deposits, savings accounts, property, and stocks and shares.

The pattern of distribution is much more unequal than that of income: the ownership of wealth is still highly concentrated. Table 2.2 reveals that the situation has not changed much over the last two decades. The wealthiest 50 per cent of the population owned 97 per cent of marketable wealth in 1971 and 93 per cent in 1987.

Redistributions within the richest half of the nation are explained partly by the spread of private home ownership and the increase in property values: 22·1 per cent of all wealth in 1971 yet 33·4 per cent in 1987. Stocks and shares represented 21·7 per cent of all wealth in 1971, slumped to 7 per cent in 1981 but climbed to 10·5 per cent in 1987. Privatisation, however, has helped to spread share ownership from 7·5 per cent of the population in 1981 to 20 per cent in 1987.

Table 2   *Distribution of wealth, UK (% and £ billion)*

	1971	1981	1986	1987
Marketable wealth				
Percentage of wealth owned by:				
Most wealthy 1%	31	21	18	18
Most wealthy 5%	52	40	36	36
Most wealthy 10%	65	54	50	50
Most wealthy 25%	86	77	75	74
Most wealthy 50%	97	94	92	93
Total marketable wealth (£ billion)	140	546	1,017	1,199

Source: Social Trends, 1990.

Social mobility

Studies have revealed a fair degree of movement within the different social groupings in Britian. Lipset and Bendix observed that over a third of those from a blue-collar background moved into white-collar jobs – a higher rate than West Germany, Japan or France but less than Australia and Sweden. Social position, then, is not determined solely by birth: it is, after all, possible for a grocer's daughter to become Prime Minister. Goldthorpe, however, revealed an important feature. He distinguished between seven different social categories and observed that the least socially mobile people in his sample were from class 1 and classes 6 and 7: the upper classes and the working classes. In fact nearly half the class 1 members and over half the class 6 and 7 members originated within their own class.

As for the really top decision-makers, they are more normally recruited from the upper levels of the social hierarchy. Boyd's study of entries in *Who's Who* revealed that in many cases those listed had parents who were also listed, e.g. 28·4 per cent of judges, 27 per cent of ambassadors and 45·4 per cent of bank directors. Heath estimates that children born to members of this elite of elites have a 1-in-5 chance of making the pages of *Who's Who*, children from class 1 parents a one-in-200 chance, children from all white-collar-worker classes a one-in-500 chance, whilst those from working-class homes have only a one-in-1,500 chance of winning some of life's glittering prizes.

Education

Education has become a vital factor in determining social mobility. Clearly, people in well-rewarded, high-status occupations can give their children the best opportunities. Education is the means whereby skills are acquired that can determine occupation. Access to higher education, which provides the long training necessary for many elite jobs, is particularly important. The small percentage of children educated at fee-paying schools (about 6 per cent), notably those attending the prestigious Eton, Harrow, Westminster, Marlborough, Rugby and Charterhouse, have the best chance of entering higher education and going on to fill the top jobs. Over 80 per cent of senior judges in 1975 had been to a public school, over 60 per cent of civil servants above the rank of under-secretary, over 70 per cent of army generals, over three-quarters of top company directors and Conservative MPs. Margaret Thatcher herself is an ex-grammar-school girl, but six members of her first Cabinet were old Etonians. The lower one is down the social hierarchy the less chance one has of entering higher education. The replacement of middle-class-dominated grammar schools with comprehensives has helped only slightly: a 1983 study revealed that, even in comprehensives, middle-class children have six times more chance of entering higher education than working-class children (*Sunday Times*, 9 January 1983).

The north–south divide

When Disraeli spoke of the 'two nations' he meant the rich and the poor. Nowadays the term is often used to denote the differences between the North and the South, but the differences are chiefly economic: the growth of new industries in the South has kept income and employment high whilst decline in the North has led to falling incomes and unemployment. The table (adapted from Moran, p. 9) indicates some of the main contrasts between the South-East and the north (the North-West, North-East, Yorkshire and Humberside).

	South-East	North
% of persons aged 16 and over in managerial/ professional occupations, 1986	17·1	11·4
Average weekly income per head (£), 1985–86	106·3	77·1
% of UK total Gross Domestic Product	35·7	23·5
% households with deep freezer	70·0	57·7
Unemployment rate (%), 1987	7·7	14·6
Perinatal mortality rate (%) 1984–86	9·1	10·3
Cars per 1,000 population, 1986	356·0	267·0
Pupils in independent schools ('000), 1982	259·5	99·1

This deepening geographical divide permeates economics and politics, producing a predominantly Labour Scotland and north of England and a predominantly Conservative or SLD-voting South (see Chapter 8). Surveys of the 'quality of life' however consistently reveal Scotland and the North as top of the scale and the South-East at the bottom.

Britain, then, has a pattern of economic and social inequality which is characteristic of Western industrialised countries. Private wealth is highly concentrated, particularly the ownership of private-sector industry; income reflects the earner's role in the economy, and whilst in theory elite occupations are open to all in practice they tend to go to those higher up the social scale. The pyramid devised by Bilton *et al.* makes a fundamental point about the relation of position in the social hierarchy to life-chances, but it must be borne in mind that:

(*a*) The working classes are no longer the most numerous occupational grouping.

(*b*) Changes in occupational structure are heavily modifying and perhaps fragmenting traditional class-related attitudes.

(*c*) There is a fair degree of movement up and down the social hierarchy despite an educational system which heavily favours the upper and middle classes.

The growth of an underclass

In recent years concern has been voiced at the growth of an 'underclass' in Britain comprising the long-term unemployed, single-parent families and pensioners living solely on state benefit.

Thatcher governments have always adduced the trickle-down argument: that the increasing wealth of society as a whole will also benefit the poor. For many years official data supported this thesis showing, for example, an 8·4 per cent increase in real income during 1981−85 for the poorest 10 per cent in society compared with an overall average of 4·8 per cent. In May 1990, however, an independent report for the House of Commons Social Services Committee revealed the figures to be 2·6 per cent and 5·4 per cent respectively. The theory was further undermined by an embarrassing report issued in July 1990 by the DHSS which revealed that the poorest families in no way shared in the 23 per cent real rise in living standards between 1979 and 1987: the typical household in the poorest 10 per cent of the population saw an income rise of only 0·1 per cent after inflation is taken into account. The report also showed that the number of people receiving below half the average income (the European Community poverty line) increased from 4·93 million in 1979 to 10·5 million in 1987. The percentage of children living in such households increased from 10 per cent in 1979 to over 20 per cent in 1987. It seems probable, moreover, than the social security changes of 1987 will have exacerbated the position of the poorest families rather than improved things as was intended.

Observers have noted that young men who have never worked are essentially not socialised into society and tend to adopt deviant lifestyles, often involving a rejection of family values and responsibilities, the use of drugs, and a reliance on crime to make up income shortfalls. Small wonder, claim such commentators, that illegitimate births soared during the 1980s from 10 per cent to 25 per cent of the whole and that the crime rate increased by 50 per cent. Certain inner-city areas are in a perpetual state of near-collapse, representing virtual no-go areas for the law-abiding majority and comprising contagious centres of subversive values and behaviour. Professor Ralph Dahrendorf has called the problems caused by the underclass 'The greatest single challenge to civilised existence in Britain' ('The Underclass', London Weekend Television, 13 December 1987).

Further reading

A. B. Atkinson and A. J. Harrison, *Distribution of Personal Wealth in Britain*, Cambridge University Press, 1978.

A. Bilton *et al.*, *Introductory Sociology*, Macmillan, 1987. (Diagram reproduced, by permission, from p. 55.)

D. Boyd, *Elites and their Education*, NFER, 1973.

D. Coates *et al.*, *A Socialist Anatomy of Britain*, Polity Press, 1985, pp. 7–99.

P. Dunleavy, *Urban Political Analysis*, Macmillan, 1980.

— *The Politics of Mass Housing, 1945–75*, Clarendon Press, 1981.

Frank Field, *Inequality in Britain: Freedom, Welfare and the State*, Fontana, 1981.

— *Losing Out*, Basil Blackwell, 1989.

Stephen Fothergill and J. Vincent, *The State of the Nation: an Atlas of Britain in the Eighties*, Pan, 1986.

John Goldthorpe, *Social Mobility and Class Structure in Modern Britain*, Clarendon Press, 1980.

Anthony Heath, *Social Mobility*, Fontana, 1981.

Ray Hudson and Allan M. Williams, *Divided Britain*, Belhaven Press, 1989.

S. M. Lipset and R. Bendix, *Social Mobility in Industrial Society*, University of California Press, 1959.

Michael Moran, *Politics and Society in Britain: an Introduction*, Macmillan, (2nd edn 1989).

K. Roberts, *et al.*, *The Fragmentary Class Structure*, Heinemann, 1977.

Questions

1. To what exent do you consider inequalities in society inevitable and desirable?

2. Do you think the removal of inequalities is best attempted via moderate or radical reform?

3. What problems for the governance of Britain are posed by the development of an 'underclass' of the disaffected poor?

POLITICAL CULTURE

A stable democracy

This chapter looks at the main features of the political culture and recent changes. Britain's political culture has long interested students of history, society and politics. Because she was the first country to industrialise (for much of the nineteenth century, the foremost industrial power) and has long been regarded as a model stable democracy, students have tried to extract lessons from the British experience. Among the admired features are:

1. The relative absence of force in resolving political differences (except for Ireland).

2. The balance between effective government, on the one hand, and respect for the rights of opposition, an independent judiciary and basic civil liberties, on the other.

3. The continuous and gradual process of change and adaptation which are important in building respect for traditions and support for the system. Compare this with the political systems of, say, the USSR, Italy, West Germany or France. Those countries have suffered ruptures in their recent political histories, e.g. the revolution in Russia in 1917, the collapse of the Fourth Republic in France in 1958 and the establishment of new post-war constitutions in Italy and West Germany.

Various explanations of political stability

1. Social and economic conditions, particularly affluence and industrialism. There is a high correlation between liberal democracy and levels of industrial development (i.e. virtually all stable democracies are highly industrialised and wealthy countries). But there are exceptions to this relationship (e.g. Nazi Germany, some East European countries before 1989). So this can be only a partial explanation.

2. *British institutions*, e.g. the two-party system (historically inaccurate – see Chapter 5), monarchy (almost certainly more a consequence of consensus and stability, rather than vice versa) and parliamentary institutions (but compare with the USA, which has a presidential system).

3. *History*. In contrast to many newly independent states, which simultaneously have to confront the tasks of building a state (boundaries, institutions), and forming a sense of nation and identity, etc., Britain was able to meet these challenges sequentially. In the sixteenth century relations between Church and State were settled, following the break with Rome; in the seventeenth century the constitutional issue was decided in favour of a limited monarchy, and so on. Similarly, the suffrage was expanded gradually between 1832 and 1928 (1969 if we count votes at the age of eighteen). Except for the question of Ulster, issues involving religion and nationality were solved many years ago. This is not just a matter of the British State having a long history. France has been plagued by disputes about the form of the regime and Church–State relations from 1789 down to this century.

4. *Social homogeneity*. Class has predominated as the basis of politics because of the weakness of other cleavages. Only 5 per cent of the population are coloured, only 5 per cent live in rural areas, two-thirds are members of the Church of England, and five-sixths live in England. Before 1922 Ireland's membership of the UK reinforced differences based on agriculture, nationality and religion. The removal of Ireland homogenised the composition and simplified the politics of the UK. For many years, therefore, there have been limited social differences to express in the political arena.

5. *Political culture* itself: the traditions and style in which politics is conducted. In their major study, *The Civic Culture*, Almond and Verba saw Britain as having the ideal civic culture, i.e. one that combined or balanced the values of citizen participation and self-confidence with a trust in the elites and a responsiveness to their laws. Such a culture, though a product of the above

four features and the political system, can itself in turn affect the way people behave in politics. British politicians have generally been pragmatic, and the extremes of the ideological left and right have not gained much consistent support.

Change

Among the changes, it is worth noting:

1. The role of government. In the 1960s and 1970s governments of both parties intervened in areas traditionally left to personal choice or the market, e.g. controls on prices and incomes, and outlawing discrimination on grounds of gender or race.

The Thatcher governments have withdrawn or reduced the role of government from many economic areas, e.g. prices and incomes, exchange controls, full employment policy and regional aid. On the other hand, they have intervened in the health service, e.g. imposing contracts of service on doctors, and education, imposing a national core curriculum and a contract of service on teachers. The political scientist Andrew Gamble has claimed that such policies combine *liberalism* in the economy with *authoritarianism* in social areas.

2. The growth of populism, which involves some diminution in the standing of Parliament. The notion of parliamentary sovereignty was associated with 'strong' government, self-confident leaders and a deferential electorate. The introduction of the referendum is one indicator of the willingness to 'let the people decide' instead of trusting to MPs. Impressive pro-EEC majorities of 117 in 1971 and 226 in 1975 in the House of Commons were still not thought to reflect the 'full-hearted consent' of the people. A referendum has been used in Ulster on the border question, and in Scotland and Wales on devolution.

The decline in the authority of Parliament is also seen in the willingness of groups to defy legislation (see Chapter 17). The effectiveness of government is not just a matter of passing legislation through Parliament: other groups have to give their consent and co-operation. The Heath government's policies on industrial relations and prices and incomes, formally approved by the Commons, were not accepted as legitimate by sections of the population outside Parliament. The conflict was dramatically (if falsely) illustrated in the 'Who governs?' election of February 1974, the 'winter of discontent' strikes in 1979 and the demonstrations against the poll tax in 1990.

3. Loss of pride in the political system. It is doubtful whether the famous satisfaction of the British with their political system is now so marked. Partly because of Britain's relative economic decline, the political institutions have also come under critical scrutiny. In the 1960s the 'What's wrong with Britain?' mood produced indictments and reforms of Parliament, the civil service, local government, etc. In the 1970s the party system and the centralisation of government in Whitehall and Westminster came under attack. In the 1980s dissatisfaction with the political system prompted calls for Britain to adopt, amongst other things, a written constitution (see Chapter 6), a Bill of Rights and a proportional representation voting system.

4. The decline of political consensus. Notwithstanding bouts of intense disagreement, e.g. over the House of Lords (1910–11), Ireland (pre-1922), and the economic crisis in 1931, foreign observers have been impressed by the extent of British agreement on:

(a) *Substance*. After 1950 the two main parties largely agreed on the mixed economy and the welfare state. The main features of these policies had been established by the post-war Labour government, with its measures to nationalise basic industries and create the National Health Service. In 1970 the Heath government tried and failed to tinker with this consensus. It was pledged to more selectivity in welfare, less government intervention in industry and wage bargaining, and a reform of the unions. Mrs Thatcher's government set out with a similar agenda and has been more successful in breaking the consensus.

(b) *Procedures*, or how politics is conducted. Nowadays there is less agreement on the Constitutional 'rules of the game', e.g. UK boundaries, local government, the House of Lords, a simple majority voting system, etc..

5. The decline of deference. 'Deference' has been used in two senses to describe British political culture. Both explain how it made Britain a relatively easy country to govern.

(a) *Political* deference, meaning respect for the government, the absence of a revolutionary tradition or a militant working class, and compliance with laws.

(b) *Social* deference, or the identification of leadership skills with high social status. This has been advanced as an explanation for the large working-class Tory vote and the continued presence in the elite of people with an upper-class and public-school background.

But political deference has declined as people and groups have become more assertive about their 'rights', e.g. campaigns against planning decisions and anti-poll tax demonstrations.

Social deference has also declined. The leaderships of Edward Heath and Margaret Thatcher have seen a more meritocratic grammar-school, middle or lower middle-class leadership take over from the 'magic circle' of old Etonians who possessed landed estates. Not only are aristocratic origins becoming less advantageous electorally for the Tories but fewer aristocrats dominate the party, in contrast to the era of Macmillan and Home.

6. Public disorder. The British have been noted for the avoidance of violence in politics, and a general willingness to compromise. But Northern Ireland has been an outstanding exception. The riots in Bristol, Brixton, Southall and Toxteth in June 1981 and in Handsworth and Tottenham in 1985 illustrate a willingness to turn to violence among the young and blacks in socially deprived areas. It is widely believed that the inner-city riots owed more to deprivation than to race. But there is also growing concern about racial discrimination and alienation among young blacks. The Brixton riots led to discussion of the role of the police and the recommendations of Lord Scarman on community policing. There were also numerous violent protests against the poll tax, which surveys showed was widely regarded as unfair.

To conclude: these changes may make the task of government more difficult: a more educated, critical electorate is less attached to the party system and elites and therefore less tolerant of failure.

B

Why the change?

This is difficult to say. Most so-called explanations merely re-describe the changes. They include:

1. Failures. Post-war Britain has experienced a sharp decline in international status and relative economic strength. In terms of gross national product per head she has steadily fallen behind other West European states (see Chapters 1 and 16). Apparent policy failures and consequent criticism have probably sapped the self-confidence of her elites. It is remarkable how many governments have assumed office pledged to tackle the economic problem. Yet, on most comparisons of economic growth, inflation, unemployment and rising living standards, Britain has usually done worse than most of her competitors.

2. Elite emphasis on the need for change in attitudes to foster faster economic growth, e.g. 'modernisation', more 'professional' government, entry to the EC, reforms in work practices, collective bargaining, local government, etc. The emphasis on change has been even more marked since Mrs Thatcher came to office. Her government has tried to weaken many planks of the post-war consensus. Mrs Thatcher has sought with some success to promote a new 'culture' in the public sector, emphasising value for money and management in the civil service, local government and in the education and health services. She has sought to extend competition in the professions, like law, extend the free market, e.g. shareowning, home ownership and privatisation of state industries and services, and reform the trade unions.

3. Changes in social class and the dissolution of old class loyalties (see Chapters 3 and 5).

4. New issues. Clearly national identity in Scotland, religion and nationalism in Ulster, and race, have weakened the validity of the old emphases on national unity and integration.

Has Mrs Thatcher changed the culture?

An important part of the Thatcherite agenda has involved changing the culture. The culture was blamed by many critics for Britain's poor economic performance. It was alleged that the welfare state undermined the work ethic and encouraged dependency; high taxes weakened work incentives; the State provided too much, e.g. guaranteeing full employment, and this sapped initiative. Mrs Thatcher wanted to restore what she called an enterprise culture and create an environment in which people would be prepared to take risks, work harder and become more self-reliant. She therefore encouraged private home ownership, self-employment, the creation of small businesses and the extension of private share ownership. Mrs Thatcher has seen herself as a crusader. In view of the electoral landslides which the Conservatives gained in 1983 and 1987 and the long period which the Conservative government has had in office, one might expect the widespread acceptance of Thatcherite values.

According to Ivor Crewe, this appears to be 'a crusade that failed'. By a margin of 5 to 1, voters say they prefer a society in which 'caring for others' is more highly rewarded than 'the creation of wealth'. The social and collective provision of welfare is preferred to the individual looking after himself. People, by large majorities, seem to prefer increased social expenditure even if this means higher taxes. In 1979 there were equal numbers of tax cutters versus service expanders. By 1987 the latter outnumbered the former by 6 to 1.

Participation

The degree of popular participation in British politics is quite small – though probably no lower than levels found in other liberal democracies. This political model is predicated upon some degree of public involvement though in practice apart from general elections most people declare scant interest in politics.

Electoral turnout in Britain at 75–80 per cent of the electorate is lower than in the Scandinavian countries but higher than the mere 50 per cent mustered in US presidential elections (see Chapter 7).

Party membership has plummeted since the war: Labour's 1 million individual (as opposed to affiliated trade union) members slumped to about ⅓ million in the 1970s. Conservative membership has nominally stood up better at around the 1 million mark but the number of committed activists is probably similar in both major parties. Between general elections it is doubtful if overall more than 2–3 per cent of the electorate can be described as genuinely active within political parties (see Chapter 5).

Pressure group activity registers a higher level of participation. As already noted, British people – though mainly the middle classes – have become used to be the idea of organising themselves to press for or prevent certain things happening. At the national level this has been noticeable quite dramatically in groups associated with the environment, as Table 3·1 indicates.

Table 3·1 *Membership of environmental groups (in thousands)*

	1971	1988
Civic Trust	214	249
National Trust	278	1,634
Ramblers' Association	22	65
Royal Society for Nature Conservation	64	204
Royal Society for The Protection of Birds	98	540

Other pressure groups, however, have suffered a fall in membership during the 1980s, especially trade unions, from 12 million to less than 10 million members (see Chapter 17).

Finally, work by Jacobs and Worcester suggests that levels of participation in the conventional political system have witnessed a slight decline over the Thatcher years. As the table below shows most measures of participation show a decrease of 1–3 per cent and a proportionate increase in the percentage of people taking no part in political activity at all. This latter group represented

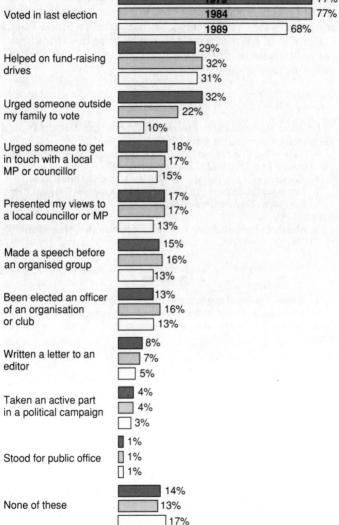

Q May I ask which of the things on this list you have done in the last two or three years?

	1979	1984	1989
Voted in last election	77%	77%	68%
Helped on fund-raising drives	29%	32%	31%
Urged someone outside my family to vote	32%	22%	10%
Urged someone to get in touch with a local MP or councillor	18%	17%	15%
Presented my views to a local councillor or MP	17%	17%	13%
Made a speech before an organised group	15%	16%	13%
Been elected an officer of an organisation or club	13%	16%	13%
Written a letter to an editor	8%	7%	5%
Taken an active part in a political campaign	4%	4%	3%
Stood for public office	1%	1%	1%
None of these	14%	13%	17%

Table 3.2 Political participation in British politics, 1979-89

Source MORI, cited in Jacobs and Worcester, p. 171.

one-quarter of socioeconomic groups C1, D and E but only one-tenth of groups A and B. Jacobs and Worcester speculate that 'one side effect of the Thatcher decade has been to reduce people's belief in the value of political activity ... just by being there for so long, she has mesmerized the nation into believing that she is an unmoveable part of the political landscape' (p. 172).

Further reading

1. Crewe, 'Has the Electorate become Thatcherite?', in R. Skidelsky (ed.), *Thatcherism*, Chatto and Windus, 1988.

— 'Values: The Crusade that Failed', in D. Kavanagh and A. Seldon (eds.), *The Thatcher Effect*, Oxford University Press, 1989.

W. Glinga, *Legacy of Empire*, Manchester University Press, 1986.

E. Jacobs and R. Worcester, *We British*, Weidenfeld & Nicolson, 1990.

D. Kavanagh, *Thatcherism and British Politics*, Oxford University Press, 2nd edn 1990.

M. Moran, *Politics and Society in Britain: an Introduction*, Macmillan, 1985, pp. 33–58.

Questions

1. Is there a political consensus in Britain?

2. What factors decide citizens' attitudes to the government?

3. Explain the relative lack of violence in Britain's post-war political history.

4

CHANGING POLITICAL IDEAS

Ever since the ancient Greeks, philosophers have been fascinated by such questions as 'Which is the best form of government?', 'How much authority should a government have over its citizens?', 'Why should citizens obey their governments?', 'How should wealth be distributed?' Over the centuries ideas about these perennial questions have been influenced by religious and revolutionary ideas, the emergence of new ruling elites and nation—states, and changes in the means of creating wealth and other technological advances. It comes as something of a shock, however, to realise that the ideas currently found in the political market-place are of relatively recent provenance. If we go back to the mid-seventeenth century we encounter a startlingly different set of dominant ideas, for example, religious dogmatism, absolute monarchical power and the divine right of kings (the notion that hereditary succession to the throne is ordained by God).

The liberal philosophers

The transition into modern frames of thinking was affected substantially by the liberal philosophers of the eighteenth century, especially John Locke, who argued for:

Rationality. Reliance upon supporting evidence for ideas rather than assertions based upon tradition.

Toleration. The belief that religious and political beliefs are a matter of personal conscience rather than a concern of governments.

Liberty. The belief that each citizen is entitled to certain liberties, like freedom from arbitary arrest and freedom to buy and sell.

Checks and balances. The idea that the main government institutions should each have a degree of independence to prevent any dangerous concentration of power.

Rights. The idea that people have rights which are personal and independent of the State and that citizens therefore have a contractual relationship with it. The revolutionary impact of this idea is that the *authority of the government is dependent upon the consent of the governed*.

In America and France these ideas were cited in support of violent revolutions. In Britain the conflict was largely non-violent but the results over time were also revolutionary. In 1832 the notion of popular sovereignty was endorsed by the Great Reform Act: elections, not monarchs would henceforward determine the colour of government.

The classical liberals

The so-called classical liberals, some of whom went on to form the Liberal Party in the mid-nineteenth century, further underpinned emergent democratic ideas by arguing for more individual freedom and representative parliamentary government elected by a much wider proportion of the population. The classical liberals, however, were not just concerned with the nature of government; they vigorously addressed the matter of what it should and especially what it should not do. They argued for *minimal government*:

1. Socially. To inhibit intervention to support the poor – as Herbert Spencer asserted, 'to protect people from the consequences of their folly is to people the world with fools'.

2. Economically To encourage a *laissez-faire* economic system. In accordance with the ideas of Adam Smith, this entailed freeing entrepreneurs from legal restraints to:

(*a*) set up businesses to produce products at prices consumers were prepared to pay;

(*b*) employ workers, take a profit and invest in other enterprises.

In this way, argued the classical liberals, the whole of society benefits. People are employed and wealth is created. The greater the wealth the higher the wages, and the more profit available for reinvestment. Competition will ensure profits are not too high and that the public will be offered the best goods at the lowest price. The 'invisible hand' of the market will ensure efficiency is rewarded and inefficiency punished by failure.

Traditional conservatism

In the mid-nineteenth century classical liberalism was pitted against the ideas of the Tory or Conservative party as it became known after the 1830s. Conservatives allege theirs is the open-minded rather than the ideological party, whilst their opponents claim they merely adopt whatever policies are necessary to gain power. Neither view is correct. Over the last century and a half a number of core ideas can be identified.

1. Human nature. Conservatives believe that man is by nature selfish, weak, corruptible, even sinful. To think otherwise, they argue, is to delude oneself and to risk disaster. Nor do Conservatives think that much can be done about this condition; attempts to change human nature – social engineering – are likely to make things worse rather than better.

2. The rule of law. Weak human beings must be protected from their own darker natures. Widespread acceptance of the rule of law is necessary to prevent anarchy. To be acceptable the law has to be impartial and to be effective it must be reinforced by penalties backed by the overwhelming force of the State.

3. Harmony and balance in society. Conservatives wish to resist whatever they see as extremist tendencies, like the unbridled capitalism of the nineteenth century or the over-mighty Socialist State of the 1970s. Like Edmund Burke, they believe 'that all government is founded on compromise'. They oppose dogmatism and prefer pragmatism: finding the right policies to stay in power and preserve social harmony.

4. Social institutions and the nations. Informal relationships like family and community, together with formal institutions such as schools, voluntary associations, Parliament and the Royal Family, play a vital role in binding society together. They provide continuity with the past, a sense of belonging. The idea of 'nation' – one's country – is a source of pride, a reason for laying down life itself in a time of war. In peace Queen and country are vital unifying symbols: Conservatives claim theirs is the patriotic party. The foreign policy corollary of this view of the nation is a concern to defend national interests first and to be suspicious of internationalism – beyond generalised support for the European Community and the Commonwealth.

5. *Liberty*. Lord Acton described liberty as 'the highest political end'. Preserving it is the fundamental purpose of government and politics. People should be allowed to do as they please – provided they do not infringe the liberty of others. Legislators must show wisdom when deciding how far individual liberty has to be curtailed in the interests of liberty as a whole. Economic freedom is central to Conservative notions of liberty: the freedom to set up in business, employ people, make a profit, and so on. Liberty must be preserved through the dispersal of power: centres of power in society will check or balance each other, creating a tension which is the guarantor of freedom. Government therefore should be limited.

6. *Government*. It follows that the executive power of government should be: *limited* in what it seeks to do; *strong* enough to maintain law and order or take steps which are necessary; *balanced* or restrained by other constitutional powers like the legislature and the Crown, and by forces within society itself, especially the owners of property. Corruptible human beings should not be allowed too much power, for their own good or for that of society.

7. *An acceptance of inequality*. Conservatives believe in equality before the law and in career opportunities but are opposed to the idea of equal rewards because:

(*a*) People are born with unequal talents. Equal rewards would be unfair to the gifted, who might otherwise not bother to develop their talents. It might also encourage people to be lazy.

(*b*) People are motivated by personal gain. If talent is rewarded, as it should be, a hierarchy of wealth and status will inevitably emerge. But this is *desirable* so that poor people will be fired to 'better' themselves by working hard. Inequality is therefore an essential element in the motor which runs a capitalist economy.

Traditional Conservatives, however, do not wish inequalities to be too dramatic otherwise the poor will become alienated from society and subversively hostile.

8. Political change. Conservatives seek to conserve; to avoid radical change; to let change occur naturally, as it will if people are free to pursue their own interests. Government's role will often be to formalise change after the event rather than promote it. Traditionally, Conservatives have agreed with the Duke of Cambridge that 'the time for change is when it can no longer be resisted'.

The impact of Thatcherism

Since Mrs Thatcher's accession to the leadership in 1975 her views have driven a battering ram through traditional Conservative ideas. She would not disagree over human nature being flawed, the primacy of the rule of law and liberty, but on most other issues her views are at once different and more emphatic. She is:

(*a*) Less interested in balance and harmony than in maximising her own ability to achieve her own clear political objectives. These include the obliteration rather than the mere containment of socialism. As a 'conviction' politician she holds compromises in contempt and seeks to build a new consensus built around her own ideas.

(*b*) Much less concerned to limit inequalities resulting from the unfettered working of a market economy: on the contrary she has defended the right of people 'to be unequal'.

(*c*) Opposed to the 'dependency culture' which she believes the welfare state creates; she vigorously advocates self-reliance.

(*d*) In favour of radical change, even describing herself as 'a revolutionary'. Her desire to promote an enterprise culture moreover smacks a little of the 'social engineering' which traditional Conservatives condemn as an unachievable socialist fallacy.

(*e*) Not keen on the Commonwealth (happy to flout its unanimity over South Africa) nor on Europe (opposed to plans for political and economic union).

(*f*) Monetarist on the economy: she wants to: control the money supply through high interest rates to keep inflation down; remove government controls over the economy; privatise state run activities; and end the power of trade unions to distort market forces.

Woodrow Wyatt, a close friend and advisor, wrote in the Conservative Party publication celebrating Mrs Thatcher's ten years in power: 'Mrs Thatcher may see herself as a Tory but I do not.' With some justification he places her in the same category as the nineteenth-century radical liberal, John Bright.

Traditional socialism

Critique
Socialism begins a critique of the kind of economy classical liberals idealised. Socialists argued that capitalism creates:

1. Exploitation. The value of a product is the sum of the labour put into it. Under capitalism the factory owner takes the lion's share whilst the worker receives a fraction. Labour is bought cheap and cast aside when no longer needed.

2. Inequality. Capitalists became fabulously and unjustifiably rich, often living off inherited wealth, whilst the mass of workers have to combat poverty.

3. Inefficiency. During its booms the capitalist economy cannot meet demand whilst during slumps millions languish unemployed, with the poorest suffering most.

4. Dominant values. Dominant groups have always used their power to inculcate values which underpin their own position. Conservative ideology is merely a rationalisation of dominant-group interests. For example, the notion that free enterprise benefits the working class does not stand up to examination: the number of workers who become rich is negligible by comparison with those who become rich via inherited wealth. The vicissitudes of the market can just as easily mean unemployment as higher wages. Moreover these are the values which do so much to inhibit man's inherent goodness, enthroning selfishness instead of fellowship, competition instead of co-operation, the urge for material goods instead of real happiness. Yet these are the values which workers themselves are induced to accept as 'common sense' in a capitalist society.

Principles

From this critique Socialists adduce a number of principles:

1. Human nature is fundamentally good. It is the distorting impact of capitalism which creates the flaws. A benign socialist economic and social environment will allow man's innate goodness to develop fully.

2. Equality and freedom. Capitalist inequalities are not only morally unacceptable but prevent all but the rich minority from becoming genuinely free. For example, how can the daughter of an immigrant family in Bradford enjoy the same choices in life as the son of the Duke of Westminster?

3. Collectivism. Individuals need to recognise their economic interdependence with and moral obligation to society as a whole. It follows that the means whereby wealth is created should be owned collectively rather than privately.

4. Efficiency and fairness. A socialist-planned economy will create wealth more efficiently and distribute it more fairly.

Post-war Labour programme

Labour's huge 1945 majority enabled it to make the transition from abstract to broad practical principles:

1. Keynesian economics had replaced classical economics as the orthodoxy of the age. Keynes argued that various forms of control and intervention made it possible for a capitalist economy to be managed and guided towards a number of desirable goals such as full employment and buoyant production.

2. Centralised planning would iron out the anarchic booms and slumps.

3. Nationalisation. Large areas of economic activity would be taken out of private hands and placed under national boards accountable to Parliament.

4. A mixed economy. Whilst the public sector was to be dominant a vigorous private sector was still thought desirable.

5. Universal social services. Following the recommendation of the Beveridge Report (1943), social services were to be overhauled, made uniform and universally applicable.

Revisionism in the 1950s

Once the 1945 programme had been implemented, socialist politicians like Anthony Crosland and Hugh Gaitskell began to re-examine the roots of socialism. In his 1956 book *The Future of Socialism*, Crosland argued that the wonders of Keynesian economic management now enabled socialists to win the fruits of revolution without the inconvenience of having one. Ownership of the economy was irrelevant when the development of the joint stock company had placed managers rather than owners in direct charge of big business. Nationalisation, moreover, was not now held to be sacrosanct. If most of the economic battles had been won, if capitalism was a tamed beast, it followed that all that was needed to achieve dignity and equality for all was a vigorous egalitarian social policy.

Left-wing revolt in the 1970s ... and failure in the 1980s

The Wilson government in the 1960s implicitly followed the revisionist line, but after the Conservative victory in 1970 a radicalised trade union movement combined with left-wing Labour MPs to mount alternative socialist policies:

1. Ownership. A reassertion of state control over the biggest companies, especially multinationals plus a call for more workers' co-operatives.

2. Democratisation of British life, starting with the Labour party and proceeding through Parliament to embrace economic activity as well.

3. Improved welfare services to remedy the failures highlighted by the 'poverty' researchers such as Professors Titmuss and Townsend.

4. Unilateral abandonment of nuclear weapons.

5. Withdrawal from the EC and a weakening of NATO ties.

A yawning chasm opened up between revisionist Labour Cabinets in the seventies and an increasingly embittered left-wing and trade union movement. The conflict took a damagingly public form in the winter of 1978–79 when the lower-paid refused to accept Labour's incomes policy norm.

Mrs Thatcher's 1979 victory gave the left the chance it had been waiting for. The 1980 and 1981 party conferences were victories for left-wing ideas, many of them inspired by Tony Benn. Left-wing policies were put in place and Labour's constitution altered. But whilst left-wing activists were faithful to socialist principles, their debates during the seventies had been rather closed intellectual affairs. Those who claimed that the British people would respond warmly to genuine left-wing socialism were brought sharply in touch with the cold reality in 1983 when Labour's manifesto was resoundingly rejected by the electorate.

Kinnock's revolution

Neil Kinnock, the new leader elected after the 1983 débâcle, resolved to move the party towards an electable programme. In practice this meant abandoning left-wing ideas and moving into the centre ground. By painful degrees he achieved a near-revolution in Labour policies by 1990. The socialist rhetoric remained more or less the same but the policies laid out in the party's May 1990 statement were unrecognisable from 1983.

1. Defence. Unilateral abandonment of nuclear weapons was phased out: a negotiated settlement with other nuclear powers (multilateralism) was preferred.

2. Public ownership. No more nationalisation, some privatised companies to be returned to public ownership, but fair market price compensation to be paid to shareholders.

3. Trade unions. No commitment to restore the pre-1979 position, substantial amounts of Tory legislation to be retained; 'our framework for industrial law will be even handed between employers and trade unions'.

4. Taxation. No return to super tax but a banded system with 50 per cent maximum.

5. Europe. Reversal of withdrawal policy: closer co-operation plus membership of European Monetary System under certain conditions. 'Britain must play a positive role in shaping the future of Europe.'

6. Economy. No radical change; a 'partnership economy' envisaged, which 'welcomes and endorses the efficiencies and realism which markets can provide'; no statutory incomes policy; 'we particularly welcome foreign investment'.

7. Social services. Restore spending and improve services, but all public spending ultimately dependent upon economic growth. 'We have to meet the bills of society out of improved performance. It cannot come out of an extra slab of taxation. That would be folly' (Neil Kinnock, 15 May 1990).

8. The constitution. An elected upper chamber (possibly via proportional representation), regional assemblies, a Scottish Parliament, plus fundamental rights protected by statute.

The May 1990 document represented a total routing of Tony Benn's socialist alternative which had been virtually endorsed in the early 1980s. He called the document 'a breathtaking revelation of the extent to which revisionism has gone in the Party'.

The diagram below reveals some of the ideological fluctuations which have taken place since the war. In 1945 a consensus formed based on Labour's programme which survived until 1970. The 1970s saw radical shifts in both parties, culminating in the victory of Mrs Thatcher. During the 1980s Labour has moved closer to a new consensus which can be seen to have formed around Thatcherite ideas.

The centre parties

In the 1983 election the SDP – Liberal Alliance mustered 26 per cent of the vote, but following the botched merger after the 1987 election the Social and Liberal Democrats (SLD), not to mention the rump SDP, had difficulty in articulating distinctive policies and getting their messages across. In 1990 the SDP formally came to an end but the SLD seems to have inherited the mantle of the Liberals as the 'third party'.

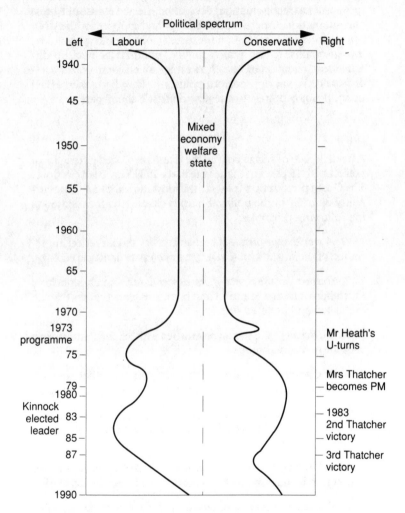

Policy tendencies of the Labour and Conservative parties, 1939–90

The SLD retains a perceived profile on liberty and individual rights, decentralisation (community politics); constitutional reform (proportional representation, devolution, elected House of Lords) and internationalism (a federal Europe and support for the UN). But its other emphases − on the mixed (social market) economy, less inequality rather than equality, multilateral nuclear disarmament, retention of Thatcherite trade union controls plus a less divisive class-war approach to politics − have been encroached upon, if not captured by the new centrist Labour party.

The Greens

After a decade of fringe politics the Greens exploded into national politics with 15 per cent of the vote in the 1989 European elections. The Green prescription is by far the most radical of all those currently on offer in the political market-place. It is founded upon the following principles:

1. A world approach. All human activity should reflect appreciation of the world's finite resources and easily damaged ecology.

2. Respect for the rights of our descendants. Our children have the right to inherit a beautiful and bountiful planet rather than an exahusted and polluted one.

3. Sufficiency. We should be satisfied with 'enough' rather than constantly seeking 'more'.

4. A Conserver *Economy*. We must conserve what we have rather than squandering it through pursuit of high growth strategies.

5. Care and share. Given that resources are limited we must shift our energies to sharing what we have and looking after all sections of society properly.

6. Self-reliance. We should learn to provide for ourselves rather than surrendering responsibility to experts and specialised agencies.

7. Decentralise and democratise. We must form smaller units of production, encourage co-operative enterprises and give people local power over their own affairs. At the same time international integration must move forward rapdily.

The implications of such principles are far-reaching and involve major changes in lifestyles, for example: a no-growth or shrinking economy; a drastic reduction in the use of cars; a new style of more primitive communal living. Whilst most people now accept the need for strict control of pollution, their 'greeness' does not extend much beyond this. However, it could be that ecological imperatives will sooner or later require all political parties to look more closely at the fundamentals of the Green programme. In a volatile and rapidly changing world today's outrageous ideas can quite easily become orthodoxies in a surprisingly short time.

Further reading

G. Almond and S. Verba, *The Civic Culture*, Little, Brown, 1964.

John Callaghan, *Socialism in Britain since 1884*, Basil Blackwell, 1990.

H. Drucker *et al.*, *Developments in British Politics*, Macmillan, 1986.

R. Eccleshal *et al.*, *Political Ideologies*, Hutchinson, 1984.

D. Kavanagh, *Thatcherism and British Politics*, Oxford University Press, 1987.

L. Tivey and A. Wright, *Party Ideology in Britain*, Routledge, 1989.

Questions

1. Drawing upon this chapter, try to describe your own political beliefs.

2. Write brief explanations and critiques of (a) Marxism; (b) Conservatism; (c) socialism.

3. 'Politicians are either warriors or healers.' Discuss.

5

THE CHANGING PARTY SYSTEM

This chapter examines the changing assumptions about, and changes within, the party system. The two-party system has long been a cornerstone of most ideas of British politics. It includes such features as a one-party majority government, a dominant executive, class voting, stable administrations and the widely accepted authority of Parliament. Because these features are interrelated it is not surprising that changes in one feature coincide with and are causally related to changes in others. Below we look at how we have changed from party system I (pre-1970) to system II (1970 onwards), and examine the prospects for further change.

Party changes

Party systems (i.e. the number and type of significant parties) usually change in response to one of three factors:

1. A party split, e.g. the Liberals in 1885 or 1916.

2. A new issue, which gives rise to a new party, e.g. Irish home rule and the Irish Nationalists after 1880, or nationalism in Scotland in 1974.

3. A change in the composition of the electorate which allows new interests to be expressed, e.g. the rise of Labour after 1918 coincided with a significant growth in the number of working-class voters.

It is difficult, however, for new parties to break in. First, the established parties (Conservatives and Labour have been the two main ones since 1918) try and adjust to new issues and interests and thereby head off a new party. Second, the electoral system penalises minority parties (see below).

Popular assumptions and the changing reality

1. There are two parties and one-party-majority governments.
This best describes the period 1945–70. For much of the twentieth century there have been more than two large parties, and between 1929 and 1945 there were either minority or coalition governments. Between 1945 and 1970 the Labour and Conservative parties together averaged 91 per cent of the vote at general elections. In 1974 this share fell to 75 per cent, falling more sharply outside England; rose to 80 per cent in 1979; then fell to a post-war low of 70 per cent in 1983. But because of the disproportional electoral system the two parties still managed to gain 95 per cent of seats in the Commons. So the two-party system more accurately describes the situation in Parliament than voting behaviour in the electorate. In 1987 the Conservatives received 58 per cent of the seats for $42 \cdot 3$ per cent of the votes, Labour 35 per cent for $30 \cdot 8$ per cent, and the Alliance only $3 \cdot 5$ per cent of the seats for 22 per cent of the vote. But the system does not hinder parties which concentrate their votes, as the nationalists did in Ireland pre-1922, or in Scotland in 1974.

2. The parties are national. Since 1974, however, there have been contrasting line-ups in different parts of the UK. Ulster now has its distinctive system; in the south of England outside London, the SLD became the main rival of the Conservatives, and in Scotland the nationalists rival the other three parties. After the 1983 and 1987 elections there were two party systems: in about half the seats Conservative and Alliance occupied the first two positions, in the other half Labour and Alliance. It was difficult to talk of a general election giving a 'national' mandate. The differentiation is also seen in the variations in election swings in different parts of the country (see Chapter 8).

3. The electorate vote on class lines. In the absence of significant religious, regional or racial divisions, class has been the decisive influence (as Peter Pulzer has said, 'all else is embellishment and detail'). Again, this has changed sharply. Since 1974 the class alignments between the parties have declined, largely because of the reduction in working-class support for Labour.

We might say that the changes above represent a shift from one party system (I) to another (II). The main contenders (Labour and Conservative) are still dominant, but their bases of support have weakened and the context of their competition has altered.

The two parties

1. Viewed in comparative perspective, the **Conservatives** have been remarkably successful. They dominate the centre-right of the political stage, and, in contrast to major right-wing parties on the Continent, they are a secular rather than a largely religious party. They have been in office for much of the twentieth century and earned the title of 'the natural party of government'. The party, like the major political, economic and social elites, has adapted to the rise of democracy and to social change and, compared with the political right on the Continent, it was not tinged with fascism in the inter-war years. Above all, since 1945, the party has managed to gain the support of about a third of the working class and has been opportunistic or pragmatic enough to embrace policies to secure that support. (For explanations of working-class Conservatism, see Chapter 8).

2. Apart from those in Scandinavia and West Germany, **Labour** has also been more successful electorally than other socialist parties. It has monopolised the cause of the political left (cf. the rivalry between Socialists and powerful communist parties in Italy and France), and the trade unions are more politically united than those in many other states. And much of the political consensus of the post-war period − the mixed economy, welfare state and full employment − was the work of the 1945−51 Labour governments (see Chapter 1) *But*:

3. **Both parties** were in trouble in the 1970s. Electorally they have seen their support crumble, and in the 1980s Labour no longer had the support of a majority of the working class. The disappointing record of both parties in government sharpened internal divisions and encouraged them to move to more extreme positions in opposition. The choice of Margaret Thatcher (in 1975) and Michael Foot (1981−83) as leaders represented this growing divergence between them. Labour's right wing lost ground after 1979 because its thinking had dominated the unsuccessful policies

of previous Labour governments. Left-wing strength was such in 1981 that a number of leading right-wingers left to join the Social Democratic Party, which in turn joined with the Liberal Party to form the Alliance.

Explanations for the two-party system

1. The electoral system. The 'first past the post', single-member-constituency system has played a part, particularly in penalising the Alliance parties in 1983 and 1987.

2. The social structure, i.e. class. Yes, but the evidence suggests this is now weakening (see Chapter 8).

3. It is 'natural'. There is an idea that political issues lend themselves to an 'either-or' treatment and that political argument is most appropriately dichotomised into government versus opposition. Duverger (*Political Parties*) has suggested that this dualism is 'natural', but in reality the two-party system is a rare plant, hardly found outside Anglo-American societies. Most Western industrialised countries which are also liberal democracies have multi-party systems, proportional representation and coalition governments.

4. The British preference for strong government, i.e. a party with a clear majority in the Commons. It is questionable whether one-party government is necessarily 'stronger' than a coalition, or that millions of individual voters consciously co-ordinate their different votes to produce this outcome. At times of crisis (e.g. the two great wars and during the 1931 economic crisis) leaders resort to coalition.

Consequences of two parties

The existence of disciplined, one-party-majority governments has made Britain distinctive (in comparison to the USA, with its separation of powers, and West European states, which often have coalitions). The party system in Britain is associated with:

1. A strong executive. The Cabinet can rely, for the most part, on its disciplined majority in the Commons to pass legislation, and the ability of Parliament to resist Ministers is accordingly weakened. But the strength of British government in relation to the Commons, and says little of its ability to impose its will on other groups. During the 1970s and early 1980s, successive Cabinets faced enormous difficulty in persuading major interest groups to agree to their polities. It is one of the measures of Mrs Thatcher's political success that she has been able to overcome such opposition and sustain the tradition of strong, executive government at even higher levels.

2. Party government. British government is concentrated (*a*) in one party, and (*b*) in the Cabinet. In the absence of federalism, a written constitution, an independent legislature or coalitions, one party with a parliamentary majority enjoys virtually complete control over the law-making process.

3. Voters have a clear choice. Because parties are disciplined and programmatic there is a good chance that the majority party can enact its proposals. It can, accordingly, be judged on its record at the next election. In contrast, the separation of powers in the USA and the need for coalitions in much of Western Europe prevent the emergence of responsible party government (i.e. voters are unable to vote directly for one party to constitute the government and hold it responsible at the next election).

4. Consensus. During the 1950s and 1960s there was broad agreement between the parties on the mixed economy and the welfare state. Because the parties were closely matched in votes and small swings decided the result, they pitched their appeals at floating voters in the 'moderate' centre. This encouraged a convergence of policies. But now:

(*a*) The electorate cannot be relied upon to return a party with a clear majority − or one sufficiently large to withstand losses at subsequent by-elections. In 1974 we had a minority Labour government, a Lib-Lab pact during 1977−78, and then another spell of minority Labour government from summer 1978 to March 1979.

(*b*) Backbenchers are more rebellious. The 1966 Wilson government was forced to abandon plans to reform the House of Lords and trade unions, and the Callaghan government had difficulties over devolution, pay policy, entry to the EEC and related issues (e.g. the referendum, direct elections). Mrs Thatcher's governments have lost a Shops Bill to permit Sunday Trading (April 1986) and faced substantial revolts over many other policies, including the poll tax and Hong Kong immigration.

(*c*) Both parties have seen a significant fall in their support. Tory support of 36·5 per cent in 1974 was an all-time low, and Labour's 1983 vote was a post-war low of 27·6 per cent.

(*d*) This decline has coincided with the rise of other parties, notably the Alliance in the 1980s. The rise and fall of the Alliance must be the greatest 'if only' of post-war British party politics. The Falklands War in 1982 distracted attention, however, at a crucial time and in the 1983 election the Alliance mustered 26 per cent of the vote − just short of the amount needed to establish genuine, multi-party politics. In 1987 the Alliance seemed poised to break through once again, but after a week of the campaign, it fell back and ended up with only 22 per cent of the poll. In the wake of the election the Liberal party pressed for an outright merger between themselves and the SDP. This was resisted by David Owen, the SDP leader. Amid much acrimony the merger was finally accomplished and a new party, the Liberal Democrats, was formed. David Owen and about a third of the old SDP refused to join. In the 1987 Parliament support for the Liberal Democrats and SDP was sharply reduced and the prospects of a third party breakthrough have disappeared − for the present at least.

Why parties?

One may justify parties on several grounds. Below we examine four supporting arguments, together with the performance of British parties.

1. Representation and choice. Parties aggregate the preferences of millions of voters and the interests of groups. For example, as issues associated with religion, free trade and nationalism waned and class became more salient after 1918, so Labour gradually replaced the Liberals as the natural alternative to the Conservatives.

In the 1980s, as class has lost some of its influence on voting behaviour, so the Alliance gained support.

Furthermore, the public has not been presented with such a clear choice. The traditional lines of division between the Conservative and Labour parties – in contrast to their leaders' rhetoric and the claims of manifestos – have not been so sharp, if one considers their record in office. That Conservatives were anti-public expenditure and anti-interventionist in industry and prices and incomes is belied by Mr Heath's government record; that Labour were pro-nationalisation is hardly supported by the performance of the Wilson government in the 1960s.

In recent years many new issues – not easily accommodated within traditional party dogfights – have developed. On electoral reform, Europe, immigration from Hong Kong, the reform of industrial relations, defence and anti-inflation policies, the divisions within parties have been nearly as significant as those between them. The parties were never as monolithic or united as was indicated in the division lobbies.

2. *Government*. Parties are important in staffing and organising the political part of the executive. But, when in government, how important are they in realising their intentions? They may achieve legislative proposals promised in manifestos, but what about the consequences supposed to follow from them – economic growth, improved industrial relations, lower inflation, etc.? Growing disillusion has been fuelled by a pervasive failure of British governments, e.g. in foreign affairs (de Gaulle's veto on applications to enter the EEC), abortive legislation (on industrial relations, prices and incomes, House of Lords reform), U-turns in policy (Heath's attitude to prices and incomes and regional subsidies; Labour's record on incomes policies), disappointing results of institutional reform (the civil service, local government, health, etc.).

If parties in government have so little effect it may be because:

(a) *Parties are poorly prepared in opposition*. In opposition, policies are formulated with little consultation with the civil service and relevant interest groups. In office, Ministers deal with permanent civil servants, who often have greater information and expertise. There are many examples of proposals which have been inadequately thought out (e.g. Labour's Land Commission in 1964, or the Conservatives' Industrial Relations Act). By applying tests of administrative (and political) practicability, civil servants confront Ministers with 'on-going reality'. And when parties come into office, it is noted, they change only a hundred or so top decision-makers. Ministers usually lack the skills (managing a large organisation, policy-making), the permanence (they change every two years on average) and the partisan commitment to impose their will on the civil service.

(b) *Power is dispersed in the modern complex British society*. In office parties have to cope with the same major interest groups and the constraints imposed by economic resources and international commitments. Labour has to take account of business opinion and foreign holders of sterling to encourage investment and maintain confidence in the pound, just as Conservatives have to live with the trade unions. After 1976 Labour's economic policy was shaped in part by the agreement with the IMF which made a large loan available to help sterling. Both parties have to deal with the same lobbies of pensioners, farmers, etc., and take account of agreements with NATO, the EEC, etc. Much public expenditure is already spoken for by ongoing programmes. So the 'realities' of group politics (Beer) again limit fundamental change. In part this explains why parties are less radical in office than they promised to be in opposition, and why the Labour left and the Conservative right, who want sharp change, feel aggrieved.

A contrary argument is that parties have too much effect. In recent years, parties have repealed their predecessors' policies in many fields, creating uncertainty in finance, industry and relations with the EEC. This contrasts with the incremental style of policy development in earlier years. Moreover this chopping and changing has been carried out by governments which claim to have a mandate even though, as in 1974, they may be supported by less than 40 per cent of the voters. Hence the complaints that groups which need to make decisions and plans over a long period of time (e.g. reorganisation of education or investment) are handicapped by the short-term perspectives of party politicians. Hence, also, the demand that some issues be 'above politics', as many defence and foreign policy questions are.

The impact of Mrs Thatcher since 1979. It is interesting to consider the record of the Thatcher government in the light of the above argument. It proclaimed its determination to break with many of the policies pursued by post-war governments. The rise in public spending and taxation as shares of GDP since 1979 provide two measures of the government's failure. But in many other respects, e.g. privatisation, refusal to reflate the economy, even with unemployment over 3 million, legislation on trade unions and industrial relations, rejection of bargaining with the 'social partners' (unions and employers) reforms of the professions, and its policies towards local governments, it has shown that a determined government can impose many of its policies.

3. Participation. The two main parties now attract fewer members, voters and supporters (i.e. strong identifiers with them) than in the 1950s and 1960s. The Labour–Conservative share of the electorate has slumped from an average of 72 per cent (1945–70) to about 50 per cent in 1987. In the past 20 years the proportion of strong identifiers with Labour or Conservative fell by half. Voters have turned away because of:

(*a*) *Social change*, e.g. the weaker class alignment. By 1987 less than half voted with their 'natural' class party.

(*b*) *The performance of the parties* in office, which led to doubts about their competence.

(*c*) *Dislike of the two main parties' policies* and their apparent identification with sectional pressure groups – business, in the case of the Conservatives, and the trade unions, in that of Labour.

4. Consent. Party government derives its legitimacy from being freely elected and being continuously accountable to Parliament.

'Ins' and 'outs'

A realistic perception of the parties must take account of the limits on what a party can achieve in government. There remain several continuities between them in actual policies and performance when they are in government. A party in opposition often presents a very different image from the government of the day and from what it itself did when last in office. It wants to oppose the government; it is relatively free to talk, to make promises and not to talk tough and unpopular decisions. There is a change, however, when it is in government, faced by the same constraints and pressures as its much criticised predecessor. May the significant difference between the parties be a consequence of 'ins' and 'outs', that is, a matter largely of rhetoric and promises, lasting only as long as each is in opposition?

Party organisation

The Labour party has a complex structure and its commitment to inner-party democracy has often proved troublesome. The party conference meets annually for five days; it represents the mass membership and in theory is the sovereign body. It elects the National Executive Council, which directs the work of the party on behalf of conference. The twenty-nine members of the NEC include twelve members elected by the entire conference, seven members elected by the constituency parties, one member for the Young Socialists, one member for the socialist society and seats are reserved for the Labour leader and Deputy leader of the party. In the 1970s the NEC and Conference came under left-wing control, and the left demanded that both bodies be given greater power *vis-à-vis* Labour MPs. Mr Kinnock has gradually asserted his control over both bodies. He plans to reduce the role of the trade union block vote and also the role of conference in making policy.

In the Conservative party the authority of the party leader is clearer. The National Union, a federation of constituency parties, organises the annual conference. It discusses resolutions but its votes are not binding on the leadership. The leader has unfettered control over appointments to senior posts in Central Office (in Labour these are made by the NEC) and over the Shadow Cabinet (which is elected by MPs when Labour is in opposition).

The future

Possibilities include:

1. *Return to the two-party normalcy of pre-1970*. This has seemed highly probable since 1987. Elections will be a 'simple' either or choice between Labour and Conservative.

2. *Continued fragmentation*, with minority governments like that of February 1974 and the deadlock of post-1977, or majority

government on less than 40 per cent of the vote. But this will give rise to demands for electoral reform. A saving grace of the British electoral system was that it manufactured party majorities in the Commons; this was widely felt to outweigh the disadvantages of its disproportionate results. Now it fails on the grounds both of providing representiveness and of securing majorities. Indeed, four of the eleven general elections since 1945 have failed to provide party governments with a commanding working majority. The Liberal Democrats have an obvious interest in seeing PR introduced. Similarly the two large parties have an interest in blocking it. PR in turn would almost certainly lead to a multi-party system and:

3. Coalitions. In Britain these have been adopted for specific purposes (e.g. war) and dissolved when the problem was solved. They have not been regarded as 'normal'. Both main parties have an interest in rejecting them, either to bring about further socialism or else to reverse it. But if no one party has a clear majority, then coalitions or bargains will be necessary for a government to get its legislation passed.

If the first possibility comes about, we shall see the restoration of the assumptions outlined at the outset of this chapter. But the second and third possibilities have important consequences for parties and Parliament. There will be new 'rules of the game', e.g. more bargaining between parties, more measures passed by cross-party majorities, perhaps a more vigorous House of Commons and some limit on the Prime Minister's power over the Cabinet. Note that parties may react to minority government either by forming a coalition (in which more than one party forms the government) or else a pact (in which one party supports the government without actually taking office).

Further reading

A. R. Ball, *British Political Parties: the Emergence of a Modern Party System*, Macmillan, 1987.

Samuel Beer, *Modern British Politics*, Faber, 1969.

— *Britain Against Itself*, Faber, 1982.

Maurice Duverger, *Political Parties*, Methuen, 1967.

S. Finer (ed.), *Adversary Politics and Electoral Reform*, Wigram, 1974.

S. Ingle, *The British Party System*, Basil Blackwell, 1987.

R. Rose, *The Problem of Party Government*, Macmillan, 1974.

Questions

1. Should there be more or fewer policy differences between the parties?

2. Consider the advantages and disadvantages of (*a*) coalition government, (*b*) minority government.

3. Analyse the pressures upon government to move away from the policies they advocated in opposition.

6

THE CHANGING CONSTITUTION

The terms 'constitution' and 'constitutional' usually refer to:

1. An authoritative document or set of rules which describes the powers and duties of government institutions and the relations between them, or

2. A spirit or style of politics, usually one in which there is a balance between the different institutions or which provides for a restraint on the holders of power.

Britain has a constitution, but not in sense 1. It is not unwritten; rather, it is uncodified. Most written constitutions are adopted by states which are newly independent or have suffered a rupture in their evolution (e.g. France in 1958). In the case of Britain, we cannot date the system of government or set of rules as being constituted at one point in time. Rather we talk about a system and style of politics which have evolved over centuries.

The British system has been widely admired. Britain prepared written constitutions for many of the colonies when they became independent and many states, in drawing up constitutions, tried to copy British features.

But the system, and therefore the constitution, came under stress in the 1970s. Most of our political institutions and procedures faced some critical scrutiny in this period and the questioning spilled over to the constitution itself. Many of the pressures came to a head in the mid-1970s. The rise of nationalist parties in Scotland and Wales and the collapse of British authority in Northern Ireland were examples of internal challenges to the constitution. Entry to the EC posed an external challenge. The Stormont parliament in Northern Ireland was suspended in 1972, and Parliament passed Bills to set up elected Assemblies in Scotland and Wales. Dissatisfaction has led to suggestions for other reforms, including a major constitutional settlement (e.g. by Lord Hailsham in the mid-1970s). Some of these pressures (e.g. from nationalism/devolution and the EC) have since weakened, though the Charter 88 movement has helped redirect attention to constitutional reforms. Before considering proposals, this chapter looks first at the British constitution today.

Sources of the British constitution

1. Common law, or traditions and customs administered by the old common law courts, e.g. freedom of expression, which have come to be accepted as constituting the law of the land.

2. Laws

(*a*) Statutory, or parliamentary, law overrides common law and provides a substantial written part of the constitution. It includes such measures as the Act of Union, 1707, successive Representation of the People Acts, the Bill of Rights, 1689, etc.

(*b*) Judges' interpretations of statute law, or 'Judicial Review', as it is called. Judges do not decide on the validity of laws duly passed by Parliament but on whether the law has been applied properly (e.g. in 1975, when the courts found against the Minister of Education's interpretation of his discretionary power in refusing to allow Tameside to select for secondary education).

3. Conventions. These are rules which, lacking the force of law, have been adhered to for so long that they are regarded as binding. Examples include the resignation of the Prime Minister following defeat on a no-confidence vote in the Commons; the Sovereign's assent to a Bill passed through Parliament. But the force of a convention depends on its being observed, and continued breaches – of the principle of the Cabinet's collective responsibility, for example – will weaken its strength.

Conventions loom large as an element in the British constitution: they are the key to its flexibility. Many essential features of the political system – e.g. ministerial responsibility, collective responsibility, occasions for a dissolution of Parliament, and constitutional monarchy are all largely the product of convention.

Consequences

1. The absolute and unlimited power of Parliament. An Act of Parliament is not constrained by any higher law; the courts cannot set aside, but only interpret, statute law; and there is no judicial review to compare with the role of the Supreme Court in the USA. Local and regional authorities only derive their powers from central government, and these may be rescinded (e.g. the abolition of Stormont in 1972; the abolition of metropolitan counties in the 1980s). The one exception is EC legislation (see below).

2. The only check on the executive supported by a majority in the House is its sense of self-restraint and the need to bargain with groups, appease backbenchers and respect opposition rights in the Commons. In a famous lecture in 1976 Lord Hailsham argued that these checks were no longer sufficient: the decline of the Lords and the monarchy, the growth of party discipline and the more interventionist legislation, and Cabinet domination over the Commons, meant that parliamentary sovereignty is actually an 'elective dictatorship'. Hailsham has argued that a party-whipped House of Commons is no longer an adequate defender of the citizen's liberties and that a written constitution which ensures a legal limitation on the powers of Parliament might now constrain the executive as the mixed constitution once did. When his party was in power however, after 1979, Hailsham's enthusiasm for change faded.

3. The British style is not legalistic. It is pragmatic, intuitive, flexible and differs from the legalism found in some West European states. Laws are expected to follow behaviour, and the courts are expected to keep free from politics. But this is changing (see below).

There are various pressures for a formal statement of the rules, i.e. a written constitution. The demand has been stimulated in part by a general dissatisfaction with the performance of the political system and the call for reform; in part by fear of a more interventionist government, against which citizens have little protection, and the spate of constitutional changes in recent years (see below). The latter indicate the flexibility of the system but also reflect less agreement on the 'rules of the game'.

Note the following:

(*a*) *Referendums.* So far these have been regarded as consultative, not binding; thus Parliament's formal sovereignty is preserved. But is there a need for rules on the occasions when referendums will be held and an authority to decide on the wording of the questions? So far the most powerful demands for referendums have been voiced in connection with constitutional matters, e.g. reform of the Lords in 1910–11, entry to and membership of the EC, and devolution for Wales and Scotland. More significantly, party leaders have usually turned to them when their own party was divided on the issue, as Labour was on the EC and on devolution in 1978–79.

(*b*) *Entry to the EC.* This means that substantial elements of a written constitution are already part of the British system. Other British authorities now have to accept rules and regulations embodied in the original treaty, commitments flowing therefrom, and further decisions taken by Community institutions. Note that all other EC states operate with written constitutions; Britain is the odd man out. And in cases of conflict between the British government and EC institutions, British courts will have to decide on the legality of Acts of Parliament.

(*c*) *Demands for a Bill of Rights* that will be entrenched (i.e. Parliament either cannot override it or can do so only with great difficulty). One step might be the formal incorporation of the provisions of the European Court of Human Rights, which Britain ratified in 1951 but has not yet been enacted into law. This would have excluded the detention (under the Prevention of Terrorism Act) of suspected IRA terrorists without trial.

(*d*) *Tutelary law*, which imposes codes of conduct. In contrast to the traditional British emphasis on negative liberty (see Chapter 3), governments have intervened more often to regulate formerly private areas of conduct, e.g. race relations, sexual discrimination and industrial relations.

(*e*) *Devolution.* The failure of devolution to come about in 1979 made it a 'dead' issue during the 1980s. But if the Scottish Nationalists attract significant support again, the issue might well return. If there was a devolution of power to Scotland the main constitutional interest would lie in how one would adjudicate in cases of conflict between the Westminster Parliament and an

Assembly in Scotland. How independent might the latter be of the former?

(*f*) *Criticism of the role of judges.* J. A. Griffith has challenged the 'myth' that judges are neutral. He argues that they are from a narrow upper-class background and, in attitudes and assumptions, support 'the conventional, established and settled interests' (*The Politics of the Judiciary*, Fontana, 1985, p. 213). This so-called 'political' role has developed as governments have enacted more interventionist legislation – sometimes carelessly drafted and often in areas which touch on the assumed 'rights' of interest groups and individuals. Appeals to the courts by aggrieved groups and the decisions and legal opinions of judges inevitably stir up political controversy. Some of this criticism is unfair. Judges deal with contentious cases, so one side is bound to feel aggrieved at the outcome.

(*g*) *The House of Lords.* There have been suggestions that it should be reformed so that checks and balances are restored, or, alternatively, that it be abolished, so that the elected government has more power. A future Labour government might choose to end its delaying powers. If accomplished, this would open up the possibility of single-chamber government (cf. Lord Hailsham). Hence demands among some Conservatives that reform or abolition of the Lords be subject to a vote by referendum.

(*h*) *Conventions are weaker.* The convention of collective responsibility was suspended by the Labour government in 1975 during the referendum over membership of the Common Market. It was suspended again for the vote over the type of electoral system to be used in the regional parliamentary elections. There has also been a growing tendency for Cabinet disagreements to become public via 'leaks'. In December 1985 and the beginning of 1986 the Defence Secretary, Michael Heseltine, publicly expressed views over the Westland dispute which were at variance with those of his colleagues.

(*i*) *Multi-partyism.* Coalitions are the norm in West European states. In Britain the Crown has only a minimal role when it comes to appointing a Prime Minister or granting a dissolution. This role may become more significant, and politically controversial, with coalitions or minority governments. Coalitions may also place collective responsibility under greater strain.

(*j*) *The weakening consensus.* There have been more conflicts between central and local government as the 1979 government took more controls, e.g. abolishing the GLC and the metropolitan counties and imposing more controls over spending and revenue. There have been allegations of some politicisation of the civil service and an increase in leaks by civil servants, e.g. the Clive Ponting affair in 1985 (see Chapter 15).

(k) *Northern Ireland*. To date this has proved to be an insoluble problem. Governments have experimented: in the last ten years there have been elections for a constitutional convention, a referendum, and PR elections. In each case these were constitutional innovations which no government envisaged for the UK. Their adoption reflected the politicians' awareness of the exceptional nature of the Ulster problem. Interestingly, during the years when governments have been prepared to consider greater devolution of decision-making for Scotland and Wales, they have moved in a different direction in Ulster. Four different forms of rule have been tried: (1) majority rule, pre-1972; (2) direct rule, 1972–74; (3) a power-sharing executive, 1974; and (4) direct rule again, 1974 onwards.

Other possibilities include:

1. Integration with the UK, so that Ulster would be like, say, Liverpool or Birmingham. This would give the British government greater powers than it had before 1972, though it would provide Ulster politicians with more local self-government, and probably rule out any possibility of an eventual united Ireland.

2. Integration with the Irish Republic, with some guarantees for the Protestant minority. But Britain has pledged that it will consider this only if the majority support it (which they do not), and there is the probability that some Protestant groups will resist it by force, as they pledged to do before 1914.

3. A British withdrawal. This would be a declaration of failure and impotence by the British government. It might lead to even more violence between Protestant and Catholic armed groups, or force the two sides to come to some political agreement in an independent Ulster.

4. *Repartition of the border*, to give one or more of the six counties to the Irish Republic. This may lessen sectarian tension in Ulster, but it still fails to meet the goal of those who want a united Ireland.

How the constitution changes

In most states the written constitution may be amended through a formal process, e.g. by referendum, or a vote by a two-thirds majority in the legislature. In Britain constitutional changes involving statute law are made in the normal way; e.g. altering the powers of the Lords in 1911 and 1949 was achieved via a simple majority in both houses. Some changes have been controversial and politically divisive, e.g. reform of the Lords, extensions to the suffrage in the nineteenth century, Irish home rule and Ulster today, devolution, etc. They came about less by general agreement than by one party using its parliamentary majority to push a change through, which was then gradually accepted. Changes in conventions tend to be more gradual and recognised as such only after the passage of time, e.g. that the Prime Minister should be in the Commons, not the Lords, or the weakening of the monarchy's political role.

Pressure for Change Charter 88 revived the issue of constitutional reform, adding the weight of its campaign to the arguments of the centre parties during the 1980s. A somewhat surprising new ally in 1990 was the Labour party, which included in its programme regional assemblies, a Scottish Parliament and a reformed upper chamber. It proposes, however, to protect civil liberties via specific laws rather than a written constitution.

The case for a written constitution

1. The view that power in Britain is too centralised and that the sovereignty of Parliament is open to abuse by any government. Demands for a written constitution are part of a broader belief that limited government is good *per se*, is under threat, and should be safeguarded. Often, these demands are advanced by opposition politicians who do not like what the government of the day is doing. Governments, on the other hand, have little incentive to restrain their own powers. Constitutional reform is often canvassed by advocates of electoral reform, devolution, a Bill of Rights,

safeguarding the House of Lords, and other devices, all of which have the effect of promoting checks and balances against the government of the day (see reference to Hailsham above).

2. *The need for statutory protection of individual liberties*, e.g. by a Bill of Rights.

3. The need for *certainty* and *clarity* about the 'rules of the game'. At present in the matter of many conventions the constitution is effectively what the government decides.

Objections to a written constitution

These may be advanced on grounds of:

1. Tradition. Having survived without one for long, why start now?

2. Redundancy. The existing system works reasonably well. The 'rules' are widely understood, and the government's sense of self-restraint and awareness of its dependence on a parliamentary majority amount to a sense of 'constitutional morality'. There is no guarantee that a completely written constitution would be better.

3. Inappropriateness to the British style of conducting politics (see above), and the difficulty of agreeing on a new constitution. But the major barrier to introducing a written constitution is the hallowed principle of the sovereignty of Parliament, which back-benchers and governments defend as and when it suits them. No Parliament (and hence no law) can bind its successors. Neither of the two major parties has shown much interest in limiting its own power in this way.

4. Practical difficulties. There is much disagreement about the contents of a proposed constitution (e.g. is the trade unions' 'closed shop' an infringement of individual freedom, and what would one say about rights of parental choice in education?). An entrenched (difficult to modify) constitution would clearly limit the sovereignty of Parliament. It would be likely to increase the political role of the courts, as they would have to decide whether the constitution had been infringed; they might come into conflict with Parliament. Because arguments for constitutional reform have often been concerned with placing limits on a government's discretion, and in the 1970s were usually designed to check interventionist governments, some Labour MPs saw these demands as part of an anti-Labour campaign.

In the 1980s, however, it was anti-Conservative figures who formed Charter 88 and called for constitutional reform. They were alarmed at actions of the Thatcher Government (e.g. the ending of trade union rights at GCHQ, the prosecution of *Spycatcher* author, Peter Wright, the refusal to allow broadcasting facilities for supporters of Sinn Fein) and the failure of weak parliamentary opposition to provide an effective check.

The main problem in a new settlement is to find a set of rules which are acceptable to different viewpoints. This is crucial if a new set of rules is to be legitimate. The first step, presumably, would be to establish a Constitutional Commission which in turn would submit proposals to Parliament, and, if these were approved, would be subject to a referendum. However, legislation affecting entry to the EC and devolution dominated parliamentary debate and the legislative timetable in the 1970s, and any future government is therefore unlikely to provide the legislative time for constitutional reform. Moreover, it would give *greater power to the unelected judiciary* at the expense of the elected Parliament.

Further reading

Mark Franklin, 'Whatever Happened to the English Constitution?', *Talking Politics*, Winter 1989.

Lord Hailsham, 'Elective dictatorship', *The Listener*, 21 October 1977.

Philip Norton, *The Constitution in Flux*, Longman, 1982.

— 'Should Britain have a Written Constitution?', *Talking Politics*, Autumn 1988.

Lord Scarman, *English Law — the New Dimensions*, Sweet & Maxwell, 1975.

Questions

1. What might be the main consequences for the conduct of British politics following the introduction of a written constitution?

2. Which features would the main parties be likely to (a) agree on and (b) find controversial?

3. Explain the advantages and disadvantages of an unwritten constitution.

7

THE ELECTORAL SYSTEM AND REPRESENTATION

This chapter examines the working of the electoral system and the cases for and against change. It also considers other problems about representation.

The electoral system

An electoral system is a set of rules for translating popular votes into seats in the legislature. It is also the established method of electing representatives, e.g. a legislature, government or head of state. There are broadly two types of electoral system:

1. *First past the post*, or the Anglo-American system. In this the candidate with the most votes wins, whether or not he has a majority of all the votes. This type of system is found, for example, in Britain, New Zealand, Canada, the United States and India.

2. *Proportional representation*. Seats in the legislature are allocated in approximate proportion to the distribution of popular votes. There are many different forms of PR (see below).

The two types of electoral system exemplify two different ideals. The Anglo-American system emphasises majoritarianism, and usually produces a majority for one party or group of parties. In post-war Britain, except for February 1974, it has always yielded a majority of seats in Parliament for one party. The proportionality systems emphasise the importance of representation. The first system works best where there are two parties or a dominant party, and consent is more easily obtained from the minority if there are not sharp divisions in society (e.g. Northern Ireland). Another way of protecting the rights of minorities is to have federalism or a separation of powers, as in the United States. The proportional system can also achieve a stable government, even though it may be a minority or coalition government.

The working of the British system. There may be a marked disproportionality between seats and popular votes, and a bias which exaggerates the 'winning' party's share of the vote. For example, consider the election result in 1987.

Party	Vote (%)	Share of seats (%)	Distortion
Conservative	42·3	58·0	+ 100 seats
Labour	30·8	35·0	+ 25 seats
Alliance	22·6	3·5	− 140 seats

The elections of 1951 and 1974 were instances when the party with most votes had not enough seats to form a government. Yet the second party is usually prepared to accept the outcome, because it has the chance of full power at the next election, and because Britain has been largely a consensual society. In recent years, however, the fall in popular support for the two main parties has produced more disproportional outcomes and fuelled demands for the introduction of PR.

Demands for Electoral Reform. PR was first raised in 1831 and attracted support throughout the nineteenth century. The Speaker's Conference recommended the adoption of the alternative vote in 1917 and the proposal nearly gained a parliamentary majority. Pressure has grown in recent years. In 1973 the Royal Commission on the Constitution recommended PR for elections to the proposed Scottish and Welsh assemblies. In 1973 and 1975 it was adopted for election to the Ulster Assembly and Convention respectively. With its electoral system Britain is the odd-man-out in the European Community. All other members have either a form of PR or, as in France, a run-off election.

The arguments examined
For the present system
1. The single-member system allows the voter to choose a single representative. The link with the constituency MP is weakened if there are multi-member constituencies and the list of candidates is proposed by the national parties.

2. PR may increase the bargaining or 'blackmail' power of a small party, if it holds the balance in a deadlocked Parliament.

3. It may provide representation for 'extremist' parties (e.g. the National Front or Socialist Workers' party).

4. If there are coalitions, then delay, avoidance of tough decisions and the absence of coherent policies are likely. Coalitions also weaken the idea of responsible party government (see below).

5. At present voters can vote directly for a team and a set of policies. But if there are coalitions the programmes will emerge only after bargaining and deals between the parties.

For PR

1. A government may exercise full power even though it is supported by a small minority of the popular vote, e.g. Labour formed a majority government in October 1974 with only 39 per cent of the vote.

2. Unfairness when a party's share of the vote is markedly underrepresented in its share of seats.

3. A majority government (probably a coalition) would be more representative of public opinion because it would have at least 50 per cent of the vote.

4. PR would overcome the geographical bias of the present system in which the North and South are respective Labour and Conservative strongholds. After 1983 and 1987 the Conservatives had 85 per cent of the seats in the south for only 50 per cent of the vote and Labour had 60 per cent of the seats in northern England and Scotland for only 40 per cent of the vote. At present only a handful of Conservatives sit for any of the great cities, and only one sits for a seat which is among the hundred constituencies which suffer from high unemployment.

5. Some critics argue that the present electoral system fuels the adversary party system. It is argued that PR would be likely to encourage consensus and continuity of policy.

Barriers to change. Electoral systems intimately relate to questions of political power, and self-interest therefore dictates the reactions of most politicians. Given that no British party has gained 50 per cent or more of the popular vote in the past fifty years, either minority or coalition governments would be the likely outcome of a more proportional electoral system. Conservative or Labour leaders would have to bargain and dilute their programmes in search of coalition partners. The effect of such a change is easily illustrated.

For example, instead of dominating the House of Commons with two-thirds of the seats, Mrs Thatcher's government would actually be in a minority if it had only 42 per cent of the seats. The other consequences for the power of the Prime Minister, the role of the Cabinet and Parliament, and the role of the monarchy are discussed in Chapter 5 on multi-partyism.

The demise of the SDP in June 1990 removed one advocate for PR from the political scene, but the Charter 88 movement has helped keep the issue alive. Increasing minorities in both major parties now support such a reform and the Labour party has evinced a more favourable attitude towards PR in respect of European elections, a reformed House of Lords and an elected Scottish Assembly. PR for elections to the House of Commons, however, is another matter.

Yet PR might come about if a third party does well in the elections or has enough seats to deny a majority to one or other of the major parties. Another way in which PR might come about could be as a result of a series of deadlocked elections; the introduction of PR would simply acknowledge that Britain had moved to a multi-party system. Yet one has to realise that some MPs, by supporting the introduction of PR, would almost certainly be surrendering their seats.

Possible effects. One can only speculate about the consequences of a move to multi-partyism, coalitions or deadlocked Parliaments, because the situations are hypothetical. Britain has had coalition governments to cope with crises, e.g. the 1931 economic crisis or the two world wars. The short periods of minority rule, as in 1974 or 1977–79, were regarded as temporary, and a speedy restoration of two-party 'normality' was anticipated. If multi-partyism and coalitions were established the likely changes would include:

1. *Individual electors would have to calculate their votes.* It would no longer be a simple choice between the government and opposition. The opportunities for tactical voting would increase (e.g. for Conservatives in a Labour seat, might a vote for the Liberal Democrats be the best way to defeat Labour?), although if a form of PR was introduced the arguments about a wasted vote would lose their strength.

2. *The House of Commons would probably become more vigorous* towards the executive and MPs more independent of the

whips. There are many reasons for the decline of the House of Commons' influence over the executive, but the dominance of the government over the legislative timetable and party discipline have been important factors. The passage of legislation has been virtually guaranteed because the government of the day has a disciplined party majority. With a coalition, however, government leaders may have to bargain more for support from backbenchers.

3. *A change in the role of the Crown.* As noted in the discussion of the constitution Chapter 6), if there is no majority for one party the monarch may be more involved in the choice of sending for a party leader to form a government and deciding whether or not to grant a Prime Minister's request for the dissolution of Parliament. The important point is that multi-partyism would challenge many accepted principles of the constitution, increase uncertainty, and might expose the Crown to charges of political bias.

4. *Limitation of the Prime Minister's powers.* The Prime Minister's powers of appointment and controlling the Cabinet agenda would be subject to bargaining with the other coalition parties.

Problems with representation

It is worth noting that some of the issues which have been raised by commentators about representation in Britain.

1. Mandate. The claim that elections give a winning party a 'mandate' for every item in their manifesto has long been suspect, because:

(*a*) Many party voters do not know the party's policies on many issues, and/or

(*b*) They disagree with these policies. For many years there has been a marked disagreement on a number of issues between Labour voters and policies of the Labour party.

As the manifestos of parties have become longer and more detailed since 1945 so it is less likely that voters are aware of the party's position on many issues. Moreover, the vote is a crude instrument; voters cannot pick and choose between rival parts of the programmes. But we can say that the party which wins the election may claim broad approval for its programme. Perhaps a more effective mechanism for testing the preferences of voters on particular issues is:

2. Referendums. These have been held in Britain once, in Northern Ireland once, and in Scotland and Wales once. They have all been held on issues which raised constitutional questions and usually on which the Labour party was divided. Referendums obviously raise problems about the status of collective responsibility and parliamentary sovereignty, although to date they have only been advisory. They are certainly difficult to graft on to the system of parliamentary sovereignty and responsible party government.

3. Local versus national mandates. The programmes of national government override the programmes of local government. But in recent years, particularly since 1979, there have been a growing number of clashes between Whitehall and local authorities. In view of the steady incursion by the centre on the independence of local government − particularly over local spending − the point has arrived, according to some critics, when local democracy has been seriously eroded (see Chapter 18).

Another case of a clash of mandates arises with:

4. Pressure-group politics. Pressure groups provide an ancillary form of representation, one that is more specific and perhaps more vital to the individual. Trade union leaders, for example, may be 'mandated' by their members not to accept an incomes policy that has been approved by Parliament. This clash of mandates was seen in 1974 when the miners broke the statutory incomes policy of the Heath government (see Chapter 17).

5. Party democracy. One criterion of democracy is that voters have a choice at periodic elections between different political parties. The critics of this view ask: what if the parties are run by elites or by leaders who are unrepresentative of members and supporters? They argue that there should be democracies within the parties as well as a choice between them.

In Britain this view is called a theory of intra-party democracy and it is associated with the Labour party. It means that the party members actually decide the policy and elect and hold the party leaders responsible for their actions. Labour party values include a great respect for the views of the grass roots, acceptance of decisions by majority vote, and anti-elitism.

The members are represented at the party's annual conference. This is the supreme policy-making body of the party, and motions approved by a two-thirds majority automatically become part of the party programme. Conference in whole or in part elects twenty-seven of the twenty-nine members of the NEC; the trade union section, the constituency section, the women's section and the socialist societies' section. In addition, the leader and deputy leader of the PLP sit as of right on the NEC.

Critics and advocates of intra-party democracy claim that Conference is supposed to instruct the PLP. An early resolution (1907) said that MPs should carry out the programme but the method and timing would be left to the PLP. Many of these ideas about the subordination of the PLP were developed before Labour had a substantial number of MPs (after 1918) or first formed a government (1924).

One view is that Labour has different centres of authority – Conference, the NEC and the PLP. They have to work together and, in practice, have done so. Only in 1960, when Conference voted for unilateral disarmament, did the party leader openly defy the authority of Conference and successfully battle to reverse the vote the next year.

Another view is that intra-party democracy is a myth, more honoured in the breach than in the observance. It is argued that the conventions of the parliamentary and Cabinet system exclude the possibility of Ministers being 'instructed' from an outside body. Moreover, it would also weaken the link between the MP and his constituents. Even when Labour leaders pay tribute to the authority of Conference, in practice they ignore it when they see fit, particularly in government.

In the Conservative party, the party leader presents a clear form of authority. She is in control of the party organisation, appoints the party chairman and director of the research department. Together with senior colleagues she decides party policy; the conference has no policy role. This simple structure limits the opportunity for disputes to persist.

There were growing pressures in the 1970s to make the Labour party in Parliament more receptive to influence from the party grass roots. Proposed reforms included:

(*a*) Election of the party leader by an electoral college, representing all sections of the movement and no longer by MPs exclusively.

(*b*) Mandatory reselection of MPs between elections. The procedure is designed to make the MP more responsive to pressure from local activists – who may or may not confirm to Conference opinion.

(*c*) NEC control of the party's election manifesto.

The first two were approved in 1981 and 1982. They increased the leverage of the extra-parliamentary elements and reduced the autonomy of Labour MPs, a shift in the power structure of the party. Given also that the political left is usually stronger in the extra-parliamentary wing, and the political right usually stronger in the PLP, there will be a shift in the political balance. Why?

1. *Disappointment* at Labour's record in office. Between 1964 and 1980 it was in office for nearly twelve years, though for some time with only a small majority or even a minority. It was particularly disappointing at improving living standards.

2. The failure was seen as a *failure of the 'revisionists'*, the right-wing social democrats, who had tried to operate a mixed economy and dispensed with radical socialist measures. Now, critics argued, the latter should be tried.

3. *Entryism*, or penetration by left-wingers of key positions in constituencies.

Problems

1. In what sense does Conference represent the nearly 7 million members? Most constituencies grossly inflate their membership returns. The actual national figure is nearer 250,000 than the 650,000 claimed by the party. Similarly, trade union votes are based on the number of members who pay the political levy. But many union members are unaware that they pay a levy, and many, of course, do not vote Labour. The block-vote system of voting by constituency parties and the trade unions may produce results which are quite unrepresentative of the aggregated votes of individuals.

2. Conference power is largely trade-union power. The unions have five-sixths of the votes and decide the composition of the NEC. The five largest unions together have a majority of the votes. By tradition, the parliamentary leadership managed to 'guide' Conference because of agreement with the leaders of the major

unions. In recent years the union leaders have not exercised the same control over the delegations and, until Kinnock's period, been less sympathetic to the policies of the parliamentary leadership.

3. How true a reflection of the views of Labour supporters are the views of members? Opinion poll evidence suggests that the latter are to the left of the former. The difference of opinion was shown in the referendum on the Common Market in 1975, when Labour voters supported membership by a narrow majority, compared to the opposition of the NEC and Conference. Here is the potential contradiction between the values of participation and representation. Increasing the participation/influence of activists may lead to policy outcomes which are quite unrepresentative of the views of Labour voters.

4. The structure of the party, with its separate arenas, helps the spread and persistence of conflict. But it is because there is a genuine and fundamental disagreement on policies and values that the structure of the party has come under scrutiny.

Further reading

A. Birch, *Representative and Responsible Government*, Allen & Unwin, 1964.

D. Butler, *Governing Without a Majority*, Collins, 1983.

Bill Jones, 'Reforming the electoral system', in *Political Issues in Britain Today*, Manchester University Press, 3rd edn 1989.

D. Kavanagh (ed.), *The Politics of the Labour Party*, Allen & Unwin, 1982, Chapters 8 and 9.

Questions

1. 'The first-past-the-post electoral system is best for Britain because it reliably provides strong executive government.' Discuss.

2. 'Political parties in Britain dominate government yet represent ideological activists rather than the average voter.' Fair comment? If so, are our political parties an adequate vehicle for democratic government?

8

ELECTORAL BEHAVIOUR

In discussing the party system (Chapter 5) we noted the change from system I (to 1970) to system II (post-1970). Not surprisingly, this change is connected with changes in the behaviour of the electorate. The shift is:

1. From such 1950–70 features as:

(*a*) The great majority of voters were stable in their party loyalties.

(*b*) Constituency swings were largely uniform across the country, reflecting the nationalisation of political loyalties.

(*c*) The Conservative and Labour parties dominated the contests throughout the UK (gaining over 90 per cent of the votes between them).

(*d*) When one of the two main parties gained support, it was usually at the expense of the other party, and vice-versa.

2. To such post-1970 features as:

(*a*) Volatility, or shifts in voting behaviour, because party allegiance declined.

(*b*) Greater variations in the electoral behaviour of different regions. Scotland, from 1979 onwards, swung to Labour, the North slightly to the Conservatives, and the South and Midlands on a much bigger scale to the Conservatives. In 1983 and 1987 Labour did less badly in the North than in the South.

(*c*) The rise in voting support and − to a lesser extent − in parliamentary seats for the Alliance. This was marked in 1983 and to a lesser extent in 1987. There is also a differentiation in the choices in different regions. In many seats in the South an Alliance candidate was the runner-up to the Conservatives. In Scotland both Labour and Conservative have to compete with Nationalists.

(*d*) In the course of time there has been a turning away from both main parties, particularly from Labour.

(*e*) The class basis of the two-party system has declined sharply. On average in post-war elections up to 1970 some two-thirds of the working class voted Labour; in elections since, the average has fallen to less than half. The decline in middle-class support for the Conservatives has also fallen, from an average of four-fifths to less than three-fifths.

During the 80s, polls suggested that the electorate had become more volatile, less predictable, more fickle and critical with a keener, more instrumental interest in issues.

How elections are decided

They are determined by the interplay of long-term and short-term factors. The former work, on balance, to stabilise voters' choices, the latter to change them. The factors include:

1. Long-term

(*a*) *Party identification* or loyalty. Some 70 per cent of voters identify to some extent with Labour or Conservative, and supporters, particularly strong ones, are likely to vote for the party in spite of misgivings about the policies or leaders.

(*b*) *Social class*. For most adults their class position will not change. Historically there has been a relationship between a person's social class and his choice of party.

2. Short-term

(*a*) *Issues* associated with elections (see below).

(*b*) *Events* leading up to and during the election, e.g. the collapse of Labour support during the 'winter of discontent' in 1979, which destroyed the party's chance of electoral success or the successful campaign in the Falklands which transformed the Conservative's prospects in 1983, or the improvement in living standards which helped the Conservatives in 1987.

In recent years the former factors have weakened, and the latter have gained in strength. (The first two, till recently, also worked in Labour's favour.) Hence the volatility in electoral support for the parties.

The 1970s and even more so the 1980s were disastrous for Labour. In general elections between 1945 and October 1974 the Labour and Conservative parties were each in office for seventeen years and their average share of the vote was almost identical. Since 1979 the position has altered drastically (Table 1). Labour in the last three general elections has trailed the Conservatives by an average of 11 per cent.

Table 1   *Con.—Lab. shares of votes in post-war elections (%)*

Years	Lab. (average)	Con. (average)	Lab. lead
1945—Oct. 1974	44·5	43·6	0·9
1979—1987	31·8	43·0	−11·2

In the next section we comment on (1) the weakening attachment to the two main parties, and (2) the decline of social class as a basis for voting.

Party loyalty and social class

1. Loss of support. The proportion of voters identifying strongly with both of the two main parties fell from 38 per cent in 1964 to less than 20 per cent in 1979. Before 1970 it was usual to think of swings only between Labour and Conservative, but in 1974 both parties lost heavily. Instead of a realignment there was a partisan *de*alignment of major party support in Britain. There is some evidence that support for the parties was becoming more fragile and conditional in the 1960s. Voters were more 'instrumental', voting for and withdrawing support according to a party's performance and promises and generally becoming more volatile. Given the country's relative economic decline in recent years, it is not surprising that more voters have doubted the competence of parties to improve conditions.

The elections of 1974 and 1979 therefore triggered long-standing doubts in the minds of many voters. The Conservative decline was associated largely with the circumstances of the first 1974 election — confrontation with the miners, the three-day week, etc. This was confirmed by the party's recovery in

1979. The collapse of Labour's incomes policy and 'social contract' with the unions in the 'winter of discontent' in 1979 produced a sharp decline in Labour support. The unions were a heavy vote-loser for the party. But Labour's problems are more long-standing.

The waning support for traditional Labour principles – links with the unions, greater spending on the social services, more nationalisation – already noted in the 1960s, continued in the 1980s. It is more marked among the Labour working-class voter (the Labour middle-class voter is more committed to these ideas). But to these were added dislike of the party's unilateralist defence policy, doubts about the party's competence to manage the economy, and worries over divisions and extremism in the party. The loss of support in the 1980s for the 'old' two-party system was largely a problem for Labour, and is connected with a sharp fall in working-class support for Labour and with:

2. Decline of the class alignment. Division between manual and white-collar workers has long been associated with the two-party system. The great challenge to this association has been the large working-class Conservative vote and the successful electoral record of the Conservatives in the twentieth century (in office either alone or in coalition for nearly fifty years since 1900).

That the traditional class alignment was waning became evident in 1974, and has been confirmed since. The decline has been explained by:

(a) The 'embourgeoisement' of the parties' leaderships. Labour Cabinets came to resemble the Conservative front bench in that they became more middle-class and university-educated. One party shed its working-class component, the other is aristocratic, grouse-moor elements. In the inter-war years 72 per cent of Labour MPs were from the working-class, compared with a quarter today (see Chapter 9).

(b) Television is the main source of political communication for most voters; it tends to be more objective and balanced in its presentation than newspapers and encourages a less partisan style.

(c) Social change and affluence, which have softened class differences and weakened class loyalties.

(d) Complexity of social class. For example, skilled workers are evenly divided between those who rent a council house and those who purchase their own home (40 per cent each). The middle class, as noted, is divided between a growing proportion who provide services in the public sector, and those in the private sector. The working class is divided into those who are in strong or weak trade unionists, are in the public or private sector, are skilled or unskilled. In turn, the parties have difficulty appealing to a single social class because its interests are so diverse and sometimes contradictory.

In sum, the social structure is more complex, 'looser', and is less important in influencing voting. If we think of an archetypal manual worker as one who also regards himself (or herself) as working-class, has received a minimum education, is not a home-owner and is a member of a trade union, then only a small minority actually possess all these characteristics. Only one-third of white-collar workers possess an opposite set of characteristics. The more 'ideal' or homogeneous the middle- or working-class person is in terms of possessing these reinforcing attributes, the more likely he or she is to vote for the party typical of his or her class.

Working-class Conservatism

Several explanations have been put forward. They include:

1. Political generations. Until recently the Conservatives had regularly enjoyed majority support among the old, and been in a minority in the younger generation. This difference had less to do with people becoming more 'conservative' as they grow older than with how people acquire party loyalties. We have to remember that Labour became a major party only after 1918, at a time when many voters had already acquired loyalties to other parties.

The main reason why the old have been less likely to vote Labour than the young is simply that they were less likely to have had Labour parents or to have voted Labour the first time they voted. As these older voters died off in the 1950s and 1960s, and new working-class voters who grew up in Labour homes came on to the registers, so Labour gained a growing share of the working-class vote. But Butler and Stokes were also to show, paradoxically, that (*a*) the class basis of voting was increasing in the 1960s, i.e. more workers were voting Labour, but (*b*) the intensity of class feeling – identification of the parties with class interests and perception of differences between parties – was declining.

2. Embourgeoisement. The spread of affluence and a middle-class lifestyle to workers was linked by commentators with the decline of Labour support two decades ago. It was effectively refuted by Labour's victory in the 1964 and 1966 elections. But there is a tendency for better-off workers and their wives to shift away from Labour, and if they buy their own house they are likely to shift to the Conservatives. What has happened among affluent workers is the growth of a more 'instrumental', less loyal attachment to the Labour Party. In the 1990s, such working class Tories may defect from the party if economic conditions worsen.

3. Social and political deference, or the belief that the Conservatives are innately more competent because of their 'better' social and educational background.

4. Policies. We should not ignore the fact that many workers prefer Conservative policies or that during the 1980s Labour was out of touch with working-class opinion on a number of issues. This was true in the 1980s on taxes, trade unions, law and order, inflation and defence. (In 1989–90 Labour rethought its position on most of these issues, and according to the polls won back much working-class support.)

All the same, Labour has made gains among the growing middle class. There are two explanations:

(*a*) A good proportion of this class are now first-generation middle-class, having come from working-class homes with Labour-voting parents. They have retained the old partisanship.

(*b*) With the growth of public-sector employment much of the expansion in middle-class jobs has occurred in local government, education and health. These services and the employees' salaries are paid largely by public expenditure. Because Labour is more sympathetic to this expenditure, whilst the Conservatives wish to limit it and make room for tax cuts, so these workers have more incentive to vote Labour.

Issues

1. 'Mandate'. The claim that elections give the winning party a 'mandate' for every item in their manifesto has long been suspect, because:

(*a*) Many party voters do not know the party's policies on many issues and/or

(*b*) They disagree with these policies (see pp. 69–70).

2. 'Position' and 'valence' issues. American students of electoral behaviour have drawn a useful distinction between 'position' and 'valence' issues.

Position issues are those on which voters and parties take different stands. The voter's choice of party is determined by his own preference and his perception of which party will further it. In 1945, for example, voters could choose between the Conservatives as the party of free enterprise and Labour as the party of nationalisation. In 1979 many voters turned to the Conservatives, in the expectation of lower taxes, and in the 1980s that party gained votes because it was seen as providing stronger defence and law and order policies than Labour.

Valence issues, on the other hand, are those on which parties and voters are largely agreed, e.g. maintaining full employment, securing peace abroad, building more houses. Here the voter is swayed by his perception of which party is more competent. In 1983 and 1987, for example, unemployment was the main issue for most voters, and they preferred Labour's policy for tackling it. But Labour gained few votes because many voters doubted whether a Labour government would be effective, or suspected that its policies would have negative side-effects, like a steep rise in inflation.

Significance of the 1987 general election

In his inaugural speech as leader of the 1983 Party conference, Neil Kinnock vowed that 'never again' would Labour suffer a defeat like that inflicted in the 1983 election. With equal measures of caution and determination he nudged the party away from a number of unpopular policies towards the centre ground which the Alliance had exploited so successfully. The Westland crisis in January 1986, followed by a host of other misfortunes, produced a healthy opinion poll lead in the summer of that year. However, Mrs Thatcher's scrupulous avoidance of banana skins from thereon, an autumn reflationary economic package from the

Chancellor and a triumphant prime ministerial visit to Moscow in the spring of 1987 reversed Labour's lead. Despite a brilliantly choreographed televisual campaign (the work, substantially, of Bryan Gould) Labour once again suffered a crushing defeat − but crucially, Labour saw off the Alliance's challenge and established the basis of a vigorous new period of opposition. The election results are shown in Table 2.

Table 2   *1987 general election (1983 figures in brackets)*

Party	% of votes	Seats	% seats
Conservative	42·3 (42·4)	375 (397)	57·7 (61)
Labour	30·8 (27·6)	229 (209)	35·2 (32)
Alliance	22·6 (25·4)	22 (23)	3·4 (3·5)
Others	4·3	23 (21)	3·5 (3·2)

Overall Conservative majority: 101 (144) (Speaker not included)

Turnout: 75·4% (72·2%)

The salient points arising from Table 2 are:

1. The Conservatives managed to reverse the tendency − charted over many previous elections − for the governing party to lose support in the last few days of the campaign. Conservative support, if anything, firmed up during this period.

2. The Alliance's challenge failed to 'break the mould', from a strong position in the polls. In terms of votes cast the 1987 result did not reassert two party politics in Britain; Labour and Conservative still won less than 75 per cent of the vote between them.

3. Despite the poor showing of the Alliance, the proportion of seats won in relation to votes still strongly supported the case for electoral reform. In the wake of the election, several Labour politicians pointed out that under proportional representation Mrs Thatcher would not have won an overall majority.

4. The campaigns seemed to have little overall effect on the outcome. Despite an imaginative and energetic campaign Labour only increased its vote by just over 3 per cent on 1983.

Studies suggested that most people had made up their minds early; the BBC Gallup survey showed a record 81 per cent of respondents who said their vote had been decided before the campaign even began.

The North—South divide

The election results reinforced the tendency for Labour to do well in the depressed North and the Conservatives to flourish in the more prosperous South. In Scotland a 7·4 per cent swing to Labour returned fifty Labour MPs, only ten Conservatives, nine Alliance, and three Scottish Nationalists. In Wales the swing to Labour was 7·5 per cent and in the North, North-West, Yorkshire and Humberside it exceeded 5 per cent. However in the West and East Midlands the swing was only 2·1 per cent; in the South-West, East Anglia and Greater London it was just over one per cent and the South-East just under one per cent. Excluding London, Labour won no seats south of a line joining the Bristol South/Oxford East and Norwich South constituencies. In London itself Labour even managed to lose three seats.

The Alliance lost votes all over the country but disproportionately more in the North than in the South — in the South-West it lost only 0·1 per cent. The Conservatives lost between 2 and 4 per cent in Scotland and the northern areas but they increased their vote in the East and West Midlands, the South-East and East Anglia. The 1987 election therefore left Britain more than ever a politically and geographically divided nation. In the South Mrs Thatcher's writ rules supreme but in the North, Conservatives command less than 40 per cent of the seats, in Scotland and Wales they have only 16 per cent of seats, and hold few seats in the major cities.

Class

Table 3 shows how far British voting behaviour has moved since the days when middle classes largely voted Conservative and the working-class Labour. The Conservative grip on the non-manual or middle-class vote weakened for the third election in succession to only 55 per cent. Middle-class voters in the

Table 3 *Vote by social class*

Party	Professional/ managerial			Office/clerical			Skilled manual		
	1987 (%)	1983– 87	1979– 87	1987 (%)	1983– 87	1979– 87	1987 (%)	1983– 87	1979– 87
Con.	59	−3	−8	52	−3	−6	43	+4	−2
Lab.	14	+2	−4	22	+1	+1	34	−1	−11
Lib./SDP	27	–	+12	26	+2	+6	24	−3	+14

Party	Semi-skilled/unskilled manual			Unemployed		
	1987 (%)	1983–87	1979–87	1987 (%)	1983	1979
Con.	31	+2	−1	32	+2	−8
Lab.	50	+6	−5	51	+6	+2
Lib./SDP	19	−8	+5	17	−9	+6

Source: Ivor Crewe, the *Guardian*, 15 June (based on Gallup survey evidence).

private sector were more pro-Conservative than those in the public sector. Crucially Labour failed to regain support among C2s (the skilled workers). In 1974, it won 49 per cent of such voters to the Conservatives' 31 per cent. In 1987 the position was almost reversed.

There is controversy about the trends in the relationship between social class and voting behaviour. According to Ivor Crewe and others, the working class has declined in size and Labour has gained a diminishing share of that smaller class. There has been not only *party dealignment*, or falling support for the two main parties, but also *class dealignment*, i.e. a weakening relationship between social class and the vote. Some part of the weakening relationship is inevitably a consequence of the rise of the Alliance in the 1980s. On the other hand, Heath and others dispute the claim about class dealignment. They agree that absolute class sizes have changed – the working class becoming smaller, the middle class larger – but that relative class voting has not. They claim that Labour's electoral decline is a consequence largely of the reduced size of the working class rather than the decline of working-class voters supporting Labour. They also claim that social change explains about half of the decline in Labour's vote since 1964, pointing out that Labour's decline in the middle class has been much slower than its decline in the working class. Crewe and others have confused the decline of the Labour party with the decline of class voting.

Conclusions

1. Weaker attachment to the party(ies) in government may further undermine support for unpopular government policies. The tendency since the mid-1950s has been for public opinion, as reflected in by-elections and opinion polls, to turn sharply against the government of the day, particularly when economic conditions were unfavourable. Governments have invariably recovered support when the economy has improved. (The possible exception is 1983, where the Falklands War success helped mask an indifferent economic record by the first Conservative government.)

2. Weakening of the class alignment allows other cleavages, e.g. nationalism or environmentalism, to become important, or helps parties which make cross-class appeals, e.g. the Alliance, or a more 'moderate' Labour party.

3. We often talk about a growing 'third force' or third-party vote in Britain. But we need to distinguish the different bases of support for the different parties. Religion is important in Ulster, and in 1974 the dozen Unionists cut themselves off from their traditional allies, the Conservatives. The Welsh Nationalist appeal is confined to the rural, Welsh-speaking areas, but the Scottish Nationalists have tapped genuine support for a more independent Scotland. Liberal support ebbed and flowed over the years, depending mainly on dissatisfaction with the two main parties.

4. Weak attachments and volatility may lead to election landslides as well as close-run results. They may lead to the fragmentation of the party system, as in the 1980s, or a restoration of the dominance of the Labour and Conservative parties.

5. The new fragility of party support increases the likelihood that campaigns can actually switch votes. Class loyalty and party identification – the forces for maintaining party loyalties – have

weakened. Voters may therefore respond more to the particular issues and candidates associated with each campaign.

6. The task facing Labour. The social and economic trends mentioned above are working against Labour. Heath *et al.* have calculated a 'normal' vote for each of the parties, based on social and economic factors. They claim that by 1980 the Conservatives had improved their normal vote by 6 per cent since 1964 (to 49 per cent), the Liberals–SDP Alliance to 13 per cent, while Labour had suffered a decline of some 9 per cent (to 37 per cent). To win a majority of seats at the next election Labour needs a swing of 8 per cent (nearly twice as large as the previous highest since 1945). It would have to gain many seats in the south and Midlands, where it often trailed third in 1987.

Some observers argue that each of Labour's last three election defeats was a product of a unique set of circumstances – in 1979 the 'winter of discontent', in 1983 the poor leadership of Michael Foot, party divisions, and the Falklands; and in 1987 the mood of prosperity. In this case it has been bad luck and political factors which have brought about the decline of Labour. If so, then improvements in policy and strategy can help Labour to regain ground: since 1989 as Labour has moved to the centre ground it has done extremely well in opinion polls.

Others argue that the social trends will prove a heavy burden for the party to overcome. In 1959, the manual working class formed two-thirds of the electorate; now it is less than half. The spread of home-ownership, the emergence of the 'new working class' (who were heavily Conservative in 1987), self-employment and the decline in trade union membership have all worked against the Labour party in recent years.

But Labour has profited from one quite unexpected development since the 1987 general election. In the 80s the rise of the Alliance meant that Labour was no longer the sole beneficiary of anti-Conservative mood. The collapse of the Alliance, however, in 1987, the demise of the SDP in 1990 and the so far indifferent showing of the Liberal Democrats has meant that Labour has more than ever become the main repository for anti-Conservative sentiment. Whether Labour can convert this recaptured support into an electoral victory remains one of the key political questions of the early 1990s.

Further reading

David Butler and Dennis Kavanagh, *The British General Election of 1987*, Macmillan, 1988.

D. Butler and R. Stokes, *Political Change in Britain*, Penguin, 1969.

Frank Conley, *General Elections Today*, Manchester University Press, 1990.

David Denver, *Elections and Voting Behaviour in Britain*, Philip Allan, 1989.

P. Dunleavy and c. Husbands, *British Democracy at the Crossroads*, Allen & Unwin, 1985.

A. Heath *et al.*, *How Britain Votes*, Pergamon, 1985.

R. Rose and I. McAllister, *Voters begin to Choose*, Sage, 1986.

Questions

1. Account for the changing importance of social class on voting behaviour.
2. Why have voters turned away from the Labour Party in recent years?
3. What influence do party leaders have on election campaigning?

9

POLITICAL RECRUITMENT

Among the questions to consider here are:

1. Who are the people who enter national politics and get to the top?
2. Is there a 'political class'?
3. Have there been changes in recent years?

There are a number of 'rules' for identifying would-be politicians. First, they are likely to be drawn from those already interested and active in politics. This factor immediately reduces the pool of 'eligibles' to some 10–15 per cent of the adult population. Then they tend to come from those occupations most compatible with a political career, e.g. lawyers, company directors, teachers, trade-union officials. The final two hurdles for would-be politicians are that they have to be selected for a constituency and, finally, be elected to Parliament.

There are several ways of recruiting people to office. The liberal democratic method, found mainly in Western states, depends on voters choosing between candidates of different parties at free competitive elections. Such election legitimises the politician's authority. However, many states are ruled by groups which have *seized* power. Military rule, for example, is often found in new (i.e. post-1945) states, and in countries which are poor (i.e. have a low gross national product). In this case the army's claim to obedience rests on its monopoly of force. Another mode of recruitment is appointment by *merit*, as in the British civil service. Competence is demonstrated here by the possession of formal qualifications and by success in examinations.

In effect our politicians are recruited through political parties and elections.

A political class?

It is well known that politicians in Britain, and in most other countries, are unrepresentative in their social and educational background. They are overwhelmingly male, middle-aged and middle-class.

1. Historically, political leadership in Britain has been exercised by men of high birth and breeding. The combined effects of universal suffrage, organised mass political parties, increasing professionalisation of political life, and the decline of the landed interest have eroded the political influence of the aristocracy. But men from an upper-class background have stubbornly retained a large toehold in Parliament and the Cabinet. Forty-three per cent of the members of Cabinets from 1884 to 1924 (the year of the first Labour government) were aristocrats (born or married into titled families). Between 1933 and 1964 the figure was still an impressive 26 per cent. For the same two periods the proportion of Ministers educated at expensive public schools actually increased from half to three-quarters.

2. MPs are increasingly drawn from the managerial and professional occupations and from university graduates. This description fits some two-thirds of all MPs. The significant post-war changes are on the Labour side. Before the war the great majority of Labour MPs were from the working class. Since 1945, however, the average has been a third, and it is still falling. Between 1945 and 1987 the proportion of university graduates on the Labour benches rose from 32 to 56 per cent (70 per cent of Conservatives are graduates). In part this reflects a change in the social and educational structure. Compared to the pre-war period, there are more white-collar or middle-class jobs, and the expansion of higher education has allowed more students from working-class families to gain degrees and enter the professions. To some extent, therefore, the embourgeoisement or social change of the Labour party in Parliament reflects a change in society.

There have been fewer changes on the Conservative side, although there has been a reduction in the number of aristocrats, big landowners and Etonians, so that the party is becoming slightly less upper-crust, as Labour is becoming less working-class. Before the war Edward Heath and Margaret Thatcher would have been unlikely choices as Conservative MPs, let alone as leaders. However, three-quarters of Conservative MPs are still drawn from public schools and most of them are products of Oxbridge.

3. Although MPs are more middle-class and better educated, differences between the two main political parties still persist. Labour MPs have usually attended grammar schools and 'redbrick' universities, and are engaged in teaching, lecturing or welfare occupations. Conservatives, as stated above, are usually from public schools and Oxbridge, and tend to be engaged in business or the law.

In both parties MPs appear to be more full-time, professional and ambitious. This may explain why they have become more rebellious over the past two decades. Traditionally there was a bloc of upper-class Conservatives 'from the shires' and a bloc of trade union Labour MPs who were strong party loyalists, neither with any great desire to make speeches or gain office.

4. Cabinet Ministers are usually of higher social status than backbenchers. This has always been more true of Conservative Cabinets but it has recently become increasingly applicable to Labour Cabinets also. Whereas half the Attlee Cabinets and Wilson's first Cabinet in 1964 were from a working-class background this element had virtually disappeared by 1970. When James Callaghan won the Labour leadership in 1976 his six rivals were all Oxford graduates. Given the tendency of bright, working-class children to go on to higher education, there are not now many MPs from working-class families who have not gone to university and are of ministerial calibre.

Does social background matter?

Critics object that the emergence of MPs from a small segment of society makes Parliament biased towards middle-class interests. This charge assumes that knowledge about a person's background enables one to predict his behaviour and values. The evidence is not clear-cut, however. The Conservative Party probably does suffer more than Labour in terms of its image because its MPs are so uniformly middle-class and public school in background.

D

Recruitment procedures for MPs

1. Labour. Party headquarters keep two lists of approved aspirants. List A consists of candidates sponsored by trade unions which are affiliated to the party. The financial help that goes with sponsorship makes such a candidate attractive to hard-pressed local parties. List B consists of other candidates. A Labour candidate has to be nominated by a group affiliated to the local party. The party executive selects a short list. The candidates appear before the general management committee, which then makes the final choice.

2. Conservative. Before the war, nominations frequently went to wealthy candidates who offered substantial contributions to local party funds. The Maxwell-Fyffe reform (1948) imposed a limit on the amount which candidates and MPs could contribute in this way: henceforth constituency parties had to become financially self-sufficient. A central body, the Standing Committee on Candidates, maintains a list of 'approved candidates', from which the constituencies may select a candidate. Aspirants apply direct to the local executive, which compiles a short list. A general meeting of members then chooses the candidate.

3. Social and Liberal Democratic procedures are similar but insist that one woman be present in each shortlist of candidates.

Problems

A growing number of disputes have arisen over the selection process. By tradition, only exceptional circumstances prevented an MP from being renominated if he so wished. Although in recent years the most publicised cases have occurred on the Labour side, since 1945 there have also been difficulties over the reselection of MPs in the Conservative party. If a Conservative association does not wish to renominate an MP, then (since 1973) the decision is left to a general meeting of all members. This step limits the opportunity for a small, unrepresentative group to manipulate the selection and has probably saved some MPs from dismissal. Sir Anthony Meyer, who stood in the leadership election against Margaret Thatcher in November 1989, was deselected by his vengeful Clwyd NW Association in January 1990.

Local Labour parties which did not wish to renominate an MP had to undergo a lengthy and cumbersome process. But since 1981 local Labour parties which have a sitting Labour MP have to begin a process of mandatory reselection, not later than thirty-six months into the life of the Parliament. This has increased the power of local management committees. But fear of not being reselected certainly influenced some disillusioned Labour MPs to defect to the SDP in 1981 and 1982.

Dismissing an MP is a lengthy and divisive business. The dismissed member may stand as an independent at the next election and help lose the seat for the party. Indeed, because MPs defeated at a general election now receive three months' severance pay, there is a financial incentive for them to stand.

There is little central control of the selection process; it is a jealously guarded prerogative of the constituencies. The party head-quarters have the 'passive' controls of maintaining a list of candidates and approving or vetoing the constituency's choice. Endorsement is rarely withheld from a nominated candidate, though Conservative Central Office managed to exclude a few Powellites between 1970 and 1974. Conservative Central Office has long wanted local parties to recruit a more diversified set of MPs, but has had little success. Under Neil Kinnock the Labour Party has tried to expel Militant activists from key positions in local parties (over a score went during 1987–88) and taken greater powers in the shortlisting of candidates for by elections (in 1986 the NEC imposed its own candidate in the Knowsley North by-election).

Reforms

Criticism arises partly because small groups have such a large say in the selection and, because most seats are safe for one party, selection is tantamount to election. Reformers suggest:

1. Primaries, as in the United States, which allow the local party supporters to choose the candidate. Critics object to the expense and the difficulties of scheduling primaries in the absence of fixed-calendar general elections.

2. Participation by more party members in the selection and dismissal process, so making it more difficult for small groups to 'take over' a local party. Labour Party moderates want to introduce 'one member one vote' selection procedures.

3. Making the MP more subordinate (and accountable) to the local party. One objection here is that as local parties become smaller so they may become less representative of the party's voters. Activists in the Labour Party, often thought to be left-wing, are frequently critical of the policies which Labour governments take up. The task of Labour leaders in Parliament would be made more difficult if 'loyalist' MPs could be more easily dismissed for not following local pressures or Conference policies.

The first two proposals are opposed by many activitsts who claim that their commitment and activity entitle them to this influence in selection. The difficulty with the third is that activists may not be representative of the party voters − who elect the MP; an MP, obviously, must try and accommodate both sets of demands, but in the case of a clash what does he do? The Labour Party moved clearly in the third direction in 1980 by changing the rules so that MPs are automatically subject to reselection by the half-way stage of a Parliament. This reform strengthened the influence of the General Management Committee, a group of forty to fifty local activists, but by the late 1980s, a strong current was running in favour of widening the basis of decision-making within constituency Labour parties.

Ministers

In the twentieth century Cabinet Ministers have on average served for fifteen years in the House of Commons before their first appointment. They usually ascend the ministerial hierarchy, working their way up from the junior posts to the major departments, like the Treasury, Home Office and Foreign Office. If MPs wish to reach the political summit they are helped by entry to the Commons at an early age. This parliamentary background emphasises the skills of managing Parliament. But some critics feel that more note should be taken of the recruitment methods of some other countries (which draw on civil servants, business executives and lawyers as well as parliamentarians for executive appointments). British

Ministers tend to lack the subject-matter expertise or skills in managing large organisations of many of their French, Dutch or American counterparts. British Cabinet Ministers' average tenure of a department, at two years, is one of the lowest in Western countries and means that at any one time many Ministers will be learning their jobs.

Party leaders

1. Conservative. Traditionally, Conservatives allowed leaders to 'emerge' by a process of 'soundings' or consultations carried on by senior figures. In fact, because the party has so often been in office, the Crown's prerogative of selecting a Prime Minister has meant that the monarch chose the party leader as well. (Balfour, Bonar Law, Stanley Baldwin, Neville Chamberlain, Winston Churchill, Anthony Eden, Harold Macmillan and Sir Alec Douglas Home were all chosen in this way). Usually the party chose 'safe' consensus-seeking men. In 1963, when Sir Alec was selected, controversy broke out, partly because he was a peer and partly because his claims were not generally regarded as stronger than those of other contenders. Both the process and Sir Alec somehow lacked legitimacy because there had not been an open, competivie election.

The new rules of 1965 provided for a formal election of the leader. In order to win, a candidate required an overall majority and a lead of 15 per cent over the runner-up. In 1975 three changes were made to the rules. First, provision was made for an annual election (providing an opportunity for MPs to dismiss a leader). Second, the party members in the country were to be consulted, though only MPs had votes. Finally, to be elected on the first ballot a candidate had to have an overall majority plus a lead of 15 per cent of all those *eligible* to vote (cf. 15 per cent of those *voting* in 1965). Mr Heath, the first leader to be elected in an open competition, was also the first to be so dismissed. The Conservative method of electing leaders was similar to Labour's until 1981. The adoption of formal election procedures strengthens the influence of backbenchers and has probably weakened the sense of hierarchy in the Tory party.

Nevertheless, the decision of Sir Anthony Meyer – an old Etonian of pro-European 'wet' political views – to take advantage of the annual opportunity to challenge the Conservative leader caused a sensation in the autumn of 1989. Mrs Thatcher's political fortunes were at a particularly low ebb at that time and party leaders urged Sir Anthony to stand down lest the contest prove disastrously divisive. In the event, just over sixty Conservative MPs either voted for Sir Anthony or abstained: too few to bring the Prime Minister down, but enough to pose serious questions about her position.

The kind of person chosen as party leader affects the type of Prime Minister. But who are the leaders? First, and most obvious, they are MPs. Second, they have long service in the House of Commons (twenty-four years on average to become party leaders, and twenty-six to become Prime Minister). This narrow background contrasts with experience in some other countries. It ensures that party leaders are well known to colleagues, and are, usually, good parliamentarians and skilled debaters. The person who emerges as leader is usually not identified with a particular faction of his party. An important task is to preserve party unity.

Interestingly, Mrs Thatcher is rather different. At the time she challenged Mr Heath she had been an MP for only sixteen years and had held only one Cabinet post, Education. She had not been a senior or influential Minister in Mr Heath's government, and was something of an 'outsider'. She was elected primarily because she was the only substantial figure who was prepared to stand against Heath. The majority of MPs, who wanted a change, had to vote for her to accomplish it.

Third, we should note that political skill in Britain is shown within the parliamentary arena. Approval among this parliamentary elite is more decisive than a popular following in the country or party conference in reaching the top. For example, both Enoch Powell and Tony Benn have attracted widespread grassroots support within the Conservative and Labour parties respectively. But they attracted minimal support among MPs. Thirteen of the seventeen Prime Ministers in the twentieth century first assumed office without the sanction of a general election.

2. Labour. In its early years the party elected its leader annually. Indeed, it was so anti-elitist that it preferred to call him a 'chairman' and give him limited powers. As Labour grew in strength, so the leader (as a potential Prime Minister) became more influential.

Since 1922 a leader has been opposed only once, when Harold Wilson stood against Hugh Gaitskell in 1960. When a vacancy occured MPs balloted until a candidate had an absolute majority. In 1976 James Callaghan gained an overall majority only at the third ballot.

Until 1981 election for the Labour party leader had no provision for participation by non-MPs. The leader was theoretically head of the parliamentary party, not the party as a whole. The 1976 party conference invited the NEC to re-examine the election methods and make the leader head of the whole party. Some wanted to have the leader elected by the annual conference (effectively by the trade unions) or by a weighted suffrage among MPs, constituencies and the unions. These reforms were defended on the grounds that the leader and the PLP would become more responsive to the wishes of conference. Most MPs, not surprisingly, wanted to keep the leadership election in their own hands, and this remained the case after the 1978 Conference vote on the issue. It was felt that MPs were the best judge of who among their colleagues should lead them day by day in the parliamentary battle and that the leader should be a person who commanded their confidence. The danger was of an unacceptable leader being foisted on them by an outside body.

Change was finally achieved by voters at the annual party conference in 1980, and a special conference in January 1981. The special conference decided to give the unions 40 per cent and MPs and local parties 30 per cent each. This particular scheme was opposed by the bulk of the PLP, who wanted at least 50 per cent for themselves. The left-wing NEC favoured a limited role for MPs. By and large the positions are determined by politics; the left, who are strong in the constituencies, favour a reduction in the influence of MPs; the right, a strong role for MPs (cf. chapter 5).

Michael Foot had narrowly beaten Denis Healey for the leadership in 1980 under the old rules, but the latter was challenged for the deputy leadership in 1981 by Tony Benn under the new ones. Healey won by a whisker. In 1983 Foot led Labour to a crushing defeat and stood down: the so-called 'dream ticket' of Kinnock and Hattersley triumphed at the resultant election and was overwhelmingly confirmed in 1988 when Tony Benn and Eric Heffer launched a last hurrah challenge.

Further reading

J. Blondel, *Voters, Parties and Leaders*, Penguin, 1980.

D. Butler and D. Kavanagh, *The British General Election of 1987*, Macmillan, 1988, Chapter 9.

M. Moran, *Politics and Society in Britain: an Introduction*, Macmillan, 1989, Chapter 6.

Questions

1. Should the composition of the House of Commons more accurately reflect that of British society?

2. What skills should potential Ministers possess?

3. Consider the advantages and disadvantages of the British convention of appointing Ministers only from the House of Commons and House of Lords.

10

THE MEDIA AND POLITICS

During the 1987 election campaign, television cameras on Mrs Thatcher's campaign bus were filming the Prime Minister talking on the telephone. She was clearly receiving good news; replacing the receiver she announced that a British diplomat held hostage in Iran had been released. In his book *Live from Number 10*, Michael Cockerell reveals that the Prime Minister had heard the news earlier: the phone call was just play-acting (p. 326). We should not be surprised: Mrs Thatcher herself has stated, 'In today's world selective seeing is believing and in today's world television comes over as truth.' Surveys show that 60 – 70 per cent of people cite television as their major source of political information with the press a poor second at 25 – 30 per cent. But whilst the press is widely perceived as reflecting political bias, television (according to poll data) is usually believed to be fair and objective.

The media has forged a revolution in the way politics is conducted. In the early days of democratic politics fiery speakers used to address crowds which nowadays could scarcely be crammed into Wembley Stadium, relying only upon their voices to transmit their messages. And they spoke at some length: during his famous Midlothian campaign (November – December 1879) Gladstone's speeches could last an hour or more. The popular press, emerging in the late nineteenth century, provided a new means of influencing political opinion and elevated newspaper owners into major players on the political stage. But the real communications revolution began in the 1920s. Stanley Baldwin (Prime Minister 1923 – 24, 1924 – 29, 1935 – 37) was the first British politician fully to exploit the potential of radio: his cosy chats into the microphone carried his relaxed persuasive charm into the homes of millions of families. Churchill was also a master of radio broadcasting but proved hopeless when confronted with television. The huge potential of this latter instrument was first exploited in America and successive developments of its use have crossed the Atlantic after an ever-diminishing time-lag.

The media: basic facts

The British press has a relatively large number of dailies which to some extent reflect Britain's social stratification. Mass circulation tabloids – the *Daily Mirror*, the *Sun*, the *Star* and *Today* – cater for the working classes; the *Daily Mail* and *Daily Express* for the lower middle classes; whilst the 'quality press', the *Guardian*, *Daily Telegraph*, *The Times* and the *Independent* are bought by middle and upper-middle-class group members. Indeed, readership of the quality press is about 80 per cent middle-class whilst the same proportion of those who read the *Sun* and the *Daily Mirror* is working-class.

As newspapers are big business and are owned predominantly by powerful business men it is hardly surprising that six of the daily newspapers are pro-Conservative whilst only two support Labour (the *Guardian* from a carefully guarded independent position). As the table below shows, political affiliations of tabloid readers (1988) are more evenly divided than those of the quality readership, suggesting that political news and comment is less important for the former group.

| | Sales (millions) | Vote of readers | | |
		Conservative	Labour	Alliance
Tory press				
Sun	4·0	41	31	19
Daily Mail	1·8	60	13	19
Daily Express	1·7	70	9	18
Daily Star	1·3	28	46	18
Daily Telegraph	1·2	80	5	10
The Times	0·4	56	12	27
Labour press				
Daily Mirror	3·1	30	55	21
Guardian	0·5	22	54	19
Non-Tory press				
Today	0·3	43	17	40
Independent	0·3	34	34	27

Broadcasting in Britain is controlled by the BBC and the IBA. The BBC was established in 1922 and in 1927 became a public corporation. Funded by licence fees, it runs two television channels plus four national radio channels as well as local and international radio services. The IBA was established in 1954 to regulate the activities of the fifteen advertising-financed television companies awarded regional franchises and those of Channel 4 established in 1982. According to statute, television and radio must handle controversial political issues in an objective and balanced fashion. Unlike America, where politicians can buy television time to advertise themselves just like any other product, Britain allocates time free of charge to political parties on the basis of their strength in the country. Parties are allowed ten minutes of television time for every 2 million votes received in the previous general election. In 1983, for example, the Committee on Party Political Broadcasting (comprising representatives of the BBC, IBA and political parties) agreed a ratio of 5:5:4 for Labour, Conservatives and the Alliance. Parties without parliamentary representation usually receive an allocation based upon the number of candidates fielded: in 1983 five minutes per fifty candidates. Party political broadcasts, however, provide only a small proportion of television's 'political' output: more important are news bulletins (20 million people watch BBC's *Nine o'Clock News* and ITN's *News at Ten*) and current affairs programmes like *Panorama, Newsnight, World in Action, First Tuesday* and *Question Time*. On radio, *Any Questions* is very popular and some 6 million people − including, according to folklore, Mrs Thatcher − listen to Radio 4's early morning *Today* programme.

The impact of broadcasting on the political process

Broadcasting has transformed the political process over the last thirty years.

1. Broadcasting has reduced the importance of local party organisation. In the late nineteenth century political parties needed strong local membership to proselytise ideology, encourage participation and sense of belonging and get the voter out on election day. Whilst the latter requirement survives, the other functions have been weakened by the ability of politicians to reach more people via two minutes on television than they could meet in a lifetime's door-to-door canvassing. This provides an important explanation for why both major parties have seen their active memberships decline drastically since the 1950s and it also helps to explain the reduction all parties have suffered in terms of highly committed support. Media messages, however, tend to be more centralised and seek to exploit the nationally known political leadership. The novelty and hopeful rhetoric of a new party attracted intense media interest when the SDP was launched in 1981. In consequence it virtually dominated British politics for over a year without any well established grassroots branch network. However, such media-based success can be short lived: the SDP never recovered after the Falklands War shifted the spotlight elsewhere.

2. *The role of the House of Commons has been usurped by the media*. The media has dislodged the House as the focus of popular political attention. Recent research has shown Mrs Thatcher ignoring the House but not television: her crucial performances are now more likely to be on Panorama than at the Despatch Box. Similarly, Ministers are more interested in announcing new initiatives direct to a mass television audience than to a poorly attended House. This and other arguments were deployed for over twenty years in support of televising the House's proceedings. Dire warnings that the unique and intimate nature of the parliamentary process would be forever sullied by the vulgar gaze of the cameras had proved wrong in the case of the House of Lords – televised since 1985. And so it has proved with the Commons when television was finally allowed in on 21 November 1989.

When it was clear that civilisation as we know it had not come to an end, some of the severe restrictions on what the camera could show were relaxed. Extracts from televised statements, debates and particularly Prime Minister's Question Time have now become a normal part of news broadcasts. Apart from smartening themselves up MPs have performed more or less as before, and despite her fears (and opposition to the scheme), Mrs Thatcher's early poll ratings were comfortably ahead of Neil Kinnock's. Through television the House has won back some of its lost ground, but as a forum for political debate BBC's *Question Time* is many times more popular. Perhaps more important in the long term is the prominence which television can now give to hitherto neglected aspects of the parliamentary process like select committee hearings or late-night adjournment debates (Emma Nicholson, MP was deluged with letters of support when her late-night motion on safety on school buses was picked up by the news bulletins). On 19 July 1990 televising the House was made permanent in a free vote of 131 to 32.

3. The form of political communication has altered. Gladstone's magisterial addresses have been replaced by relaxed television performances where politicians strive to persuade us of their competence, commitment and sincerity within the time constraints of television schedules and audience attention-spans. To be successful requires special attributes and skills possessed by few politicians. Mrs Thatcher was carefully coached from 1970 onwards by (now Sir) Gordon Reece to lower the tone of her voice, wear non-fussy clothes and change her makeup and hairstyle. She is still undeniably herself on television but training has helped play down her weaknesses and point up her strong points. As *The Listener* (23 June 1983) commented on her 1983 campaign performance, 'Whilst many may recoil from the hectoring style, know-it-all manner and quasi-regal airs and graces, she is undeniably crisp and clear, confident mistress of the facts and figures which underpin her simplistic world view.' Attendance at a television 'charm school' has now become an automatic requirement for ambitious politicians.

4. Political leaders must be good on television. Attlee and Churchill were cheefully dismissive of television; Eden and Macmillan were more attentive and responded to its demands; Wilson and Callaghan deployed their relaxed folksiness to good effect; Heath tried hard but when Prime Minister could never relax; and Mrs Thatcher triumphed over her shortcomings, as we have already noted. Michael Foot, however, elected Labour leader in 1981, scored badly on a number of important counts: his clothes and spectacles were wrong, he looked frail and elderly, he had a number of nervous twitchy mannerisms and tended to ramble and waffle instead of answering questions confidently, concisely and persuasively. Hitherto Labour had tended to resist television coaching as too close to the business or capitalist advertising world but after Foot attitudes changed; Neil Kinnock was chosen as his successor principally because he was believed to be good on television. Looking at possible successors to Mrs Thatcher, Mr Heseltine and Mr Baker have a clear advantage over Sir Geoffrey Howe, for example, in terms of televisual skills.

5. *The government has made more use of television to sell its policies*. Under the influence of Lord Young, annual spending on government advertising increased from £35 million to £150 million between 1979 and 1989. Television was used extensively to sell privatisation policies and the White Paper on the NHS, *Working for Patients*, in January 1989. In September 1989 a *Panorama* programme claimed that public money had already been used to sell the idea of water privatisation *before* the measure had been enacted into law thus using government funds for political purposes.

6. *The media has transformed the conduct of elections*.

(*a*) *Political hustings* where candidates met voters of all parties and displayed their political talents by dealing with hecklers have largely died out. Political meetings involving party leaders are now all ticket affairs with everything choreographed and carefully rehearsed for the television cameras. The leader arrives to ecstatic cheers from a crowd bedecked in party colours and rosettes. He or she steps up confidently to the microphone to deliver (in Mrs Thatcher's case, with the assistance of the invisible one-way autocue first used by Ronald Reagan) a speech in which carefully written passages have been strategically inserted for media attention. Campaign organisers hope to create the impression of a united party, a charismatic leader, a euphoric unstoppable march to victory. They hope the cameras will briefly capture this essence for news bulletins, together with one or two of the prepared 'sound bites'.

(*b*) *Campaigns have become presidential*. Because television news conveys political news in such an abbreviated form, it is inevitable it should focus upon party leaders who also inevitably have come to represent their party's brand image. The emphasis is increasingly upon the person rather than the party: whatever the leader says or does is, perhaps too slavishly, reported. Packs of reporters consequently form royal processions behind the party leaders who have learnt to eschew impromptu press conferences in favour of symbolic 'photo opportunities' involving them in activities like driving a tank (tough on defence), playing with disabled children (caring on social policy) or visiting a re-training workshop (concerned about unemployment). However, if the leader does make gaffes, as Thatcher and Kinnock both did in 1987, they are leapt upon with delight by the media and loudly exploited.

(c) *Campaign and media managers now play crucial roles.* The Conservatives have tended to take the lead in employing advertising agencies like Saatchi & Saatchi and media advisors like Reece and Tim Bell. Labour, however, appointed an ex-television producer, Peter Mandelson, as Communications Director and have employed the talents of such media professionals as the playwright Colin Welland and the film director Hugh (*Chariots of Fire*) Hudson, who produced a stunning party political broadcast in 1987 focusing upon Neil Kinnock. Labour indeed ran a highly televisual American-style campaign in 1987 which most commentators judged to be more professional than the lacklustre Conservative campaign.

(d) *Personal attacks in the tabloid press have grown in frequency and intensity.* In 1987 especially the private lives of certain politicians were subjected to an inquisition perhaps more merciless than any previous election. Many criticise this as dishonourable and unjustifiable − which it is − but most people are interested in the pecadilloes of others, especially those in the public eye, and there is much evidence from both sides of the Atlantic to suggest that the victims of such character assassinations also suffer in the ballot boxes.

The media influences voting behaviour

Research into this topic is inconclusive and a little confused. One school of thought is that the media merely reinforces voter preferences because of the 'filter effect': people tend to watch, listen and read what they want to hear and remember what they want to remember. Whilst this may well be true of newspapers in that people tend to read those which coincide with their views, it ignores the role which newspapers might have over time or on people whos views are undecided. And it also ignores the more balanced treatment provided by television. It is impossible for viewers of *Question Time*, for example, to be oblivious to the arguments put forward by representatives of parties with which they disagree.

Research also reveals that 20−30 per cent of voters can switch parties during an election campaign and media messages almost certainly play a causal role in influencing them, especially 'new' and uncommitted voters. But it is hard to disentangle the media from the other causal factors like family, work, region, class and so forth and it is hard to separate the media from the message. For example, Michael Dukakis's sanctioning of the release of Willie Horton from jail (a black rapist who thereupon raped again) was exploited by the Republicans during the 1988 presidential election. But was it the covert racist message which helped destroy Dukakis's opinion poll lead or was it the particular form and distribution which television gave it? Common sense tells us that a medium which can sell so many products should surely be able to sell politicians. Politicians clearly agree, otherwise they would not spend so much money on the activity – at the very least they fear they will lose by default if they fail to use television whilst their opponents do – but the precise impact of the medium defies accurate measurement.

Political control of the media

Once the widely accepted pluralist theory of how our democracy should (and to some extent does) work predicates media which are independent, free of sectional interest and thus able to give fair and accurate reportage. Given the power which the media clearly have this is an important political issue.

The press is independent of government control in that all newspapers in Britain are privately owned. However, it is widely asserted that because the press is owned by big business concerns which exist to make a profit the press is bound to favour the party of capitalism, the Conservatives. About 80 per cent of newspaper circulation is in the hands of three big conglomerates. Robert Maxwell and Rupert Murdoch, who control two of them, are the modern-day press barons and both take an interventionist editorial line. Maxwell dictates a pro-Labour line for the *Daily Mirror* but he is unusual. The majority of daily and Sunday newspapers urge readers to vote Conservative at elections, from the raucous populism of the *Sun* to the more sedate but no less committed injunctions of the *Daily Telegraph*. Murdoch is a confidant of Mrs Thatcher and a strong supporter. There is some evidence of co-ordination of editorial policy during elections between Conservatives and sympathetic newspapers but usually the support is so strong no encouragement or direction is needed.

Some critics claim the *lobby* system tends to favour the government of the day – whichever part is in power. One hundred and fifty Westminster journalists belong to this organisation whereby unofficial confidential briefings are given by Ministers and information officers, provided no specific attribution is made. Often information is transmitted via this system which would not otherwise see the light of day but, argue critics, it is inimicable to democracy in that it enables the government to manage the news and set the political agenda, and it encourages laziness amongst journalists who come to prefer dictated government briefings in exchange for challenging investigative journalism.

Television comes much closer to the requirements of a democratic system in that it is legally required to avoid bias and offer a balanced treatment of political issues. It is still possible for the government to influence television, however, and both Labour and Conservative governments have striven to do so. Harold Wilson was convinced of an anti-Labour bias within the BBC and fought an extended battle with its governors and staff. Mrs Thatcher is likewise convinced that the BBC and some independent television companies, especially Granada Television, are strongholds of leftish sentiment. In common with her predecessors she has sought to apply pressure in the following ways:

(a) *Power of appointment.* Advised by the Home Secretary, the Prime Minister appoints the Chairman of the IBA and the BBC together with Board members for given periods of office. The appointment of Marmaduke Hussey, ex-Chairman of *The Times*, as Chairman of the BBC, was widely interpreted as Mrs Thatcher's attempt to 'sort out' a supposedly leftward-leaning BBC. Shortly afterwards Alastair Milne, the Director-General with whom Mrs Thatcher had been in dispute, was fired. But experience suggests even political supporters, once appointed, can oppose the government as Hussey has done over a number of issues, including the restrictions on reporting from Northern Ireland.

(*b*) *Financial support*. Several governments have used their control over the licence fee as a lever with which to pressurise the BBC. Mrs Thatcher was known to favour the introduction of advertising to finance the BBC but the Peacock Commission on the financing of television refused to produce the hoped-for recommendation. Currently the government is trying to deregulate independent television, reduce the power of the IBA and sell off the regional franchises to the highest bidder. This, however, is more to do with Mrs Thatcher's free-market principles than any attempt to influence editorial control over news and current affairs programmes.

(*c*) *Opposition to particular programmes*. The BBC has come in for much criticism, especially in relation to programmes concerned with defence, the security services and Northern Ireland. During the Falklands War some Conservative MPs actually accused the BBC of 'treason' because their reports of the action were couched in objective rather than committed or patriotic terms. The Corporation fought its corner on this and other programmes like the *Real Lives* series on Northern Ireland in 1985 but was forced to give substantial ground; the sacking of Alasdair Milne over the Zircon Satellite programme in 1987 badly hit morale in the Corporation. Independent television companies have also come under intense pressure. The government did its best to prevent the broadcasting of Thames Television's *Death on the Rock* in 1989 which suggested that the SAS shooting of three IRA terrorists in Gibraltar was part of a shoot-to-kill policy. The IBA resisted the onslaught and the programme was shown. The government was doubly furious when an enquiry headed by Lord Windlesham, an ex-Conservative minister, completely exonerated the programme and the reporting techniques employed.

(*d*) *Political campaigns*. In 1986 a monitoring unit was set up in Conservative Central Office and in the summer of that year a critical report of the BBC's coverage of the American bombing of Libya was published, together with verbal onslaughts from the then Conservative Party Chairman, Norman Tebbit. BBC executives complained of 'intimidation' in the run-up to the election and despite their claims to the contrary, they were almost certainly affected by the pressure. In January 1990 another Conservative Party campaign became evident when the early morning *Today* radio programme was accused of giving Conservative ministers the third degree whilst Labour spokesmen were subjected to much milder inquisitions. The presenters denied any bias and pointed out that the party which actually disposes of power, the government of the day, will naturally attract the toughest questioning from any medium which is truly independent.

Do the media favour the left or the right in British politics?

As we have seen, Conservative politicians and commentators perceive the BBC as a stronghold of left-wing and post-war consensus points of view. They point out that the present generation of senior management began their careers within the BBC during the radical 1960s and cite any number of news, current affairs and radical dramatic productions in support of their case. Indeed amongst Conservative MPs a belief in the left-wing bias of the BBC has become virtually a litmus test of Thatcherite orthodoxy. The left can mount a powerful rebuttal. Indeed, the case that the press has a rightwing bias is virtually undefended, but the issue of bias amongst broadcasters is more controversial. Bryan Gould argues that 'Everything is referred to a presumed standard of normality and therefore anybody who is outside the mainstream, who takes a different view, who is a bit radical, inevitably looks on television or radio to be something of an eccentric or a maverick.' This tendency to marginalise left-wing points of view, in Gould's opinion, is 'not their fault, it is just intrinsic to the way that they operate' (interview on Tyne Tees TV, April 1986). The Glasgow University Media Group, however, in a book called *Bad News* (Routledge, 1976) and successive volumes, argue that in some areas, especially the reporting of industrial relations, television producers reflect a right-wing bias: as members of the upper middle class they have a vested interest in presenting working-class arguments in an unfavourable light.

Marxist critics go a step further. They argue that the media is just one element in the complex web of mystification which the ruling economic group in society utilises to buttress their position. Just as the educational system, Parliament and the government bureaucracy implicitly transmit dominant values, so also do the media.

Which argument is more persuasive? At the party political level there may well be something in the case for the BBC as a repository of consensual views but when they are not being paranoid, party politicians are often playing a shrewd political game in which they believe advantage can accrue from attacks upon the media. The Marxist critique is more difficult to answer, but whilst it may contain elements of truth British broadcasters are surely not the supine instruments of capitalist propaganda. Recent history reveals that they jealously guard their independence and successfully resist a great deal of pressure to conform from politicians of all persuasions.

Further reading

M. Cockerell, *Live from No. 10*, Faber & Faber, 1988.

J. Curran and J. Seaton, *Power Without Responsibility: The Press and Broadcasting*, Routledge, 1988.

Glasgow University Media Group, *Bad News* (1976), *More Bad News* (1980), both Routledge.

Martin Harrison, *TV News: Whose Bias?* Hermitage Policy Journals, 1985.

Ralph Negrine, *Politics and the Mass Media in Britain*, Routledge, 1989.

Colin Seymore-Ure, *The Political Impact of the Mass Media*, Constable, 1974.

John Whale, *The Politics of the Mass Media*, Fontana, 1978.

Questions

1. Do you think that the impact of media advisers and 'charm schools' have enabled politicians to mislead the public as to their true natures?

2. Assess the impact of televising the House of Commons.

3. Do you think the impact of television has overall been beneficial for democratic government?

11

THE MONARCHY AND THE HOUSE OF LORDS

This chapter deals with the 'dignified' parts of the political system, i.e. those which outwardly look the most impressive but in reality have least effect. Arguments for and against each of these ancient institutions are considered, together with the recent renaissance in the power of the House of Lords.

The development of a constitutional monarchy

Over a thousand years ago the king's right to rule was absolute; he dominated all the functions of government. Parliament existed to advise, endorse and provide revenue for the king's needs. But as his needs became greater Parliament began to sell its support more dearly. A great struggle for power ensued between king and Parliament which only a civil war could resolve. Finally the 1832 Reform Act gave the electorate the ultimate deciding power, and the king was now forced to act, in accordance with the developing party system, upon the advice of Ministers commanding a majority in Parliament. By Queen Victoria's time the monarchy had been gently eased into a position which had dignity and occasional influence but no power.

Republican sentiment has never reached the heights of Cromwell's day, but criticisms of the monarchy are raised from time to time.

Arguments against the monarchy

1. Heads of state should be elected. Inherited titles, it is argued, cannot be justified in a democratic age. In most other developed countries heads of state are popularly elected.

2. It reinforces conservative values. The monarchy is not non-political in that it reinforces conservative values like inherited privilege and wealth, deference to social status and tradition, and support for the status quo. The Queen may be non-partisan but her influence and advice are bound to reinforce the values which sustain the position of the traditional ruling elite.

3. It is expensive. The Queen used to receive an annual grant of nearly £6 million – the Civil List – to meet the expenses of the nearly 400-strong royal household.

In July 1990 a new arrangement was introduced whereby the Queen receives an agreed sum over a ten-year period with more money being made available in the early years (£7.9 million in 1991–92). Similar arrangements were made for other members of the Royal Family.

Critics argue that the State should not have to pay the Queen's personal expenses, let alone those of Royal 'hangers-on', when the Queen is the richest woman in the world. The *Sunday Times* (8 April 1990) calculated her personal fortune at £6.7 billion: £3.0 billion from art treasures; £2.4 billion from stocks and shares and £1.2 billion from property.

4. The absurdity of the honours system. The Queen is the cornerstone of what is often called an absurd system of elevating some men and women above their fellows. Mainly on advice from the Prime Minister, the Queen dispenses honours such as peerages, knighthoods and sundry medals.

5. Its functions are meaningless. In theory there are many things the Queen can do without consulting Parliament – declare war, conclude treaties, grant pardons – but in practice these powers do not exist. Moreover, it is argued, most of the other functions are meaningless:

(*a*) The Queen's annual opening of Parliament is a time-wasting ceremonial; even her opening speech is written by the Prime Minister.

(*b*) In theory the Queen can select her own Prime Minister, but in practice she always chooses the leader of the majority party (coalition politics could change this).

(*c*) The Queen has a large number of appointments at her

disposal – Ministers, Permanent Secretaries, bishops, Lords of Appeal, the Governors of the BBC – but in practice they are prime-ministerial nominations usually arrived at through some measure of consultation with the bodies concerned.

(*d*) The Queen can refuse to sign Acts of Parliament, but for some 200 years no monarch has seriously attempted even to delay legislation.

6. *The royal prerogative has been usurped by the executive* in virtually every respect. Whilst Parliament can influence Ministers, anything done in the name of the Crown is immune from democratic parliamentary control, nor can it be challenged in the courts. Thus, for instance, NHS hospitals are run by the State (in theory by the Crown) so they cannot be prosecuted if their kitchens are a health hazard. Tony Benn has long campaigned against the government's usurpation of the Royal Prerogative and for greater accountability to the Commons.

Arguments for the monarchy

1. *A unifying influence above party*. Elected heads of state usually have a party colour, whilst the Queen is a permanent, non-partisan symbol of national unity. The British system also offers an advantage over the US system, where the President has to combine onerous chief executive functions with time-consuming head of state duties; in 1980, for example, the Queen was able to perform no fewer than 325 engagements, including four overseas visists. She is a full-time head of state and is very experienced and skilled at her job.

2. *The Queen tenders non-partisan advice to the Prime Minister*. Bagehot wrote of the sovereign's 'right to be consulted, the right to encourage and the right to warn', and most Tuesday evenings the Queen discusses matters of state with the Prime Minister for over an hour. We are told she takes an active interest in Cabinet business, and perhaps her long experience of public affairs – she has advised eight Prime Ministers – proves of value. The Queen is scrupulously neutral in party political terms but occasionally she does hint at personal views, as in May 1977, when she inserted into a public speech some implied criticism of devolution proposals.

In June 1986 it was rumoured that the Queen disapproved of Mrs Thatcher's opposition to economic sanctions against South Africa.

3. *The ceremony of monarchy 'legitimises' government*. Some argue that the solemnity and symbolism of ceremony are essential ingredients in public life in that they strengthen awareness of national identity and respect for the authority of government. According to this view, most people are not so rational that they remain unmoved by the splendour and mystery of the monarchy.

4. *A touchstone of social behaviour*. The Queen's personal and family life are above reproach and, it is held, act as a model for the nation. She lends her moral weight to countless charities and good causes.

5. *The monarchy is popular*. Opinion polls regularly show high endorsement of the monarchy: the Jubilee celebrations in 1977 and the royal weddings in 1981 and 1986 gave spectacular evidence that support has never been higher.

6. *Head of the Commonwealth*. As a ceremonial head of the Commonwealth the Queen acts as a focus and a binding influence for this loose association of states. Her constant contacts with other heads of state must be of value to the government.

7. *The monarchy earns money*. Thousands of tourists are attracted to London by the pageantry and glitter of the monarchy, thus earning valuable foreign currency. In addition, the Queen makes superb 'public relations' visits abroad. Hundreds of thousands flock to see her, and business deals often follow in the wake of these visits.

8. *The monarchy is good value*. It may cost more than its equivalent in Holland or Scandinavia but the essence and appeal of the monarchy lie in its more 'splendid' nature. Even allowing for the extra costs, the social, political and economic benefits make it good value: after all, the NHS spent more on appetite suppressants alone in 1975 than the entire cost of the Civil List.

The public seem to agree: a Marplan poll (July 1981) showed that 76 per cent believed the advantages outweigh the cost. A Gallup poll in December 1988 also revealed high public endorsement for a number of important functions.

Table 1   *The importance of the monarchy, by function*

Function	% responses Importance				
	Very	*Quite*	*Not very*	*Not at all*	*Don't know*
Represent the UK at home and abroad	67	25	4	2	1
Set standards of citizenship and family life	59	26	8	4	3
Unite people despite differences	52	30	8	6	4
Ensure armed forces owe allegiance to the Crown rather than government	52	24	10	7	7
Maintain continuity of British traditions	51	34	9	3	2
Preserve a Christian morality	43	26	17	10	4

Source: *Daily Telegraph*, 28 December 1988.

The monarchy arouses powerful feelings. To John Cunningham (the *Guardian*, 2 August 1980) its expense characterises our 'muddle of sentiments, privilege and national inability to be rational about an embarrassing historical legacy'. To Enoch Powell the continued existence of a 'prescriptive, hereditary consecrated monarchy is the definite assertion of those supernatural elements ... which bind society together and endow it with a claim on the service and obedience of its members which transcends their individual lives and interests' (the *Guardian*, 27 July 1981). Whilst few would take such a mystrical view, most people enjoy the monarchy and believe it to be worthwhile.

The House of Lords

In 1407 Henry IV agreed that money grants were to be initiated in the Commons, but throughout the Middle Ages the House of Lords was able to use its influence to control the Commons through its widespread control over elections and nominations to Parliament. Relative harmony between the two Houses in the eighteenth century was shattered in 1832. The Great Reform Act ended the Lords' control over the Commons by extending the vote to the lower middle classes and removing the Lords' ability to nominate members. The Commons now came to represent wider interests than the landowners who sat in the Lords – the growth of the Liberal Party reflected the change – and these conflicting interests were manifested in a series of clashes between the Liberal-controlled House of Commons and the Conservative-dominated Lords.

In 1909 the Liberal Chancellor, David Lloyd George, introduced a budget which declared 'implacable warfare on poverty and squalor' via a package of tax increases. The Lords threw it out, 350 votes to 75. Two elections in 1910 reaffirmed the Liberal majority in the Commons and when the new King, George V, threatened to create sufficient non-Conservative peers to shift the balance of power in the Lords, the diehards caved in. The Parliament Act of 1911 reduced the Lords' power over legislation to one of delay only for a period of up to two years after the second reading of a bill. In 1949 Labour's Parliament Act halved the period to twelve months.

In 1958 the Life Peerages Act made it possible for men, and women for the first time, to be elevated to the peerage during their own lifetimes. The Peerage Act of 1963 made it possible for hereditary peers to give up their peerage and become eligible for the lower House. These two measures have helped transform the Lords: average attendance has doubled since the 1950s to about 300 a day, and average length of sittings has increased from three and a half to six and a half hours per day.

Harold Wilson stopped creating hereditary peers in 1964 but Mrs Thatcher renewed the practice after 1983, though on a limited scale – three so far. In November 1988 there were 784 hereditary peers, 353 life peers (by far the most active element in the Chamber), 24 bishops, 2 archbishops and 22 Law Lords. Total membership was 1,185 (of whom 65 were women) but when those who declared they wish to take no part in proceedings are excluded, the potential actual strength of the Lords is reduced to 932.

The political complexion of the Lords broke down as follows:

Table 2 *The House of Lords, by political allegiance*

		%
Conservative	538	45·4
Labour	117	9·9
Liberal	60	5·1
Social Democrat	25	2·1
Communist	1	0·1
Independents		
Crossbench	220	18·6
Non-party	54	4·5
Non-political affiliation	168	14·2
Total	1,185	100

These strengths, however, are very theoretical. Shell (1990) shows that whilst a majority of Labour, Liberal and Social Democrat peers attend at least one-third of sittings, the figure for Conservatives and crossbenchers is only 30–40 per cent. The government's Chief Whip in the Lords, Lord Denham, therefore cannot count on a majority when opposition peers unite with crossbenchers. Indeed whilst Mrs Thatcher's governments have suffered only three defeats in the Commons, she has sustained scores in the Lords (see below).

Arguments for and against the House of Lords

1. The hereditary principle
For. Enoch Powell defends the hereditary principle as no worse than any other method of appointment. John Stokes, Conservative MP, admires hereditary peers: 'their behaviour is impeccable. They are trained for the job from youth onwards and they are truly independent, being answerable to no constituents' (*Hansard*, 10 April 1981). Those of a practical rather than romantic frame of mind point out that the services of their lordships – hereditary and life peers – are given cheaply: they are not paid a salary but are entitled only to an attendance allowance of up to £64 (overnight) plus £25 per day secretarial expenses (1990 rates).

Against. It is argued that (*a*) *the hereditary principle is totally indefensible* in a democracy: legislators should be accountable to society as a whole. Hereditary peers in any case have a poor attendance record compared with life peers. (*b*) *It represents outdated values* like inequality, inherited privilege, wealth and the right to rule. No one would deny that the Lords is heavy with respect for tradition and the established way of doings things.

2. The constitutional function

For. The House of Lords still retains an absolute veto over any proposal to extend the lifetime of a Parliament beyond the present limit of five years. Supporters of the Lords argue that its powers of amendment and delay provide a useful check against ill thought-out or over-radical legislation, particularly when the government is elected with a thin or no overall majority. The 1949 Parliament Act has never been formally used to overrule delay by the Lords: in a dispute the Commons have usually reached a compromise with the upper chamber.

Against. It is argued that it is indefensible for a body of non-elected peers to frustrate the will of the elected chamber. Moreover the Conservatives have a permanent majority over Labour (though not overall) and if necessary can increase their number by summoning less regular attenders (or 'backwoodsmen'). This enables the Conservatives to delay and amend for party political reasons, particularly in the later years of a Labour Government.

3. Useful for the Prime Minister

For. The Lords provide a useful way for the Prime Minister to recruit Ministers direct without an election. In addition it is an honoured resting place for politicians who have retired or who need to be moved to one side.

Against. It is argued that Ministers should be accountable to the Commons and that the patronage of the Prime Minister is already dangerously excessive. Moreover the majority of life peers are past retirement age, and even the active members are elderly. It is not unusual to see their Lordships doze off in the somnolent atmosphere of the upper House: younger blood is needed to make it effective.

4. Deliberative function

For. The Lords represent a protean mix of wisdom and experience. Their thoughts upon certain public issues, unfettered by constituency or party pressures or the harsh timetable and restrictive procedures of the Commons, are often illuminating and occasionally provocative. Televising debates has generally been judged a success; about ⅓ million on average watch the daily 'highlights'.

Against this it is pointed out that, however excellent they may be, few bother to read reports of Lords debates; nor do viewing figures tell us how attentive the television audience is.

5. Legislative function

The Lords does not interfere with bills concerned primarily with finance (about one-quarter of all legislation) but it has a key role in other respects.

(*a*) *Non-controversial legislation*

For. By introducing non-controversial legislation, particularly in connection with local government, the Lords relieve the burden on the overworked Commons. About 40 per cent of all government legislation was introduced via the Lords during 1974–79.

Against. Sometimes controversial Bills are introduced in the Lords for tactical political reasons. In this way MPs were denied first consideration of sweeping proposals under Michael Heseltine's Local Government Planning Bill in 1980.

(*b*) *Revision and amendment*

For. The Lords revise and improve Bills on their way to the royal assent, and the government often uses this stage of the journey to introduce its own amendments and improvements. The Labour Party, which often has a 'large and contentious legislative programme, probably gains more than it loses from the second chamber in terms of valuable and relatively non-partisan scrutiny of its Bills, the anomalous composition of the House notwithstanding' (Drewry, in Walkland and Ryle, p. 106). During the 1987–88 session the Lords made amendments to legislation originating in the Commons all but one per cent of which were subsequently agreed by that body.

Against. It is sometimes argued that a reformed chamber would perform this task more effectively.

(*c*) *Select committee work*

For. It is often overlooked that the Lords has a European Communities Committee with a wider remit than its Commons equivalent. One hundred peers are involved in its six subcommittees. The Lords also set up a number of *ad hoc* committees on specific topics and take particular care to consult expert opinion.

Against. Once again, a reformed Chamber with younger members might perform these tasks more effectively.

6. The judicial function

For. The House acts as the highest court in the land, but this function is performed by the Law Lords, who include the Lord Chancellor, ex-Lord Chancellors, and Lords of Appeal in Ordinary (including those retired). They do not pass judgement but rather clarify the law and give their opinion upon appeals.

Against. Critics point out that this function could be performed by a separate institution completely unconnected with a second legislative chamber.

Concluding comment. Enoch Powell believes that the house of Lords is 'at worst a useful device' but one of its members, Lord Foot, is not convinced. 'It really can do very little. It performs a minor useful function of looking at matters in detail which the Commons has not got the time to do but that is no satisfactory bi-cameral system' (*Hansard*, 18 November 1980). Readers must make their own judgement but may find their views influenced by the way the Lords have reacted to the Conservative government, especially since 1983.

The Lords and Mrs Thatcher

Since 1979 the Lords have voted down Mrs Thatcher's legislation over 150 times. Government defeats themselves are not unknown: Mr Heath suffered twenty-six between 1970 and 1974, and Labour 355 between 1975 and 1979. What makes this state of affairs unusual, of course, is the preponderance of Conservatives in the Lords and the severity of some of the defeats. They have included the exclusion of special cases from the council tenants' right-to-buy scheme; the rescinding of transport charges for school-children in rural areas; and, most important, the reform of local government. On 28 June 1984 the Local Government (Interim Provisions) bill, designed to pave the way for the abolition of the GLC and the metropolitan counties, crashed to ignominious defeat in the Lords by 191 votes to 143. What their lordships could not accept was the proposal to abandon the May 1985 elections to those bodies a year *before* abolition had become law. The Conservative

Lord Alport described the Bill as 'morally, intellectually, politically and constitutionally indefensible ... a contempt for the tradition of local government in Britain'. The government was forced to *extend* the life of existing councils by a year instead of *nominating* interim successors. The Commons, of course, can reverse Lords' amendments and do so when the issue is deemed sufficiently important, for example in 1988, over proposed increases in dental charges and charges for eye tests.

This record suggests that the Lords − free of constituency and re-election pressures − do take their role seriously as guardians of the constitution. The huge Conservative majorities after the 1983 and 1987 elections gave added point to this concern that an 'elected dictatorship' should not 'railroad through any old measure which takes the fancy of the Prime Minister' (Beavan). Ironically the Lords have become, in some ways, more important as a counter to Mrs Thatcher's government than the opposition in the Commons. Interest groups have reacted accordingly. 'They have deluged individual Lords with immaculate scripts produced on word-processors, furnished them with draft amendments, telephoned them and lunched them, though, before, they never thought them worth a cup of tea' (Beavan).

Reform or abolition?

Since the 1950s, the Lords has undergone something of a rennaissance. The injection of life peers into the work of the upper house has transformed its work rate so that: 525 peers spoke at least once in the 1985−86 session compared with 283 in 1957−58; 631 questions were placed for oral answer compared with 184; 1,182 questions were placed for written answer instead of 48; 250 divisions were called instead of 19; the House sat for 1,213 hours instead of 450 and average daily attendance was 317 instead of 136. In June 1990 the Lords roused itself to reject emphatically the Nazi War Crimes Bill (to facilitate the prosecution of war criminals living in Britain) after the Commons had passed it equally emphatically on a free vote. In spite of this vigour, or in some cases because of it, many people agree that the Chamber should not remain as it is.

Opinion, however, is divided. Some want to abolish it and end for good its ability to interfere with the decisions of the Commons. Others believe the functions at present ill performed by the

Lords are of crucial importance and would be done better by a reformed chamber.

The Labour Party and the Lords have had a long and difficult relationship. In 1918 Conference resolved to abolish the second chamber and Labour's 1935 election manifesto promised to carry this into effect. In power after 1945, however, Labour found legislative revision in the Lords valuable and its 1949 Parliament Act was only a mild reform. In fact Labour politicians have always willingly sat in the Lords and taken part − though when Ramsay MacDonald offered him a peerage R. H. Tawney replied, 'What harm have I ever done the Labour Party?' Richard Crossman's 1969 proposals were embodied in the Wilson government's Parliament (No.2) Bill, but an 'unholy alliance' between the Labour left (led by Michael Foot), who feared a strengthened chamber, and the Conservative right (led by Enoch Powell), who opposed the direction of the changes proposed, led to the withdrawal of the Bill.

In 1976 Labour's difficulties over the Lords reached a new climax. Denis Skinner's Bill for abolition was defeated 168−153 in the Commons, but the party conference in 1977 voted overwhelmingly for it. During question time on 3 August 1978 Mr Callaghan denounced the unelected Lords as having no legitimate authority but it was he who insisted that a commitment to abolition be withdrawn from Labour's 1979 election manifesto. Reaction within the party helped strengthen the left, and at the 1980 conference Tony Benn urged immediate abolition by a new Labour government even if it meant creating a thousand Labour peers to vote for their own extinction.

According to the eminent lawyer Lord Denning, in his 1980 Dimbleby lecture, the Lords have a constitutional safeguard against such action. Whilst allowing that Parliament had the right to reform it, he doubted whether it could lawfully abolish the second chamber altogether, at least without a referendum. 'I would expect any such legislation to be challenged in the courts.' This view was strongly challenged by the law professor John Griffith, among others. A referendum might well vote to retain the Lords, if an NOP poll in November 1980 is any indication. Only 16 per cent of respondents wanted abolition, and a majority wanted to retain the House, though over a third favoured reforms.

Notwithstanding, Labour's 1983 election manifesto contained a pledge to abolish the Lords. By 1987 this had been dropped, and in 1989 Labour's policy review proposed the establishment of a reformed upper chamber, probably called a Senate. Members would be elected to it possibly via a different system to election for the Commons. The role of the chamber would be to scrutinise legislation, especially that relating to the EC and to delay bills which altered citizens' fundamental rights for the lifetime of a Parliament. Whether Labour could push such reforms through is a moot point. Neil Kinnock has said it would be foolish to try during a first term of office for Labour. Changing constitutional arrangements is exceptionally time-consuming and a new Labour government might find it hard to find the necessary legislative time.

This impasse is not unfamiliar. The House of Lords is one of a series of structural political questions, like electoral reform or devolution, which are so contentious and divisive that they are left untouched. One of our fundamental political problems seems to be the system's inability to reform itself even when there is a strong consensus in favour. Because reform has implications for devolution and the voting system the upper House is likely to be with us in its present shape for some time. No one believes it to be particularly useful, relevant or efficient, but the truth is that attempts at change carry heavy short-term penalties. In Britain bad reasons can always be found to defend the status quo, and more than good reasons are needed to change it.

Further reading

A. Adonis, 'The House of Lords since 1945', *Contemporary Record*, Vol. 2, No. 3, 1988.

— *Parliament Today*, Manchester University Press, 1990.

John Beavan, 'At bay in the Lords', *Political Quarterly*, Autumn 1985, pp. 375–81.

Janet Morgan, *The House of Lords and the Labour Government, 1964–70*, Oxford University Press, 1975.

Donald Shell, 'The House of Lords', in D. Judge (ed.), *The Politics of Parliamentary Reform*, Heinemann, 1983.

— 'The evolving House of Lords', *Social Studies Review*, March 1990.

— *The House of Lords*, Philip Allan, 1988.

S. A. Walkland and M. Ryle (eds.), *The Commons Today*, Fontana, 1981.

Questions

1. Argue the case for abolition of the Lords.
2. Discuss Enoch Powell's view that the hereditary principle is no worse than any other method of appointment to a legislative chamber.
3. Construct your own plan for a reformed upper chamber.

12

THE HOUSE OF COMMONS

This chapter traces the decline in the power of the House over the last century and considers the substantial functions it retains, together with proposals for reform.

The development of the House of Commons

In theory Parliament, comprising the House of Lords and the monarchy as well as the House of Commons, is the ultimate source of power in British government. A majority vote in both Houses endorsed by the Queen's signature can make or change any law; there is no written constitution to place limits to this power (see Chapter 6).

It is often said that Britain has the 'Mother of Parliaments'; its history dates back to the Witan, the council of the Anglo-Saxon kings. Its subsequent history has been one of struggle against the power of the monarchy, with Parliament winning the battle by the eighteenth century, and struggle between the elected House of Commons and the hereditary House of Lords, with the former gaining dominance in the nineteenth century when a series of reform Acts increased the number of people with the right to vote.

The idea of 'representative government', as elaborated by J. S. Mill and others, replaced the notion of an inherited right to rule. According to this view, ultimate authority would rest with an educated public electing representatives who would control the process of government in the interests of society as a whole. In the mid-nineteenth century, with a small electorate, loose party discipline and MPs with private incomes who did not rely heavily upon party affiliation for re-election, theory accorded closely with reality. The House 'sacked Cabinets, it removed individual Ministers, it forced the government to disclose information, it set up select committees to carry out investigations and frame Bills and it rewrote government Bills on the floor of the House' (Mackintosh, p. 613).

The decline of the House of Commons

Since those days the power of the House has been lessened by:

1. Expansion of the electorate and growth of a disciplined party system. Political groupings in the House realised that the new mass electorate responded to a coherent programme and that co-ordinated voting enabled them to pursue such policies more effectively. Parliamentary government became party government. Typically, two large parties now competed for the popular vote, striving to achieve an overall majority of MPs which would enable them to govern for the maximum term. MPs ceased to play the same intermediary role: the executive bypassed Parliament and dealt more directly with the electorate. Opportunities for free debates virtually vanished as the timetable was geared to the achievement of manifesto programmes; the majority of amendments and even many private members' Bills could now succeed only with the support of government. The MP's role was now dominated by support for his own party and opposition to others. Debates ceased to unseat governments, and the real debates took place off stage in the meetings of the majority parliamentary party. Strict party discipline was enforced: MPs knew that without the party label their re-election would be virtually impossible.

2. Growth in the power of the Prime Minister. As the role of backbench MPs has diminished, ministerial office has become an even more fiercely sought-after prize. The Prime Minister has control over the hundred or so Cabinet and Junior Ministerial appointments that are made from within the majority party, and MPs are loath to jeopardise prime-ministerial favour by acting independently. There is some justification for Neil Kinnock's jibe that the House has become 'little more than an Edwardian fan club for the Prime Minister' (see Chapter 14).

3. Extension of government activities and growth of the bureaucracy. The numbers employed in the civil service have grown enormously as government responsibilities have expanded in scope and complexity: under 50,000 were employed at the turn of the century compared with some ⅔ million at present. The number of Ministers had only doubled during the same period, and the relatively temporary, part-time, amateur politicians have found it increasingly difficult to challenge or even critically assess the advice offered by their highly professional permanent civil servants. A growing volume of legislation, moreover, is now 'delegated'; Parliament agrees a framework and the often important details are worked out by civil servants.

4. Loss of control over finance. Historically the House controlled the purse strings of government, but this function has passed almost wholly into the hands of the executive. Even in the late nineteenth century debates on supply – which in theory consider proposed expenditure – had degenerated into party political exchanges over economic policy. The old Estimates Committee, set up in 1912 (and reformed in 1971) to scrutinise spending proposals more closely, never exerted more than a minimal check. For MPs to exert control over a sum representing about half the gross national product was difficult enough, but it became more so in 1961 when the government began to plan public spending five years in advance via the work of the Public Expenditure Scrutiny Committee (PESC). Parliament, in contrast, still strove to 'approve' expenditure on a twelve-month basis.

5. The growth of pressure-group influence. As government's powers and responsibilities have increased it has come to rely upon pressure (or 'interest') groups for advice, information and co-operation in its day-to-day running. Moreover new legislation is often formulated jointly by Ministers, civil servants and pressure group representatives before Parliament has any chance to see it. The capacity of MPs to challenge the corporate wisdom of this 'triumvirate' is limited.

6. The increasing influence of the media, particularly television, has distracted public attention from the floor of the House. In an hour-long interview with the Prime Minister broadcasters like Brian

Walden have more chance to probe and challenge than the elected chamber has in most weeks. (The televising of the Commons since November 1989 has helped redress the balance — see below.)

7. EC membership since 1972 has caused many decisions affecting the UK economy and way of life to be taken by Community institutions rather than the House of Commons.

8. Challenges to Parliament, such as the Clay Cross council's rebellion against the 1972 Housing Finance Act and the trade union refusal to accept the 1971 Industrial Relations Act, brought the authority of the elected chamber into question.

9. The referendum was used in 1975 by Harold Wilson as a device to counteract opposition in the House — mostly in his own party — to continued membership of the EC. The devolution referendums in 1978 were again an extra-parliamentary device, through, interestingly, this time used by MPs who wished to frustrate government legislation on devolved powers for Scotland and Wales.

Critique of the House

By the mid-1970s some commentators felt that the House had reached a nadir of impotence (e.g. see Walkland and Ryle, pp. 279–304); pushed offstage into a peripheral, almost ritual role, regarding the formulation of government policy, the control of public expenditure, the passing of legislation and informing the electorate about public affairs. According to this view the democratic chain of accountability from the electorate to the legislature to the executive and back again to the people had been hopelessly short-circuited. Instead of helpfully collaborating with the chamber to which they were accountable, Ministers, once appointed, behaved purely defensively, aided and abetted by civil servants and pressure-group representatives.

According to this view ready-made legislation is presented by Ministers for Parliament's formal imprimatur; opposition attempts to alter or amend are resisted as a matter of course, and any dissatisfaction within the government party is branded as disloyalty; debates have become a futile series of party political assertions and counter-assertions.

One study calculated that of the forty-eight government Bills passed in 1967–68 only 12 per cent were 'substantially amended' (Rush, p. 81). Professor John Griffith reported that during three sessions in the early seventies 99·9 per cent of government amendments to Bills were passed, whilst only 10 per cent of government backbench and 5 per cent of opposition amendments were approved. MPs allegedly responded by deserting debates after the opening speeches, and the public with low electoral turnouts and withdrawal of support from the two main parties. Having spent centuries winning its independent powers from an executive dominated by the king and the nobility, the House had meekly surrendered its powers to an executive controlled by its own representatives; governments had become in effect an 'elective dictatorship', in Hailsham's phrase. This is a powerful critique, but it oversimplifies and neglects the considerable functions which the House still performs.

Functions retained by the House

1. It sustains government. Its efficacy may have declined but it is still elections to the House that decide the political complexion of the government, and it is the majority party in the House that provides its publicly endorsed support. Ironically the mid-1970s critique was followed by a period when Labour's lack of an overall majority injected vigour and significance into the Commons' activities. Ultimately the House defeated the government in March 1979 on a vote of no confidence – the first time this had happened since 1841. True, it was due to an unusual distribution of seats and in the May 1979 general election the traditional pattern was reasserted, but MPs had proved that the way they vote can still defeat governments.

2. It sets limits to government action. It follows that when governments frame legislation they have to be aware of what is acceptable. Apparently loyal voting often masks bitter divisions within parties, and what the majority party will accept from its leaders sets the boundaries within which policy is made. Government whips play a crucial mediating role here in reconciling what the government wants with what the party will accept; the difficulty of their task is just one measure of democracy in the House.

Furthermore the prospect of a violent reaction from the Opposition, with associated delaying tactics, may also deter governments from taking certain decisions.

Finally, the government has to explain and defend its policies convincingly in the Commons; it cannot afford to lose the argument regularly or its credibility will be threatened and the morale of its supporters diminished. This was well illustrated by a comment in the (Conservative-supporting) *Daily Telegraph* on some lacklustre parliamentary performances by Transport Minister Cecil Parkinson in June 1990: 'It is dismaying to notice that Mr John Prescott, Labour's front bench spokesman, has sounded considerably more convincing than his government counterpart in his analysis of the transport issue this week.' The House's reaction does matter.

3. *As a 'sounding board of the nation'*. Some argue that the House is unfit for this task in that it is unrepresentative. Enoch Powell believes, however, that the House's good geographical representation is more important and that MPs in close contact with their constituencies can accurately reflect what the country is thinking. They can represent these views in a wide variety of ways: in major debates, on Ten-Minute Rule Bills, in emergency debates under Standing Order No.9, in adjournment debates, via private members' Bills and motions and through written and oral questions. They can also see Ministers privately, publicise their views in the media or demonstrate them through abstention or crossvoting in a division.

4. *Legislation*. Most legislation passes through Parliament as the government wishes but on a significant number of occasions MPs do rouse themselves to say emphatically, 'No.' The defeat of the Wilson government over House of Lords and trade union reform in 1969 is well known, but the Heath government suffered six defeats in 1970–74, and the Labour governments in 1974–79 no fewer than forty-two. Even Mrs Thatcher's large majority has not prevented Conservative backbenchers from rebelling on numerous occasions, over MPs' pay, proposed increases in parental contributions to student grants, and the Shops Bill, when they inflicted a humiliating defeat on the attempt to fulfil a manifesto commitment to Sunday opening.

Moreover the hurdles placed in the way of private members' legislation have not prevented a number of resourceful MPs from clearing them and contributing towards an important body of law, including divorce, homosexuality, capital punishment and the disabled (see Morris).

5. *Financial control*. Scrutiny of public expenditure was improved by the introduction in 1971 of an annual White Paper with an accompanying debate and by the replacement of the Estimates Committee by the strengthened Expenditure Committee: further reform of select committees took place in 1979 (see below). Whilst these innovations have increased the House's *influence* rather than its *control* over expenditure, far greater control is exerted over the taxation proposals in the Chancellor's budget speech. Often unpublicised, many concessions are made to special interests during the legislative stages of the Finance Bill.

6. *Recruitment and training of Ministers*. All Ministers must be Members of Parliament, and so service in either chamber is a form of apprenticeship for ministerial office. As the executive has become so powerful the recruitment and training of the hundred or so government Ministers and the smaller number of opposition Shadow spokesmen is one of the House's most important functions. MPs usually have to serve several years – making their mark in debates, select committees, etc. – before being rewarded with junior ministerial office. It is in the Commons that the ambitious MP still has to establish a reputation, e.g. Gordon Brown in debates against Chancellor Nigel Lawson in 1988–89. The skills of the parliamentary performer are not necessarily those of the able Minister, but the House can undoubtedly be a testing stage. Speakers must be in command of their subject and their audience and have a ready wit.

The House is also a socialising influence. It has a curious mixture of formality and informality – rather like the gentlemen's club it is often compared with. The dignity of the Speaker's procession at the start of the day's proceedings contrasts with noisy interruptions and occasional uproar during debates. Similarly, MPs who oppose each other bitterly in debate may be on first-name terms outside the chamber.

Whatever the differences, there is a strong sense of belonging which, in time, seems to affect even the most radical new members. After a few years this influence becomes as important, if not more so, than any previous background a member may have had.

7. Political education. Despite the encroachments of the media the House still plays an important role in political education. The various stages of debate — formal first reading, second reading debate, committee stage, report back, third reading debate and then a similar process in the Lords — provide opportunities for informing the public and for challenge and scrutiny. Ministers have to justify their actions on the floor of the House or in the standing committee rooms. Few people read the verbatim Hansard reports, but edited extracts appear in the quality press and on the radio. In addition much of the content of news stories and features draws upon the proceedings of Parliament, and the media seem almost lost when it is in recess. 'Parliament remains', according to David Wood (*The Times*, 7 August 1980), 'the great democratic educator, the sounding board without compare.'

8. Private grievances. Each of the 650 MPs represents a constituency — usually around 60,000 voters — and anyone may contact their MP. MPs can write to government Departments to seek explanations, lobby Ministers or meet them on their constituents's behalf, put own questions for a written or oral answer, or raise the topic on a motion for the adjournment (i.e. instituting a half-hour debate at 10.00 p.m.). If the issue relates to maladministration by a government Department for which a Minister is directly responsible, an MP may refer it to the Parliamentary Commissioner for Administration, or 'Ombudsman', as he is popularly called (see Chapter 13).

9. The House 'legitimises' political decisions. All societies seem to adopt some formal procedures for publicly endorsing government decisions. The House is particularly appropriate for this function in that its ancient traditions and esoteric procedures lend it a special mystique. Supporters of Parliament claim that this helps to reinforce consensus in society, whilst the left argue that it can serve to cloak inequalities and injustices.

10. Scrutiny of the executive. In addition to debates MPs can challenge Ministers via:

(a) Question time. From Monday to Friday between 2.35 and 3.30 p.m. MPs can receive oral answers from Ministers to questions submitted in advance. On Tuesday and Thursday the Prime Minister answers questions, and her brushes with the leader of the Opposition have become one of the highlights of the House. MPs are allowed one supplementary question, and, with skill, an MP may catch a Minister out, though this is rare. Usually Ministers are briefed so effectively by civil servants that they are able to take on all comers with confidence.

(b) Party committees. All parties have a wide range of committees, for the most part shadowing government Departments. they are frequently addressed by Ministers, and backbenchers have considerable chances to challenge and influence. Similar opportunities arise during the twice-weekly party meetings.

(c) Select committees, as opposed to standing committees, which scrutinise legislation during its committee stage, usually have an investigative remit into a particular area of government, with power to collect evidence and summon witnesses. About a third of all MPs are involved in them.

The most powerful is the Public Accounts Committee. Its task is to ensure that government funds have been properly spent and its existence is thought to deter inefficiency or malpractice by civil servants (see below). Of the other three dozen or so committees, some relate to internal or procedural matters, but since 1978 most of the remainder now either concentrate on a particular function or department of governmenet (see below).

The power of the Commons. If power has shifted away from the House over the last century it does not mean that no power, influence or worthwhile role remains. The House is far from being a rubber stamp, and indeed underwent something of a renaissance in the late 1970s.

Assessment of this changed role depends very much upon the balance thought desirable between the legislature and the executive. If one takes a minimalist view of Parliament as a forum for public debate on the activities of government, with the power to influence occasionally when it thinks fit – a passive watchdog – then its present functions fulfil or even exceed the requirements; if it is expected to perform an active interventionist role, then it will still be found wanting. Those who support the former view argue that the functions of government in running a complex, changing technological society whilst performing a wide range of welfare roles have properly placed more power in the hands of Ministers supported by expert advisors. The government, according to this view, must be allowed to govern, and the House should recognise that it best serves the public when it occupies a responsible, supporting, watchful but essentially secondary role.

However there are those who, whilst accepting that the House can never regain its former eminence, have argued strongly that the balance has shifted too far in the direction of the executive and that the House needs to be strengthened to ensure that the nation's elected representatives have a greater say in executive decisions and that government is more answerable to them.

Reform of the Commons

The movement for reform gained momentum in the 1960s, when a number of academics — Crick, Hanson, Wiseman and Mackintosh — adopted it and wrote widely upon it. In the House, Richard Crossman carried the banner for Labour and Norman St John Stevas for the Conservatives. Throughout its history, however, the movement has been vitiated by a number of fundamental contradictions.

1. There is a tacit agreement between the government and ambitious MPs who, whilst wishing to assert the power of Parliament, do not want to limit their own freedom when they themselves become Ministers.

2. The champions of parliamentary power are split between those who favour the growth of small specialist committees and those who resist this tendency as a distraction from the floor of the House, where, it is maintained, the great issues should be publicly debated.

3. Proposals for reform generate great dissent and absorb valuable legislative time. In the 1960s and 1970s, House of Lords reform and devolution both obsessed Parliament for ages and both ultimately failed.

4. Reformers often support conflicting aims. Walkland points out (p. 285) that Labour reformers have tended to favour strong executive government to achieve socialist objectives while urging that Parliament be strengthened. They cannot have it both ways, e.g. in the late 1970s the House's enhanced effectiveness was won at the expense of the Callaghan government's authority.

Recent reforms. In 1978 the Select Committee on Procedure reported that the relationship between the House and the government 'is now weighted in favour of the government to a degree which arouses widespread anxiety and is inimical to the proper working of our parliamentary democracy'. The report signalled a sea change in the attitudes of MPs. Party politicians they may all be, but there is also a collective sense in which they are all legislators and share a concern that Parliament should be more than a rubber stamp to executive action. A number of reforms have followed this watershed report (see Norton's *Teaching Politics* article for an excellent summary).

Two minor reforms recommended in the report were adopted in 1980: Friday sittings now begin at 9.30 a.m. instead of 11.00 a.m., and in an attempt to curb garrulity the Speaker was empowered to set a ten-minute limit on speeches during second-reading debates from 7.00 p.m. to 9.00 p.m. Other reforms since 1978 have included:

1. *House of Commons Commission*. Set up in 1978, this body gave the House a greater measure of political and financial control over its own administration and personnel appointments. The Speaker is its *ex-officio* chairman, and it comprises the Leader of the House plus three backbench MPs.

2. *The Public Accounts Commission and the National Audit Office*. These two bodies were set up as a result of a private member's Bill steered through by Norman St John Stevas in 1983. The NAO was established to replace the Exchequer and Audit department of the Comptroller and Auditor-General: the agency entrusted with the task of ensuring the government has spent its money properly and effectively. Now the C and A-G operates independently of Treasury control, and on the basis of statutory authority, not convention, as hitherto. The Public Accounts Commission (PAC) was also established as an independent body to help supervise the NAO. It comprises the chairman of the PAC, the Leader of the House and seven – usually senior – backbenchers.

3. *Special standing committees.* In 1980 the House agreed to a new type of standing committee — the *ad hoc* groupings of MPs which scrutinise Bills in detail during the committee stage — whereby four 2½-hour hearings could precede normal business so that evidence could be taken and witnesses heard. Only five committees became 'special' in the years up to 1983, but in the event they were generally regarded as a successful experiment.

4. *Estimates days.* In July 1983 it was agreed that three days would be allocated each session for the debate of specific items of proposed expenditure (estimates) to be chosen by the Liaison Committee (comprising chairman of select committees).

5. *Opposition days.* Traditionally twenty-nine Supply days were made available each session for debates on topics to be chosen by the leader of the Opposition. However, several of these days were always taken up by regular subjects like the armed forces, Europe, etc. In 1981 the regular topics were accordingly allocated to government time and the Supply days reduced to nineteen. In May 1985, the number was increased to twenty, but three were now placed at the disposal of the leader of the second largest opposition party — at that time the Liberals.

6. *Televising the House of Commons.* In 1966 the proposal that the House of Commons be televised was heavily defeated chiefly on the grounds that such an intrusion would rob the House of its distinctive atmosphere. Successive votes in the 70s sustained this position. In the 80s Mrs Thatcher's opposition helped tip the balance against the cameras until November 1989, when the House finally bowed to the inevitable. Contrary to dire predictions, the world did not end and a limited experiment will now continue as established practice. Severe restrictions on what the camera could show were relaxed somewhat as early as February 1990. The Labour Party had hoped the cameras would show them to advantage, but initial surveys showed Mrs Thatcher (despite her nervousness at the prospect) outpointing Mr Kinnock. A Leeds University study, moreover, revealed that Conservative MPs received 50 per cent more of broadcast time than opposition parties; researchers pointed out that this merely reflected party strengths in the Chamber.

The biggest hit of the televised proceedings has been the twice-weekly clash between Thatcher and Kinnock at Prime Minister's Question Time. Some MPs have complained, however, that

Conservative whips have been increasing the number of 'planted' friendly questions to which Mrs Thatcher has been able to provide virtually scripted answers. Only 150,000 people watch the summarised highlights at 8.15 a.m. on BBC, but ¼ million tune in to Channel 4's afternoon programme. Much more important, however, are the extensive excerpts used in the major news bulletins which are watched by up to 20 million people each day. Despite the politicking for good exposure, few have suggested that the House's distinctive character has been seriously affected by the televising process.

7. *Select committees*. This reform, set in train by the 1978 report, has been the most significant and far-reaching. Previously, select committees – charged with investigating areas of government activity of their own choice – had been regarded lightly for the most part, and their reports were regularly ignored by other MPs, press and government alike. The new broom in 1979 abolished most of the old committees and fourteen new ones were established – for Agriculture, Defence, Education, Employment, Energy, the Environment, Foreign Affairs, Home Affairs, Trade and Industry, Social Services, Transport, Treasury and Civil Service, Welsh and Scottish Affairs. All have eleven members, except the last, which has thirteen; 156 MPs in all. Since 1979 the committees have been busy, producing over 350 reports on a whole range of topics – some of them very broad, like the Treasury Committee enquiries into economic policy, and others more specific, like the Home Affairs report, which prompted the abolition of the 'sus.' law.

Opponents of the new system argue that:

(*a*) It has further diverted attention from the floor of the House, contributing to sparse attendances.

(*b*) MPs are being choked with information.

(*c*) It imposes strain upon civil servants and Ministers.

(*d*) Committees concentrate upon neutral consensus topics and deflect MPs from winning the really important debates in the House and the country.

(*e*) Many of the committee reports are still ignored, and real legislative power is still controlled by party whips and leaders.

(*f*) Members fail regularly to attend meetings and others ask ill-informed questions.

Supporters reply that:

(*a*) The committees have achieved some real successes, e.g. the repeal of the 'sus.' law.

(*b*) They have extracted much more information from government departments than would otherwise have been divulged.

(*c*) Ministers and civil servants have been forced to defend their policies before skilled and informed questioning and have consequently become more accountable. Before the reform Ministers frequently ignored committee requests to give evidence with impunity: now they usually comply.

(*d*) The widespread publicity which their reports receive help inform the public and influence the climate of opinion.

(*e*) Chairmen of committees have enhanced their authority and stature: MPs have been given an additional way of acquiring expertise and proving themselves.

(*f*) MPs have been encouraged to find common cause as legislators and cross the often artificial party lines on specific issues.

(*g*) The televising of the Commons has won a national audience for Select Committee work.

It is true that select committees do not command legislative power but they have done a great deal to redress the imbalance of power in relation to government. In the wake of the Westland crisis the Defence Committee held the limelight for some time, especially when it probed the facts surrounding the famous leak of the Solicitor General's letter, but the limitations of select committee power were also revealed. Mrs Thatcher refused permission for two of her key aides to testify, and in their evidence Sir Robert Armstrong (Secretary to the Cabinet) and Leon Brittan (former Industry Secretary) were shamelessly evasive or unforthcoming. The government's response to the committee's scathing July 1986 report was to rule the questioning of civil servants out of order in future. However, the report *was* debated in the House, and the Liaison Committee gained government recognition that Westland was 'an aberration'. Business has proceeded more or less as normal.

As the work of the select committees has become more important, leaks of papers and conclusions have proliferated. Calls have also grown for better professional support. In May 1990 the Social Services Committee scored a direct hit by revealing that government statistics had been wildly overestimating the extent to which poor people's standard of living had improved during the early 1980s. They were able to do so through a commissioned report by the Institute for Fiscal Studies.

Further reforms

1. *Devolution* advocates urge greater autonomy for Scotland, Wales and the English regions to assuage local feeling and take some of the pressure off the House, which sits twice as long as any other legislature in the world. However, Labour's ill-fated attempt to set up regional Assemblies in Scotland and Wales, and the part the issue played in the fall of the Callaghan government, are likely to deter action in this direction for some time.

2. *Proportional representation* would enable small parties with thin national support to gain representation in Parliament which reflected their support. The big parties jealously guard the simple-majority system, which benefits them, but growing minorities now favour change.

3. *Full-time members*. Many MPs carry on their parliamentary duties without giving up their normal jobs, and in consequence less than half could be called full-time members. Labour MPs tend to favour measures which would discourage a second occupation, e.g. morning sittings, but others, like the Conservative Sir David Renton, are opposed to MPs being full-time, which would tend to produce 'an inward-looking ... and rather narrow-minded Parliament. It is far better that we keep our contacts with life.' The marked tendency of certain (mostly Conservative) MPs to accept outside consultancies which could influence their role as MPs has intensified calls for stricter controls over such activities.

4. *MPs' pay and facilities*. At 1 January 1990 MPs received £26,701 per year plus up to £24,903 Office Costs Allowance. Some MPs claim this is not enough if they are to do their job properly, and cite West German and Japanese MPs who receive twice their incomes. But judged by market forces, they arguably receive too much: after all, scores of applicants compete for every nomination!

5. *Labour's Reform Package*. In 1989 Labour issued its proposals on reforming the Commons: review the use of the Royal Prerogative to increase the accountability of government to Parliament; a Freedom of Information Act to improve the ability of MPs to question government policy; a reduction in the obscurity

of Commons' language and procedures; the introdcution of new Legislative Committees which would take expert advice; the extension of the remit and powers of Select Committees and the provision of more professional support; the transfer of certain appointments from No. 10 to the Commons; the improvement of pay and conditions; and the introduction of measures to encourage more women to stand for the House.

In July 1990 a PLP review group recommended that the Commons should start three hours earlier at 11.30 a.m. and finish at 7.00 p.m. instead of 10.00 p.m. as at present.

6. *Charter 88* represents a movement in favour of structural change in British politics. Its 18,000 signatories (as of June 1990) call for sweeping reforms like PR and the placing of the executive 'under the power of a democratically renewed Parliament'. Many of its supporters would agree with Ewing and Gearty that

> The structure of government has stood still, but about it all has changed. Because of this failure to develop, the great debate about Liberty and the control of power in the technological age, which we see in other western nations, is passing the country by, almost unnoticed. The result is that, in international terms, where once it was a paradigm, Britain is little more than a jaded footnote.

Further reading

A. Adonis, *Parliament Today*, Manchester University Press, 1990.

K. D. Ewing and C. A. Gearty, *Freedom under Thatcher: Civil Liberties in Modern Britain*, Oxford University Press, 1990.

Bill Jones, 'Select committees and the floor of the House. Du Cann v. Kilroy Silk', *Teaching Politics*, September 1982.

Labour Party, *Meet the Challenge, Make the Change*, 1989.

John P. Mackintosh, *The British Cabinet*, Hutchinson, 2nd edn 1977.

— *The Government and Politics of Britain*, Hutchinson, 4th edn 1977.

Alf Morris, 'The Chronically sick and Disabled Act', *Teaching Politics*, September 1981.

Philip Norton, *The Commons in Perspective*, Martin Robertson, 1981.

— *Teaching Politics*, January 1986.

Enoch Powell, 'Parliament and the question of reform', *Teaching Politics*, May 1982.

Michael Rush, *Parliament and the Public*, Longman, 1976.

S. A. Walkland and M. Ryle (eds.), *The Commons Today*, Fontana, 1981.

Questions

1. 'In the House you can say what you like but you do as you are told.' Is this a fair description of democracy in the House of Commons?

2. Can a socially unrepresentative House still be a democratic one?

3. 'Parliamentary government in Britain was designed for the nineteenth century and is wholly inappropriate to the twentieth.' Discuss.

4. Comment on Labour's prescription for a reformed House of Commons.

13

THE REDRESS OF CITIZENS' GRIEVANCES

The citizen has many opportunities to try and influence the government, e.g. by voting, joining a pressure group, writing to his MP, and so on. Indeed, the opportunity to choose the government (via elections), and to influence it, is an essential feature of a democratic system.

But what protection does the citizen have against the government, civil servants or the activities of other groups? Another feature of a liberal democracy is that there are limits on what a government or a majority of the population can do, and rights or liberties are guaranteed for individuals and groups. In contrast, there are no formal limits on what a totalitarian government may do.

Some countries with written constitutions (e.g. the USA, France) give citizens formal guarantees of freedoms – from arbitrary arrest, the right of free speech, the right to a free trial, etc. Such a Bill of Rights is often part of a larger constitutional settlement.

There is no such settlement in Britain, and the Bill of Rights, dating from the seventeenth century, deals largely with the rights of Parliament against the monarch. At the time it was a far-reaching check on the monarchy or executive. For example, it declared that in peacetime an army could be raised only with the consent of Parliament. In Britain we rely on the rule of law, or the rights enshrined in common law and upheld over time by judges, and the general culture or climate or public opinion. If there are few guaranteed rights for individuals, there is a general freedom to do as one wishes, as long as it does not transgress the law or interfere with the rights of others. Many of our freedoms (speech, organisation, demonstration, etc.) exist as long as, and to the extent that, they do no infringe the law. No particular freedom is absolute, because if it is pushed to the limit it may limit the freedom of others.

Freedom of speech is limited by laws against defamation, obscenity and slander.

Protections for the citizen

There are many ways in which the citizen may be protected against the exercise of arbitrary power by the government and other public authorities, and his freedoms maintained. They include:

1. The rule of law. The basic idea of this concept is that governors as well as the governed should be subject to clear and promulgated law, and that government cannot act in an arbitrary manner. Its most famous exponent was the nineteenth-century constitutional lawyer, A. V. Dicey. He suggested that the English constitution rested on three major principles which amounted to a 'rule of law'.

(*a*) The equality of all before the law, with disputes decided in ordinary courts.

(*d*) No man is punishable except in the case of a distinct breach of the law. No one is above the law.

(*c*) The laws of the constitution, especially the liberties of the individual, are the result of judicial decisions. The rights of the individual do not derive from the constitution but precede it, and are backed by the law.

He claimed that this rule dominated the constitution in the sense that the principles were the result of judicial decisions made under common law. In other countries these rights were granted by the written constitution and could be withdrawn.

But Dicey's formulation is now widely criticised. First, it is hardly compatible with the sovereignty of Parliament, which means, as some observers have noted, that it is unchecked (see below). Parliament may choose to give the government arbitrary powers, as in wartime or in Northern Ireland today. Many public authorities (e.g. Ministers and the police) have special powers, and trade unions enjoy special immunities, e.g. from claims for damages by firms or other groups due to breach of a contract while acting in 'furtherance of trade dispute'.

So Dicey's principles may be important as ideals rather than a guide to actual practice. And the courts may bring the executive to order, as in the Tameside case in 1976 (see Chapter 6), or when it allowed Freddie Laker to fly his Skytrain, so overturning a decision of the Minister.

2. *Questions in the Commons* or approaches by an MP to the Minister concerned. The Minister (according to the convention of Ministerial responsibility) is accountable for the actions of his civil servants. But with the growth in the activity of the State, and the number of civil servants, many doubt the efficacy of this procedure today.

3. *Appeal to the Ombudsman*. The Parliamentary Commissioner for Administration (1967) was modelled on Scandinavian practice. He deals with private citizens' complaints that the authorities have not carried out the law or have not observed proper standards of conduct, e.g. in income tax assessment or the conduct of an eleven-plus examination. Examples of maladministration would include such features as bias, delay and arbitrariness in making a decision. Initially the complaint must be channelled through an MP. Many of the complaints the Ombudsman receives prove to be outside his terms of reference, e.g. about the police, local authorities, or the Health Service, all of which have their own complaints procedures. (Indeed, the last two and Northern Ireland have their own Ombudsman.) In investigating a complaint the Commissioner is empowered to call for the relevant files of the Department concerned. If he finds a case of maladministration, the Department is invited to rectify it. (A successful case was the Sachsenhausen claim, in which the Foreign Office belatedly agreed to pay compensation to former inmates of that prison camp.) If the Department refuses, then the PCA lays a report before Parliament and a select committee will consider the case. Of some 300 cases the PCA actually deals with each year, he usually finds some maladministration in about 10 per cent.

Some critics have complained about the narrowness of his remit; they say it is too concerned with maladministration, i.e. failure to follow the established procedures and rules. Critics want him to comment on the rules and policies themselves if he thinks they work unfairly, and apart from dealing with procedural errors he should deal with cases of unfairness. In Sweden and New Zealand the Ombudsman has broader scope. To date, most holders of the office have been former civil servants. Critics allege that this limits the Commissioner's independence; defenders claim that personal experience of administration and of how the government machine works helps his judgement and ability to operate effectively.

4. *Administrative tribunals*. Breaches of civil rights can clearly be dealt with by the courts (see above). But in the twentieth century the growth in the size of government (e.g. regulations, laws and civil servants), its intervention in society and the economy, together with the proliferation of duties and rights among citizens, have led to problems. Many regulations and statutory instruments are left to civil servants to work out, applying administrative discretion to statutory instruments.

In the event there are many disputes: about planning permission for motorways and slum clearance, hospital treatment, the allocation of housing rents, dismissal from work, and entitlements to pension, unemployment and National Insurance benefits.

The ordinary courts would be overwhelmed if they had to decide on the details of all these cases. Adjudication of queries and complaints is therefore left to the appropraite administrative tribunals, e.g. on Supplementary Benefits, or Commissioners of the Inland Revenue on tax matters, or local valuation courts on rates queries. Members of tribunals are appointed by the appropriate Minister, and he usually accepts their advice. But critics say that this form of appeal still falls short of providing an effective check on the civil servants' possible abuse of their discretion.

Rights

These include, for example:

1. *Freedom of meeting*, subject to laws on obstruction, nuisance and trespass.

2. *Freedom from arbitrary arrest and imprisonment*. This includes such principles as a person's presumed innocence until he is proved guilty, the right to a fair trial, no detention without trial (i.e. a person has to be charged with a specific offence if he is to be detained and brought before a magistrate within twenty-four hours — but cf. IRA terrorists).

3. *Freedom of speech*, subject to laws on blasphemy and obscenity. A further limit has been imposed in the form of the Race Relations Act, which forbids statements to be made in public which are designed to stir up racial hatred.

4. *Freedom of conscience*, e.g. to practise religion, or exclusion from military service on grounds of conscientious objection.

The above are *civil* rights. In recent years Parliament has been active in promoting *social* rights, e.g. to work, against unfair dismissal from work, to abortion, and has also given some protection to women, consumers and racial minorities. But many rights are not absolute. They may conflict with other rights, e.g. the freedom to join a trade union versus the freedom not to be a member and retain one's employment (the 'closed shop' may be inconsistent with the latter), or the freedom of some strikers to picket in large numbers and the freedom of others to work. The police have had to face growing physical attacks and political criticisms for protecting the strike-breaking workers and meetings organised by the National Front. In the case of the latter, how does one strike a balance between the NF's freedom of speech (however objectionable the views) and the disorder and obstruction to which NF meetings invariably give rise?

Reform

A combination of such trends as (*a*) the growth of bureaucracy, (*b*) more interventionist government, (*c*) the subordinate role of the courts to Parliament and (*d*) the imbalance in the constitution, particularly the power of a party majority of the House of Commons (see Chapter 6), has led some to call for a Bill of Rights, or even a written constitution, to provide greater protection for the individual's rights.

Parliament may act in a liberal way and grant rights. Equally a parliamentary majority may pass illiberal laws against which there is no appeal. Lord Scarman, among others, has argued that reliance on the common law and the political culture is no longer adequate in the face of the above trends. In recent years there have been two blatant exceptions to the rule of law (see above).

In 1972, when a High Court decision left doubt about the

legality of the army's actions against civilians in Ulster, the Home Secretary introduced a Bill to legalise them retrospectively, and it became law the same day. The rule of law is clearly not in force in Ulster, e.g. the detention of IRA terrorists without trial, under the Northern Ireland Special Powers Act, 1972, or trial without jury.

In 1983 the government withdrew the right of workers at GCHQ, the military surveillance centre, to belong to a trade union. The decision was later upheld by the courts on the grounds that only government could decide whether national security was endangered. The case was considered by the European Court of Human Rights but was rejected.

There is some all-party support for a Bill of Rights (the Alliance officially supports it) and for the replacement of section 2 of the Official Secrets Act, so that there may be greater information about the work of central government. There is some support too for the incorporation into British law of the European Convention of Human Rights. The convention is enforced through the European Court of Human Rights, whose jurisdiction Britain recognises. To date, more appeals have been received, registered (i.e. regarded as suitable for the court) and upheld against Britain than against any other member state. About a quarter of all cases in which a breach of the convention was found involved Britain. The court, for example, has ruled against the use of torture in Northern Ireland, telephone tapping, and in favour of prisoners' rights to correspond in confidence with their lawyers.

However, the legislative sovereignty of Parliament and the inability of courts to set aside any move authorised by the government of the day 'make it difficult for the legal system to accommodate the concept of fundamental and inviolable human rights' (Scarman).

Further reading

J. Benyon (ed.), *Scarman and After*, Pergamon, 1984.

F. Ridley, 'British approaches to the redress of grievances', *Parliamentary Affairs*, 1984.

H. Street, *Freedom, the Individual and the Law*, Penguin, 1982.

Questions

1. Write a critical appraisal of the role performed by the Ombudsman in the political system.

2. Consider the arguments for and against a Bill of Rights.

3. Do you consider that opportunities for the redress of individual grievances are adequate?

14

THE ROLE OF THE PRIME MINISTER

Much, probably too much, of the analysis of the Premier's role has been devoted to his or her 'power', and whether it has grown to such an extent that we should now talk of 'prime-ministerial government' rather than Cabinet government. Critics of this development claim that it is unconstitutional and that the Cabinet is being bypassed.

In 1867 Walter Bagehot argued that effective power lay with the Prime Minister and the Cabinet. The Monarchy was only a 'dignified' part of the constitution, i.e. did not have effective power but only the appearance of it. During this century commentators have claimed the House of Lords and the House of Commons have joined the dignified part of the constitution. In the nineteenth century the theory was that the Prime Minister was first among equals in Cabinet. In the 1960s Richard Crossman and John Mackintosh (*The British Cabinet*, Stevens, 1962) claimed that we had also entered the era of prime-ministerial power and that the Cabinet had also been relegated to the dignified part of the constitution. More recently, Tony Benn has adduced similar arguments, describing the Prime Minister as a 'medieval monarch living in No.10'.

Power

Claims that we have moved into the era of Prime-ministerial dominance rest on a number of grounds: the Prime Minister is leader of the majority party and *de facto* head of the civil service; the media increasingly portray politics and elections in terms of personalities; and the Prime Minister is invariably a central figure in most of the major policy areas.

It could also be added that the sheer increase in the volume of work facing the Cabinet (the *overload* phenomenon) has limited the scope of collective discussion. The Cabinet only meets weekly, but decisions have to be taken all the time. Increasingly, matters are left to the Departments or to the Prime Minister, with the Cabinet less important as a decision-making body.

This line of argument has intensified under Mrs Thatcher's stewardship at No.10. She is seen, and to some extent has presented herself, as a figure apart from her Cabinet. Many of the resigning Ministers, notably Michael Heseltine, have complained that she has been dominant to the point of behaving unconstitutionally. Mrs Thatcher and a small group of Ministers allowed the American bombers to fly from British bases and bomb Libya, decided to purchase Trident and banned union membership at GCHQ. There was also little or no Cabinet discussion on economic policy in the first years of the Thatcher governments. Other indicators, according to Peter Hennessy, of the declining role of the Cabinet under Mrs Thatcher, are that fewer papers are circulated and fewer committee meetings are convened compared with the 1950s and 1960s. Mrs Thatcher, therefore, has been cited as a classic case of a strong Prime Minister and as conclusive proof of the prime-ministerial thesis.

Constraints

But we should note:

1. Dominant Prime Ministers are not new. Lloyd George, Churchill (1940–45) and Neville Chamberlain were probably each more dominant *vis-à-vis* their Cabinets than any post-war successor. This relationship was a product both of their personalities and skills and, in the case of the first two, of war crises.

2. The Prime Minister's shortage of time. Many broad departmental policies and most specific decisions are decided in the departments. The PM will usually be concerned with a few areas, usually the economy and foreign affairs (the major preoccupations, from Macmillan to Thatcher). But, even here, attention will be distracted by other matters, and the PM's own initiatives, if not well informed in particular subjects, may be counter-productive. For support there is a small 'kitchen Cabinet' of political advisers, in the form of No. 10's Policy Unit (the 'Think Tank' was abolished in 1983), but on the whole the PM lacks the expertise and background to reverse or even monitor all but a few departmental policies.

And however energetic a Prime Minister might be (Mrs Thatcher is rumoured to work anything up to eighteen hours a day), there are limits to the extent any individual can govern a large and complex country.

3. *The Prime Minister needs the support of party*. Joe Haines, a former No. 10 aide, once emphasised the key limitation of party upon prime-ministerial power:

> At the end of the day, a Prime Minister cannot survive without the support of Party in the House of Commons. It's quite unlike the power of the American President ... It's an exaggeration to think we have presidential government in this country. We've seen this Prime Minister (Mrs Thatcher) take a number of reverses ... when her power could not be exerted (Jones, 1986).

4. *Cabinet does restrain*. Strong prime ministers may dominate Cabinets and bypass them when they can, but Cabinet government is still very much alive. According to *Guardian* columnist Hugo Young, there is 'a collective mood of those who are in the Cabinet which acts, maybe often, as an inexplicit veto on what Prime Ministers want to do ... they may decide not to do things because they know they might not get approval'. Certainly the office of Prime Minister has become more presidential, especially during the Thatcher era. Because there are so few formal constraints upon the office Prime Ministers can literally do what they can get away with. A dynamic and dominant personality can command immense power, especially when things are going well – but ultimately a Prime Minister must command party loyalty.

Finally, it is worth remembering that power over colleagues does not necessarily extend to decisive power over events. As Hugo Young observes, 'The Prime Minister exists on a diet of insoluble dilemmas. All the most difficult problems in the end finish up with the Prime Minister and very few of them have an obvious answer; so that, at least, is a very great limitation on their power' (Jones, 1986).

Prerogatives

Most of these have been transferred over the years to the Prime Minister from the monarch. They are often called 'powers', yet they are also 'responsibilities' and, depending on how they are exercised, may undermine the PM's position. Possession of the prerogatives is important in distinguishing the Premier from colleagues. The power to appoint and dismiss them, after all, demonstrates that the PM is more than *primus inter pares* ('first among equals').

1. Appointments. A Prime Minister today disposes of over 100 Ministerial appointments. They include Cabinet Ministers, non-Cabinet Ministers, Junior Ministers and other MPs in paid posts. If the governing party has around 330 MPs and the Prime Minister eliminates some of them on the grounds of old age, inexperience or sheer incompetence, then some sort of office will be offered to about a third of the party's MPs. The criteria for appointment will usually include:

(*a*) *Personal and political loyalty.* Most leaders will want to reward some MPs who have shown personal loyalty. Critics have claimed that Harold Wilson's first Cabinet in 1964 contained a number of second-rate appointments who were there mainly because they were loyal; their votes in Cabinet ensured that his position would not be threatened. In Mrs Thatcher's 1979 Cabinet such Ministers as John Biffen, Geoffrey Howe and Sir Keith Joseph were generally regarded as 'loyalists' both to her personally and to her policies. By 1983 the Cabinet consisted to a great extent of people (King, Brittan, Parkinson, Tebbit, Lawson) who owed their promotions to her.

(*b*) *Competence* is difficult to measure, for the criteria will vary with the office. Leadership of the House of Commons, for example, requires tact in dealing with people, mastery of procedure, and a range of parliamentary skills, including firmness and ability to help the House conduct its business. A Chancellor of the Exchequer obviously requires a mastery of economics. Law officers will be drawn from among senior politicians who also have standing in the legal profession. More generally, certain politicians acquire a reputation as skilful debaters, effective communicators and efficient administrators over the years. Their 'political weight' and reputation ensure their consideration for appointment.

(c) *Representativeness*. The Prime Minister will also wish a Cabinet to be broadly representative of the main interests in the party. National figures will be needed for the Scottish and Welsh Offices, there must be at least one woman, and so on. Because the Labour Party more obviously contains political factions, the Labour leader must also seek a balance between the political wings. The Prime Minister will be aware that potential leaders of an opposition or 'troublemakers' may be restrained by the ties of collective responsibility and secrecy of the Cabinet. Let loose on the back benches, a critic may become a focus of opposition. Mr Benn was retained in office even though he was out of sympathy with many of the last Labour government's policies. Mrs Thatcher gradually dismissed critics of her economic policy but retained the two most dangerous for some time (Heseltine until he resigned in 1986 and Peter Walker until his resignation in May 1990).

But the PM also has to think of the cohesiveness of the Cabinet; after all, it has to arrive at collective decisions and then defend them. Mr Heath was excluded by Mrs Thatcher in 1979 because he was so obviously out of sympathy with many policies. A PM may seek to 'isolate' or outmanoeuvre the potential dissidents, e.g. most of the so-called 'wets' in Mrs Thatcher's Cabinet were kept out of the major economic and industrial departments.

2. Dissolution of Parliament. Claims that the PM can use this as a 'big stick' to overcome opposition in the House of Commons are wide of the mark. Of the twelve dissolutions since 1945, the incumbent Premier has lost five. It is not credible to threaten rebellious backbenchers (as Mr Wilson did over opposition to his plans for trade union reform in 1969), for a divided government is hardly likely to inspire confidence among the voters.

Most PMs are now careful to consult colleagues before deciding on the election date. The fact that Mr Heath in February 1974 and Mr Callaghan in 1979 got their dates wrong certainly subsequently weakened their position in the party. Dissolution is a two-edged weapon, and nobody has more to lose from defeat than the PM. Because public opinion is so much more volatile and the economy more difficult to manage, it may now be less easy to manipulate an election-year 'boom' in the economy as in the 1950s and 1960s.

3. *Control of the Cabinet agenda*. A skilful PM can certainly exploit the right to schedule items for Cabinet discussion, call Ministers to speak, sum up the views of the meeting (which is then a decision), decide whether an issue should be referred to a Cabinet committee (usually yes, if the issue is divisive) and choose the members of the committee.

But much of the Cabinet agenda is fairly predictable, e.g. reports from the Foreign Secretary, statements about the following week's parliamentary business, reports on Ulster and EEC matters, recommendations from the committees. And it is difficult for a PM to keep important matters off the agenda, e.g. Wilson eventually gave way to pressure to discuss devaluation of the pound in 1967 and in 1981 Mrs Thatcher agreed to allow full Cabinet discussion of general economic strategy. Cabinet Ministers in the Callaghan and Thatcher governments have shown determination to have full discussion of proposed cuts in public expenditure. Spending Ministers in the present government have managed to resist the pressure of Mrs Thatcher and her Chancellor for greater cuts in programmes. Mr Heseltine's resignation in 1986 was on the grounds that Mrs Thatcher was trying to prevent Cabinet discussion of the full range of policy options for the rescue of the Westland helicopter company. The episode harmed the PM's position and it was widely reported that she was later outvoted by a Cabinet which opposed the sale of Land Rover to a US firm.

The Prime Minister's role

1. *Image*. A PM has many opportunities for self-presentation as *the* government or, strictly speaking, as its spokesman. On the mass media, on foreign tours, and in the Commons, the Premier is seen as the authoritative spokesman for Cabinet policy. At times Mrs Thatcher has appeared to 'make policy' in this way, almost committing her Cabinet in advance. One has to remember that it is the PM's Cabinet; Mrs Thatcher appoints Ministers, and they hold office at her pleasure. If one PM is overthrown or resigns the resignation of the whole government follows. So the PM dominates public coverage of politics and we regularly talk of 'Mrs Thatcher's' or 'Mr Wilson's' government.

2. *Power*. The difficulty here is: how do we measure the power? It is pointless to see it as something the PM gains and the Cabinet loses, or the reverse as a sign of the PM's weakness. A PM who frequently faces a divided Cabinet is heading for trouble, and no Premier can afford to be isolated in Cabinet discussions; he or she has to speak for a collective Cabinet viewpoint, and provide a lead for the party and the nation.

If getting one's way in Cabinet is an indicator of power, then a successful PM need only ask what is sure to be granted, or never give a lead for fear of being overruled.

Security of tenure is not a good indicator, either. Since 1945 Prime Ministers have lasted an average of nearly four years. No acting PM has been sacked; although there was pressure on Churchill (in 1955), Eden (to 1957) and Macmillan (to 1963) to go, each retired in his own time. It is difficult to organise a *coup*, simply because the obvious rival, if there is one, risks splitting the party, alienating influential Ministers, and thereby undermining his own position. In opposition, however, it is easier to remove a leader. The Conservatives now provide the opportunity to contest the leadership, and this is how Mrs Thatcher replaced Mr Heath in 1975.

A PM may sometimes prevail against strong Cabinet opposition. But to push for your own view all the time entails political 'costs'. The power of the PM is, effectively, the power he or she has *in* and *with* the Cabinet. British government is a collective enterprise, and a weak Cabinet weakens the PM.

3. *Political management*. This occupies a good part of the PM's time. The PM does not want resignations, which reflect a failure of management and advertise disagreements to the opposition. Therefore it is important to anticipate the reactions of fellow Ministers, the mood of backbenchers, the views of party activists, and public opinion. A Prime Minister who is publicly committed before the Cabinet decides an issue risks loss of face if overruled.

Ideally, outsiders should not be able to separate the PM's position on an issue from that of the Cabinet. But, according to the many press 'leaks' of Cabinet proceedings, Mrs Thatcher appears to have been overruled on several issues, e.g. MPs' pay (1979), teachers' salaries (1980), Rhodesia, Vietnam boat refugees, and expenditure cuts.

The doctrine of collective responsibility binds the PM as well as Ministers; it means that members have to make compromises and settle for a policy that is broadly acceptable in the group as a whole. After all, Cabinet Ministers have to publicly defend the policy. Consideration of different points of view and different interests – which should be reflected in Cabinet discussions – should promote more coherent and acceptable policies. No PM wants to lose a Foreign Secretary or Chancellor through resignation (Mrs Thatcher strenuously tried to dissuade Lord Carrington from resigning in 1982, Leon Brittan in 1986 and Nigel Lawson in 1989). Some Ministers occupy a symbolic position and their resignation would weaken the government (e.g. Mr Foot, 1974–79, who was believed to represent the support of an otherwise hostile left wing).

4. The art of management. Ideally the PM wants to let decisions 'emerge'. But if the Cabinet is divided, the matter may be refered to a committee. There is no appeal against the committee's decision unless the chairman agrees to reopen the matter. This is one factor invoked by those who claim the Cabinet has lost power. Mrs Thatcher refers many economics issues to a sub-committee which is balanced in favour of her line of policy.

Another way is to try and agree a policy line with senior Ministers (e.g. an inner Cabinet which was formalised by Mr Wilson before 1970) or the appropriate departmental Minister, or to make concessions to critical Ministers beforehand. This process is sometimes called 'squaring' or 'fixing'.

Finally, the PM may mould a common Cabinet line, through force of argument (the Premier does have the opportunity to take a broad view, and because many Ministers are preoccupied with their department duties they may be only too willing to concede the initiative) and strength of personality. Prime Ministers avoid votes on issues; it formalises divisions and makes consensus more difficult to reach.

A Cabinet is a collection of colleagues – drawn from the same party and wanting the government to 'succeed' in its policies and win the next election. It is also a collection of rivals – aspiring for the leadership now, five years or ten years hence, and advocates of different policies. It is a political body which, when making decisions about policy, is arbitrating between different deparments and reflecting differences in the parliamentary party, the party activists and public opinion.

5. *The case of Mrs Thatcher*. Margaret Thatcher has been a remarkable Prime Minister. The key to how she operates lies both in her personality and in how she came to the party leadership. Her political beliefs – less state spending and personal taxation, support for the free market, suspicion of the trade unions, of much of the public sector, and of incomes policies – were not shared by many in the Conservative leadership in the 1970s. She was in a minority among the leadership on some economic questions, and promised a change of direction not only from previous Labour policies but from Conservative ones as well. She became party leader by accident in 1975 because she was the only major figure to stand against Edward Heath (see Chapter 9).

It seems clear that Mrs Thatcher has been more than first among equals. She has been the most dominant of post-war Prime Ministers. But this has largely been because of her agenda and her personality, both of which are unique to her. She is associated with her own 'ism', a set of values and a set of policies. Her Cabinet was bound to be divided because she wished to break with so many of the policies of her predecessors. To get her policies through she had to fight with the Cabinet or bypass it.

An examination of her record will provide some clues about how Prime Ministers manage to dominate the Cabinet. All Prime Ministers have certain fixed powers, including the right to recommend a dissolution, the right to sum up Cabinet meetings and the right to appoint to and dismiss from Cabinet. Mrs Thatcher has used these fixed powers to expand her influence. For example, she gradually dismissed many 'wet' critics of her policies, including Gilmour, Soames and St John Stevas, 'exiled' Prior to Northern Ireland, and over time also managed to lose more independent-minded ministers such as Carrington (1982), Heseltine (1986) and Lawson (1989). In their places she gradually appointed ministers who owed their promotion to her. They included King, Tebbit, Parkinson and Brittan. Gradually she acquired a Cabinet that could be relied on to support her. But Cabinet appointments have to represent the significant elements in the party also. The PM does not have a completely free hand.

Second, she has used this power to set up Cabinet committees and 'fix' their composition. For example, the key economic policy-making Cabinet committees have always been dominated by supporters of the Thatcherite approach. Although these decisions are reported to the full Cabinet it is very difficult for individual Ministers in Cabinet to overturn the recommendation of a Cabinet committee.

- Mrs Thatcher has also been successful in elections. Although she consulted over the timing of dissolutions, the final responsibility was hers. Elections are increasingly seen as personal mandates for successful party leaders and this increases their authority over their colleagues. Mrs Thatcher has also made good use of her Policy Unit and other advisers to second-guess policies in departments. Her reliance on the advice of her economic adviser, Sir Alan Walters, caused Mr Lawson to resign in 1989. One way in which she makes policy is to summon an individual Cabinet Minister and his Permanent Secretary to No. 10 and, supported by her Policy Unit advisers, grill the departmental minister. She commissions papers for herself, holds seminars on subjects, and in several ways helps to make policy free from the full Cabinet. Many policies of her government bear her imprint. They include some of the trade union reforms, the abolition of the GLC, the poll tax, the ending of trade union membership for GCHQ workers, and some of the economic policies, notably in 1990 the refusal to join the EMS despite the views of senior Cabinet colleagues, the City and the CBI.

Yet it would be foolish to generalise from Mrs Thatcher's experience. Such a style of premiership requires extraordinary energy, personal commitment and ideological zeal. Very few other politicians will have this. She has also been successful in many areas, e.g. reforming the unions, lowering inflation – until 1990, curbing strikes, increasing Britain's international standing, etc. Success builds on success. It remains true to say that the relationship between a Prime Minister and Cabinet varies over time. Because Mrs Thatcher has been more dominant than other Prime Ministers, it does not mean to say that others will follow her. British government has tilted more to being prime-ministerial than Cabinet, but it is not presidential.

The following table provides a revision checklist and a framework for examining an individual Prime Minister. The table is adapted from Geoff Hall's in the first edition of *British Politics Today* (1979), pp. 86–7.

DIMENSIONS OF PRIME-MINISTERIAL POWER

I. Prime Minister and government: the power of appointment

Sources

1 Appoints all Ministers and subsequently promotes, demotes, dismisses
2 Decides who does what in Cabinet
3 Appoints chairmen of Cabinet committees (now increasingly important)
4 Approves choice of Ministers' Parliamentary Private Secretaries
5 Other patronage powers, e.g. appoints chairmen of commissions, recommends knighthoods, peerages and sundry other awards

Constraints

1 Seniority of colleagues demands their inclusion and sometimes in particular posts
2 Availability for office – experience, talent, willingness to serve
3 Need for balance:
    (*a*) Ideological, left + right
    (*b*) Regional
    (*c*) Occupational
    (*d*) Lords
4 Debts to loyal supporters
5 Shadow Cabinet expectations

II. Prime Minister and Cabinet: direction

Sources

1 Summons meetings
2 Determines agenda
3 Sums up 'mood' of meeting
4 Approves minutes
5 Spokesman for Cabinet to outside world
6 Existence of inner Cabinet (intimate advisors)

Constraints

1 Needs Cabinet approval for controversial measures
2 Determination of groups of Ministers to press a case or oppose a particular policy
3 Power of vested departmental interests backed up by senior civil servants
4 Convention dictates certain items will appear regularly on Cabinet agenda

III. Prime Minister and Parliament

Sources

1 Commands a majority in House [usually]
2 Spokesman for government
3 Twice-weekly Question Time provides platform upon which PM can usually excel

Constraints

1 Activities of opposition
2 Parliamentary party meetings
3 Question Time: not always a happy experience

IV. Prime Minister and party

Sources

1 'Brand image' of party, especially at election time: PM's 'style' is that of the party
2 Control over appointments
3 Natural loyalty of party members to their leader and their government
4 Threat of dissolution (but seldom a credible threat)
5 Fear of party members that opposition will exploit public disagreements

Constraints

1 Danger of election defeat: can lead to loss of party leadership
2 Existence of ambitious alternative leaders
3 Need to command support of parliamentary party, particularly when majority is thin or non-existent
4 For Labour Premiers, some constraints from party outside Parliament, e.g. National Executive Committee and Party Conference

Further reading

P. Hennessy, *Cabinet*, Blackwell, 1986.

B. Jones, *Is Democracy Working?*, Tyne Tees TV, 1986.

— 'The Thatcher Style', *Political Issues in Britain Today*, Manchester University Press, 1989.

D. Kavanagh, 'Mrs Thatcher: a study in Prime Ministerial style', *Teaching Politics*, 1985.

Anthony King, *The British Prime Minister*, Macmillan, 2nd edn, 1985.

Hugo Young, *One of Us*, Macmillan, 1990.

Questions

1. 'The power of the Prime Minister has increased, is increasing and ought to be diminished.' Discuss.

2. Would you say that we have 'prime-ministerial' or 'Cabinet' government in Britain?

3 Using the chart on 'Dimensions of prime-ministerial power', compare and contrast two post-war Prime Ministers.

15

THE CIVIL SERVICE

The British executive has two parts. There is the *political arm*, which consists of elected politicians who lead the departments and sit in Cabinet; and the *administrative arm*, staffed by permanent, expert civil servants. The linchpin of the relations between the two – and the key to understanding the constitution – is *ministerial responsibility*. According to this doctrine the Minister is answerable to Parliament for the conduct of officials in his department. As long as it is assumed that the civil servants are acting as his agents he can be questioned in Parliament on their activities and on policies. He is expected to protect the civil servants if they have acted on his instructions, and to take the credit for the good and the blame for the bad.

According to one view of relations between Ministers and civil servants, Ministers decide policies; and civil servants, whilst they do play an advisory role, are mainly concerned with carrying them out. In fact it is now widely acknowledged that the civil servants' role in defining policy options and attaching recommendations to their reports is important in deciding policy itself. Even the way a programme is implemented may have an important policy component. A good example is immigration, where the officials have a good deal of discretion in applying the rules. Other factors which strengthen the position of the civil service include its permanence compared with the way Ministers come and go, and the disparity in size between the eighty or so departmental Ministers and almost 570,000 civil servants, or even the top 4,000 or so concerned with high policy matters. In recent years the conventions governing relations between Ministers and civil servants and ideas about the role of the civil service in policy-making have both been questioned.

Principles of the civil service

Three interlinked principles which shape the role of the civil service are:

1. Impartiality. The civil servant is a servant of the Crown, and thus he is responsible for some higher purpose than that reflected by the government of the day. As a corollary he is subject to limits on his political activity and freedom of expression. For example, he is required to resign once he has been adopted as a parliamentary candidate. At senior levels a civil servant may not take part in national politics. The principle of impartiality means that promotion is on criteria of professional competence, not on political grounds.

2. Anonymity. Civil servants are expected to remain publicly silent on political and other controversial matters. It is Ministers, in line with the doctrine of ministerial responsibility, who answer questions in Parliament. In the wake of the Westland crisis in January 1986, the Thatcher government tried to argue that it is Ministers and not civil servants who should answer policy questions raised by select committees.

3. Permanence follows from the idea that members of the civil service are servants of the Crown, and not of the government of the day. The civil service is much more of a closed corporation than is the case in the United States. There is little tradition of 'outsiders' coming in at top levels, except in wartime.

We can readily understand how these principles are interlocked. The principle of permanence depends upon impartiality, and this in turn is helped by anonymity. Because civil servants only advise, they remain anonymous: Ministers are responsible to Parliament for policy.

In the last twenty years or so there have been demands for major reform. One aim has been to make the civil service more efficient, in particular to encourage more businesslike and economic methods of working. A second has been to make it more responsive to Ministers. It is important to keep these two considerations separate.

The Fulton Inquiry

The Fulton Committee was established in 1965 to report on the management and structure of the service. To some extent the civil service of the day suffered from the general critique of British institutions. A 'What's wrong with Britain?' mood was in the air. In 1968 the Fulton Report came up with four main criticisms:

1. Narrow and unrepresentative social background of senior civil servants.

2. Narrow educational background. In 1959–63, for example, 85 per cent of senior civil servants were Oxford or Cambridge graduates.

3. Lack of outsiders. It was argued that the appointment of people from other walks of life – notably business, finance and the law – would broaden perspectives.

4. Amateurism. It was noted that there was no provision for training once people had joined the service. Recruitment by interview and competitive examination from well qualified university graduates meant that new recruits had no experience of the outside world and received only 'on the job' training. The civil service was still dominated by the nineteenth-century idea that senior civil servants should be qualified for general and not specific responsibilities. The view was fondly and widely held that someone with a high quality mind and a sound education (preferably an Oxbridge Classics degree) was able to master the essentials of complex administrative problems and bring wise judgement to bear. The Fulton Committee did not necessarily agree. It made five recommendations:

1. The promotion of more specialists, and the recruitment of graduates 'with relevant specialisms'.

2. The unification of grades and classes.

3. The establishment of a civil service college which would provide training in management, data analysis, economics and other skills.

4. The creation of a Civil Service Department.

5. The appointment of more outsiders.

A Civil Service College was set up to provide post-entry training. A Civil Service Department was created and made responsible for recruitment, training and pay as well as for organisation and efficiency. More political advisers were brought in, but there was little progress in the recruitment of outsiders or late entrants. The administrative and executive grades were united to form the 'Administration Group'.

Many observers feel that the report's recommendations were not fully implemented. One reason may be that the task of putting them into effect was left to the service itself. Another is that in some ways the report may have been unsatisfactory. For example, the sensitive question of relations between Ministers and civil servants was excluded from consideration; the government insisted that the constitutional convention of ministerial responsibility governed relations between the executive and Parliament and between Ministers and civil servants. The report may have erred in levelling the charge of amateurism; senior civil servants are highly professional in running the machinery of government and judging the feasibility of policies. The civil service may be generalist but that is not to say it is amateur.

Persisting problems

Since 1979 a number of developments have undermined the traditional role of civil servants. Anonymity has been challenged as select committees have questioned them about matters of policy and the officials have become known to the public. In the collapse of the Vehicle & Accident Insurance Company (1972), senior civil servants were named and disciplined for administrative failures (raising doubts about the responsibility of Ministers). In the Westland case (1986) civil servants were named and blamed for leaking information to the press. Some officials have acted in ways which have led people to doubt their impartiality. Moreover, critics ask, how can Ministers be responsible for activities of which they may have little knowledge? James Prior refused to resign as Secretary for State for Northern Ireland over escapes from the Maze prison on the ground that he was not personally responsible. The increasing visibility of civil servants makes it difficult to protect them from comment and criticism (which was one object of ministerial responsibility). Kathy Massiter was charged with leaking defence information to the *Guardian*. Clive Ponting leaked a document concerning the sinking of the *Belgrano* during the Falklands War to Tam Dalyell, an Opposition MP. He was dismissed and charged with breaking the Official Secrets Act but after a sensational trial the jury found him not guilty.

Ponting leaked his document because he believed the Minister was misleading Parliament and hence the country. But in 1985 the head of the civil service, Sir Robert Armstrong, stated, 'The civil service as such has no constitutional personality or responsibility separate from the duly elected government of the day.' In other words, the government of the day represents the interests of the nation – a proposition which worries some critics.

Ways in which politicians may feel that the civil service is not co-operating with them include:

1. Obstruction, through delay, inadequate briefing, presentation of biased information, or overloading the Minister. Such complaints have more often come from Labour politicians (compare the diaries of Richard Crossman, Barbara Castle and Tony Benn). Another example was the eleventh report of the Expenditure Committee on the Civil Service (1976–77). It called for the appointment of more party political advisers, and personal aides for each Minister, and greater political direction generally.

But right-wing Conservatives have also complained, in particular, about the centrist tendencies of the service. Sir John Hoskyns, a former head of Mrs Thatcher's No. 10 Policy Unit, has called for the appointment of more politically sympathetic civil servants by the government of the day.

2. Co-ordination. Departmental officials serve on committees which shadow the Cabinet committees. Their job is to reconcile different departmental views and to secure agreement about a policy before it goes to the Cabinet. Some Ministers may feel that this practice tends to leave them exposed and vulnerable in Cabinet.

3. Overload. The sheer pressure of work (as general spokesmen for the government, in their constituency, in Cabinet, as well as running the department) means that Ministers have to delegate and let civil servants exercise their discretion. It is also argued that the work of the civil service in sifting information, analysing options and making recommendations gives it too much influence on policy.

4. Permanence. On average Ministers remain in their department for about two years. At any one time a number of Ministers are likely to be new to their job and looking to their officials for guidance. In support of the claim that the civil service can obstruct politicians and/or play too great a role in policy formulation, critics point to the continuity of policies in many departments since the war. According to this view, radical governments are held back by consensus-inclined civil servants.

On the whole the idea that civil servants fail to obey their masters is far-fetched. Some of the criticisms smack of special pleading, or of politicians seeking a scapegoat for their own failures. One has to remember, moreover, that civil servants cannot reply to this sort of criticism. It is worth bearing in mind that:

1. Ministers and governments may not really want to effect radical changes in policy. The Wilson and Callaghan governments, for example, accepted the status quo in many fields. Governments respond to electoral mood, or economic imperatives, or party pressures, as well as to civil service advice.

2. The policies of a government may fail because they were inadequately prepared in the first place. Consider:

(*a*) The curtailment of Labour's ambitious social programmes after 1964 and 1974, largely through lack of the necessary economic growth.

(*b*) The ineffectiveness of the 1971 Industrial Relations Act. The Heath government never expected that so few trade unions would register.

(*c*) The disastrous introduction of the community charge (or poll tax) as a substitute for local rates in April 1990.

3. The civil service should not be partisan but should point out the pros and cons of different policies in a reasonably detached way. The experience of Mrs Thatcher's government has raised particular difficulties for this line of analysis. After all, her administration has brought radical change in many areas, e.g. trade union reform, privatisation, local government changes and reforms in education and the health service.

The impact of Thatcher

The party normally associated with the establishment has challenged the civil service to a greater extent than Labour ever has:

1. Reduction in the number of civil servants, from 750,000 in 1979 to under 600,000 in 1990. In part this reflects the government's dislike of the public sector (seen as a 'drag' on the rest of the economy) and its quest for greater efficiency.

2. Abolition of the Civil Service Department in 1981, following the civil servants' lengthy strike over pay. Responsibility for pay and recruitment was transferred to the Treasury (likely to be less generous) and the Management and Personnel Office of the Cabinet.

3. The pursuit of financial savings. Instead of leaving it to civil servants to find economies Mrs Thatcher appointed a businessman, Lord Rayner, who had direct access to her.

4. Mrs Thatcher's use of her Policy Unit to question Ministers and senior civil servants about policies.

5. Her close interest in high-level promotions, particularly at the level of Permanent Secretary and Deputy Secretary. It has been alleged that she promotes 'Thatcherites', politicising the civil service. If true, this would put a question mark against the principles of impartiality, permanence and anonymity. Mrs Thatcher, however, seems to be more concerned with overturning the tradition of seniority and promoting people who will get things done.

6. The sheer number of policy changes which have broken the old consensus, e.g. in local government, privatisation, trade union reform.

There are still critics on the right of the Conservative Party who criticise the civil service (and Ministerial timidity), notably for failing to cut public spending or to privatise more (school vouchers for example). But the extent of Mrs Thatcher's changes in policies hardly supports the claim that civil servants rule, and none would claim that she personally was in their thrall. Indeed the opposite is a more persuasive argument. After several years of power in which she has vigorously promulgated her relatively simple messages, civil servants have been more effectively permeated by a Prime Minister's views than ever before.

Further reforms?

Reforms are still being canvassed – a comment on Fulton's lack of impact. They include strengthening political or Ministerial control, dismissing many senior figures ('too defeatist', according to Sir John Hoskyns) or making civil servants accountable. Ways of doing this include:

1. Increasing the number of political aides, so that a Minister has a cabinet of political supporters who can put forward alternative views.

2. More explicit political appointments at the top, so that the administration is more responsive to politicians.

3. Making individuals directly responsible for particular policies. Indeed, the Thatcher government has introduced Financial Management Initiatives since 1982 to give civil servants more autonomy over spending. In this way they can be held accountable.

4. Greater accountability of Ministers and civil servants to Parliament. The 1979 system of select committees has regularly called ministers and civil servants to present papers and answer questions. The committees are often vigorous in their questioning. After the Defence Committee inquiry into Westland (1986) some Ministers wanted the committees to be forbidden to interview senior civil servants. They claimed that since they were servants of the Ministers it was the latter who were accountable to Parliament.

5. The introduction of agencies. The Ibb's programme, *Next Steps* (1988), envisages that the civil service will in future consist of a small, policy-making core of 20,000–30,000. Most departments would be converted to free-standing agencies delivering services directly to the public. The agencies will be independent and no longer subject to ministerial direction or ministerial repsonsibility. They will be led by powerful chief executives with wholly delegated powers over finance and staffing as well as goals to achieve. The senior civil servant in charge of *Next Steps*, Peter Kemp, is hopeful that within ten years, three-quarters of all civil servants will be transferred to such agencies. By the summer of 1990, twenty-seven agencies had been set up involving 50,000 civil servants. Since becoming an agency in October 1988, Companies House has reduced the time for processing documents from twenty-four working days to four.

The first two suggestions would weaken the idea of a 'career' service and might raise a barrier between the political appointees and the rest. The third, fourth and fifth are likely to weaken the convention of Ministerial responsibility. A major, though little discussed, problem is that the appointment of 'better' (i.e. more able or more expert) civil servants will perhaps create pressure that they be allowed more influence over policy in relation to Ministers who remain formally responsible for policy.

The old style of Minister/civil servant relations has certainly come under strain. Some of it has been provoked by general dissatisfaction with the political system or the country's poor economic performance. This mood dates back to the 1950s and 1960s at least, but the new factor which has weakened the relationship has been the collapse of consensus. Thatcherism, with its challenge to so many policies and rejection of continuity, has obviously created problems for many civil servants.

Strains

1. An increase in leaks – some of them very damaging to the government (e.g. Ponting on *Belgrano*) – of documents to the Opposition. In the Westland affair, civil servants were instructed by Downing Street staff to 'leak' documents calculated to damage Mr Heseltine. Following this, new rules governing these matters were drawn up by the then head of the civil service, Lord Armstrong. Armstrong claimed that, as servants of the Crown, civil servants were effectively servants of the government of the day; it was not for them to decide to leak documents. Ministers effectively decided what was in the national interest and what was constitutional. If officials had doubts about a course of action they were recommended to raise it with their permanent secretary or the head of the civil service.

2. There has been a growing debate over politicisation, which is potentially damaging for the service. Some critics fear that civil servants may lose their detachment and become too eager to please their political masters. If this is so, then a future Labour government may have less confidence in the civil service it inherits.

3. There has been a loss of talented civil servants in their 30s and 40s.

The ethos of the civil service has probably changed under the Thatcher influence. There is more emphasis on good management, value for money and the emulation of practices of the private sector. Yet in many respects continuity is also evident, notably in recruitment, and the scale of change does not compare with that achieved in local government and the trade unions. It may be that civil servants, wedded to impartiality and to continuity in many policy areas, will always experience difficulty at a time of sharp political divisions.

Further reading

Leslie Chapman, *Your Disobedient Servant*, Chatto & Windus, 1978.

Joe Haines, *The Politics of Power*, Cape, 1977.

Peter Hennessy, *Whitehall*, Secker & Warburg, 1989; Fontana, 1990.

Sir John Hoskyns, 'Whitehall and Westminster', *Parliamentary Affairs*, 1977, 1983.

— 'Conservatism is not enough', *Political Quarterly*, 1983.'

Questions

1. 'The ability of Ministers to control their civil servants is the acid test of democracy.' Discuss.

2. Do you think it is possible for civil servants to carry out the wishes of Ministers, unaffected by personal political beliefs?

3. Criticise the notion of the 'generalist administrator'.

16

GOVERNMENT AND THE ECONOMY

Most important political issues are economic. This chapter examines the reasons for Britain's relative economic decline, the kind of instruments available to government for managing the economy, plus the two main economic philosophies in theory and practice.

The political importance of economics begins with the high priority which most people attach to improving their standards of living. Popularly elected governments will naturally seek to meet this demand. The result of this 'electoral bidding' has been a growing expectation – possibly unfounded – that governments are responsible for running the economy successfully and a corresponding disillusion when they fail. Opinion polls suggest that the popularity of governments closely follows the ups and downs of the economy. The delivery of prosperity has become the most important expectation people have of their politicians.

Economic decline

In 1939 British income per head was second only to that of the USA. After the war the economy soon recovered, expanding at about 2½ per cent a year. Production had more than doubled by 1970. At about £400 billion per annum in the early 1990s, gross national product is the fifth largest in the world, and Britain ranks among the richest 10 per cent of countries. This absolute improvement is seldom stressed; it is *relative* performance that commands attention.

The growth rates of West Germany and Japan were, respectively, 7·9 and 7·7 per cent in the 1950s; and 4·6 and 10·5 per cent in the 1960s. Both countries are now close to producing twice as much per head as Britain. Still among the richest ten countries in the late 1950s, we had slumped to the twenties by 1981. During the 1970s all countries suffered economic recession but, despite the considerable advantages of North Sea oil, Britain suffered more than most. Growth was negligible, and, towards the end of the decade, contraction set in. Between 1975 and 1984 Japan's manufacturing output increased by 61 per cent, the USA's by 42 per cent, Italy's by 22 per cent − but Britain's declined by 4·3 per cent. Our manufacturers could no longer outsell foreign goods in their home market: industries in which Britain once excelled, particularly electrical goods and motor vehicles, became dominated by imports. Awareness of this relative decline became a potent, almost obsessive element in politics. Shorn of empire and economic pre-eminence, the country indulged in gloomy introspection. Diagnoses of the 'British disease' were plentiful.

1. Historical explanations

(a) The first country to industrialise, we became burdened with obsolete plant and attitudes which other competitors were spared.

(b) Two world wars exhausted Britain economically. Overseas investments were sold to pay for the war effort.

(c) The end of empire, with the economic growth of former colonies, lost Britain many of the advantages she once enjoyed. Some emphasise the 'cushioning' effect of imperial preference and date the real decline from as early as the middle of the nineteenth century (see Weiner).

2. Geographical explanations.

For an island with few natural resources, but for coal and oil, dependence upon exports is greater than for any other developed country. This helps explain why world economic recessions hit Britain particularly hard.

3. Cultural explanations

(a) *Poor industrial relations* reflect the deep class divisions in society. Trade unions have felt it necessary to defend their members' interests to the point where productivity suffers from insistence on unnecessary jobs (overmanning) or work procedures (restrictive practices). Strikes were frequent. Between 1968 and 1977, 850 days were lost per 1,000 employees through strike action, compared with 241 in Japan and 53 in West Germany.

(b) *The education system* reflects prejudice against business as a career. The ablest young people often turn to the media, the civil service, the law or banking rather than industry. Managers are frequently undertrained compared with their overseas competitors and lack flair in identifying new products and markets – e.g. missing out on TV games and pocket calculators – and exploiting them effectively – e.g. salesmen are rarely good at foreign languages. Moreover, top decision-makers have little experience or direct knowledge of business: senior civil servants have usually studied non-economic subjects and only one or two members of the Cabinet, as a rule, have had substantial business experience.

(c) *Immobility of labour*. Over 60 per cent of houses are owner-occupied. Problems of moving house and the higher price of housing in the more prosperous parts of the country restrict the mobility of labour from areas of low to high employment and from declining to expanding industries. In 1990, the average cost of a semi-detached house in inner London was two to three times that of a similar house in the North. The quarter of houses which are council owned, with their endless waiting lists, compound the problem, whilst the small, privately rented sector is often too expensive and unsuitable for families.

4. Political explanations

(a) *The social policies* pursued by Labour and to some extent Conservative governments since the war have encouraged the growth of employment in the service sector, e.g. central and local government, education and the health service.

(b) *Adversary politics*. The tendency of successive governments in the last decade to reverse the measures of its predecessors has diminished the confidence of businessmen in the future of their own country's industries. This has affected planning and investment.

5. Financial explanations

(a) *Industrial investment* – crucial for competitiveness and growth – has regularly been lower in Britain. Between 1966 and 1976 it was 19·9 per cent of gross domestic product per annum, compared with 21·5 per cent in West Germany, 23·4 per cent in France and 30·9 per cent in Japan. Over half Britain's investment is by private individuals and firms; in 1981 the former Labour Cabinet Minister, Harold Lever, and the economist, George

Edwards, blamed British banks for denying the private sector
the long-term finance needed to develop imaginative or 'risky'
projects. Unlike those in Germany and Japan, British banks
favour short-term loans.

(b) *Relatively low investment in research and development*
compounds the problem. Whilst Japanese spending on R&D
increased by 90 per cent since 1967–80 and by 40 per cent in
France and West Germany, the British figure actually declined
by 10 per cent during the same period.

6. Economic explanations

(a) Low investment and R&D, combined with poor industrial
relations, help explain why productivity is low. Productivity
(the ratio of output to number of persons employed) inevitably
suffers when investment is low. In 1967–76 it increased by
3·1 per cent a year, compared with 4·8 per cent in West Germany
and 8·9 per cent in Japan. America's rate, at 2·1 per cent,
was actually lower, but that is scant comfort, as in 1971 US
productivity per man was already double the UK rate.

(b) Inflation of prices and wages never used to be a serious
economic problem in the 1950s and 1960s, when it ran at 3
or 4 per cent, but in the 1970s inflation took off. in 1974 prices
rose by 19 per cent and wages by 29 per cent. After a decline
in the late 1970s it began again to climb and Mrs Thatcher
made its reduction her prime economic objective. Inflation
is harmful in that it: (a) reduces competitiveness; (b) reduces
the values of savings; (c) hits those – the poorest – who cannot keep up with it; (d) creates uncertainty and ultimately
chaos if it develops into hyper-inflation, as in Germany in the
1920s.

It should be stressed that none of these explanations stand
independently. They all *interact* to form a vicious circle: low
investment causes low productivity, which causes traditional
industries to decline and new industries to remain stillborn,
which causes falling living standards and social bitterness, which
exacerbates industrial strife, which helps promote rival political
antidotes, which a bewildered electorate vote in for alternating
periods of office, which saps business confidence, which causes
low investment; and so it goes on. Politicians, as we have seen,

assure the electorate that their policies will work − but what can a government do to control the economy?

Instruments of government control

1. Monetary policy. The supply of money and borrowed money (credit) in the economy will influence the level of economic activity. The more money available the greater people's capacity to buy things (demand), hence the need for the production of goods, which in turn creates employment. Similarly, the lower the supply of money, the less demand, production and employment. The government can generally control the amount of cash available throught the Bank of England and the Royal Mint; but credit, available from many sources − banks and finance houses − is harder to control. One important way is to regulate interest rates: the higher they are the more expensive repayments become and the less attractive the loan; the lower the rate the easier it is to borrow money. Government raises interest rates when it wishes to reduce the money supply and lowers them when it wishes to increase it.

2. Fiscal policy aims to control and demand and supply (the ability of the economy to meet demand) through taxation and government expenditure. The Chancellor of the Exchequer can reduce demand by increasing taxes or increase it by lowering them. This sort of exerciseis often called 'fine tuning' the economy. The Chancellor must be careful, for if he allows demand to rise too rapidly industry may not be able to meet it, and imports will rise. If they exceed exports by too much, too regularly, an adverse balance of payments may ensue. This can have several deleterious effects; the most obvious is that the rate at which other countries are prepared to exchange their own currency for pounds − the exchange rate − declines, making imports dearer and nudging inflation up.

Government revenue in the past has rarely been sufficient to meet expenditure, and in most years the deficit known as the public-sector borrowing requirement (PSBR) had to be covered by borrowing from financial markets in the City of London. However, banks can use government 'bills' and 'bonds', issued in exchange for the loans, to finance other loans to several times their value. Government borrowing therefore has a disproportionate in influence on money supply.

3. Direct control and intervention. Between 1939 and 1945 the government assumed control of almost every aspect of production and employment. In peacetime not all these controls were abandoned. For example, regular attempts have been made to keep prices in line with wages by means of prices and incomes policies, to achieve a more geographically balanced growth by subsidising depressed regions, and to regulate specific sectors of the economy by special institutions.

Economic philosophies

The combination of measures government chooses will depend upon its view of how the economy works. Two broad economic philosophies can be discerned.

1. Keynesianism. Unemploymnet was the most acute problem between the wars, and it is no coincidence that J.M. Keynes's *General Theory of Employment, Investment and Money* (1936) was, to a large extent, addressed to it. Keynes believed that in times of slump, when unemployment was high and investment low, the government could reverse the downward spiral by spending money. Its expenditure might exceed income for a while, the deficit being made good by borrowing, but the injection of funds into the economy would increase demand, stimulate production and hence employment. Government spending, or 'demand management', would therefore transform a vicious circle into a virtuous one. Full employment and economic growth were simultaneously possible. Keynes was in favour of using the full range of economic controls to achieve this. His followers believed that keeping wages in line with prices would restrain any inflationary tendency. By 1944 Keynesian thinking had become so widely accepted that it was enshrined in a White Paper committing the post-war government to 'maintain the highest possible level of employment'.

2. Monetarism owes much to pre-Keynesian classical economists like Adam Smith, but in its modern guise has emerged as an answer to the more recent economic bane, inflation. Its chief protagonist is Professor Milton Friedman of Chicago University. He perceives deficit spending *à la* Keynes as at best only temporarily effective. As soon as businessmen realise that people have more money to spend on consumer goods they will push prices up rather than increase production. Higher prices mean pressure for higher wages, and so the inflationary spiral begins. 'Inflation occurs when the quantity of money rises appreciably more rapidly than output, and the more rapid the rise in the quantity of money per unit of output the greater the rate of inflation' (Friedman, p. 299).

Government should therefore concentrate on strict control of the money supply. Apart from that, advises Friedman, it should leave the economy alone. If companies can produce goods at prices people can afford they ill prosper; if not, they will give way to those who can. Give market forces free rein and, as the Japanese and American economies prove, everyone will grow rich. If money is kept tight, trade unions who insist upon inflationary pay rises will bankrupt their employers and lose their jobs; the threat of unemployment will consequently be an effective substitute for incomes policy.

To summarise: Keynes believed that by injecting money into the economy the level of demand would be stimulated, production increased and more people employed. Friedman argues that, on the contrary, such injections merely stimulate price increases by business and wage demands by trade unions: in other words, inflation.

Naturally, each approach has proved attractive politically. Keynes appealed powerfully to socialists as a justification for intervening in the economy to: (a) refuce the power of privately owned business; (b) encourage equality by channelling government money to the lower-paid; (c) promote economic prosperity through planning and state investment.

He seemed to offer a route to economic prosperity which also led to social justice.

Friedman appeals to Conservatives, the party supporting business, because: (a) he stresses more freedom for businessmen from government controls; (b) he places the logic of market forces before the need for full employment; (c) he justifies the role of business in terms of the overall public good. However, since the war Conservatives have been heavily influenced by Keynes, just as Labour in the 70s absorbed, to a degree, the teachings of Friedman.

The philosophies in practice

From 1945 to 1970 both Labour and Conservative governments put their faith in Keynesian 'demand management' and set up a variety of prices and incomes controls plus measures to stimulate investment and plan future growth. In 1970 Mr Heath's new government experimented briefly with a monetarist approach but, when major bankruptcies threatened, reverted to a Keynesian 'dash for growth', combining heavy investment with statutory controls over incomes. It foundered hopelessly when the miners challenged such legal controls, and Labour won the resultant general election in February 1974.

The runaway inflation of the next two years, combined with growing unemployment and stagnant growth, seemed to bear out Friedman's analysis rather than Keynes's. In 1976 the Labour Chancellor, Denis Healey, adopted policies of monetary control, urged on by the International Monetary Fund (IMF), which had advanced massive loans to support the collapsing pound. Healey's blend of monetary control − resulting in public expenditure cuts and increased unemployment − and Keynesian intervention through incomes restraint and government cash for ailing industries was not unsuccessful: in 1978 inflation was down, real incomes (helped by North Sea oil) were up, and there was a mood of some confidence.

However, Callaghan's attempt to win acceptance of a 5 per cent wages guideline resulted in the industrial chaos of the 'winter of discontent', 1978−79: his government stuttered to ignominious defeat in May 1979 and Mrs Thatcher was given the chance to apply her stricter brand of monetarism. She always claimed that she would need two terms in office for her policies to have full effect. After eleven years, the balance sheet is a mixed one. Mrs Thatcher can claim with some justice that:

1. Inflation has been drastically reduced. When she came to power it was running at 10 per cent; in 1980 it soared to 22 per cent but gradually went down to 3 per cent in 1987.

2. Privatisation of British Telecom, the TSB, British Gas and other concerns has proved popular with the public, has earned billions for the Exchequer and has − according to the Conservative perspective − freed sections of the economy back into the private sector.

3. Real disposable incomes for those in work have increased by 25 per cent over the period 1981−88, meaning that the vast majority of people have enjoyed higher material prosperity under Mrs Thatcher.

4. Employment. Over a million new jobs have been created, many of them in new industries.

5. Unemployment soared to $3\frac{1}{2}$ million in the early 80s, but thanks to sound economic policies (say Conservatives) and changes in the ways unemployment is calculated (say Labour) the figure stands at $1 \cdot 6$ million in the summer of 1990.

6. Industrial relations. Between 1985 and 1988 only 178 days per 1,000 employees were lost through strike action.

7. Business investment as a proportion of Gross Domestic Product (GDP) increased from $11 \cdot 2$ per cent in 1977 to $16 \cdot 4$ per cent in 1988. Investment in plant and equipment rose from $32 \cdot 1$ per cent in 1977 to a little over 40 per cent in 1988, reflecting the extent to which British industry has restructured and re-equipped during the 1980s.

8. Productivity (output per person employed) rose by $1 \cdot 3$ per cent during 1970−80; during the period 1980−88 the figure was $2 \cdot 5$ per cent, compared with an average of $1 \cdot 8$ per cent for the seven biggest economies belonging to the Organisation for Economic Cooperation and Development (OECD). Productivity was especially impressive in the manufacturing industry at $5 \cdot 2$ per cent, compared with an OECD average of $3 \cdot 6$ per cent.

9. Overseas investment has climbed dramatically from £3 billion in 1976 to £80 billion in 1986; Britain is now second only to Japan in terms of net external assets and, largely in consequence, has built up impressive 'invisible' overseas earnings.

10. Public expenditure has steadily decreased as a percentage of GDP since it reached a peak in 1982. In 1988 it stood at 38·2 per cent, the lowest figure since 1966 (for details of how government money is spent, see Table 1).

Table 1 *Public expenditure by function (1987–88 prices, £ billion)*

Function	1981–82 outturn	1988–89 estimated outturn
Defence	16·9	18·1
Overseas services, including overseas aid	2·1	3·0
Agriculture, fisheries, food and forestry	2·2	2·2
Industry, energy, trade and employment	10·0	6·4
Arts and libraries	0·9	1·1
Transport	6·9	5·6
Housing	5·7	3·0
Other environmental services	5·4	5·4
Law, order and protective services	6·0	8·1
Education and science	19·5	21·2
Health and personal social services	21·4	25·4
Social security	39·7	46·3
Other expenditure	4·3	4·1
Privatisation proceeds	−0·7	−5·7
Planning total	140·4	144·4
Of which expenditure by:		
Local authorities	35·9	40·6
Nationalised industries	4·8	0·2
Other public corporations	1·4	0·5

Source: Social Trends, 1990.

11. Economic growth. After the 1979–81 recession, the economy recovered rapidly and expanded on average by 2·9 per cent per year until 1989, a better performance than any of our leading competitors except Japan.

Criticisms of Thatcher's economic record

A number of economists and opposition politicians argue that the Thatcher years have not been successful ones for the British economy.

1. Inflation began to increase steadily after 1988. Most economists agree that the reason for this was the extended period of low interest rates which followed the 1987 stock market crash. Chancellor Lawson was anxious to avoid a recession, but low interest rates unleashed a consumer boom based on credit. Billions of pounds were cheaply borrowed (a large proportion on the vastly enhanced house values, which low interest rates had caused), enabling the whole nation to go on a spending spree. The result was that a 'blip' (Lawson's term) in inflation became a steadily upward trend until it reached 9·7 per cent in June 1990. Interest rates were hoisted high (15 per cent) by the government to bring inflation down, but the cure was slow to take effect and, to the extent that it led to vastly increased mortgage rates, the policy fuelled demands for higher wages and was therefore itself inflationary.

2. Balance of trade deficits began to reappear after 1987 and when imports were sucked in by the consumer boom, the deficit rose to an alarming £20 billion in 1989, with a similar figure forecast for 1990. 'There is scarcely an industry in which we are not outsold on balance by foreigners' (Will Hutton, the *Guardian*, 22 June 1990). Such a poor trading performance places downward pressure upon sterling. If the exchange rate falls, foreign goods will be more expensive and inflation will tend to rise. Critics of Mrs Thatcher blame the size of the deficit partly upon the savage 1979–81 recession, which her policies precipitated: the destruction of nearly one-fifth of Britain's manufacturing industry at that time, they assert, made it impossible for the economy to meet the boom in consumer demand later in the decade.

3. North Sea oil. Mrs Thatcher's critics point out that without the windfall of North Sea oil, large trade deficits would have been an acute problem much earlier. As it is, the potential which this asset represented for renewal investment in British industry has been largely wasted.

4. *Economic growth* slowed down in 1989 and in 1990 was running at a mere 1–2 per cent per annum – only a whisker away from recession. Other OECD economies, by comparison, were still enjoying steady expansion. Critics also point out that despite the improvement in Britain's economic performance:

(*a*) Manufacturing output did not exceed the 1979 level until 1987.

(*b*) Britain's real GDP per capita is still the lowest of the OECD's big seven, having fallen behind that of Italy in the late 1980s.

(*c*) Productivity was eroded by alarmingly high wage settlements in the late 1980s and early 1990s.

(*d*) Japan invests twice as much as the UK proportionally and West Germany invests one-third more.

5. *Control of the money supply* has proved elusive, to say the least. Contrary to Friedman's theories, the rate of measured monetary growth has not correlated at all with the rate of inflation.

6. *Privatisation* in most cases has merely changed public monopolies into private ones. The intention to introduce competition has not been fulfilled.

7. *Public expenditure* may have declined as a percentage of GDP, but in absolute terms it has increased and plans for 1990–93 anticipate a further 8 per cent increase.

8. *Distribution of disposable income.* The well-off have done very well out of the Thatcher years, but the poorest one-third of society have received only marginal benefits and in many cases families are now worse off than they were before Mrs Thatcher came to power (see Chapter 2).

9. *Taxation*, despite cuts in income tax from 33 per cent to 25 per cent (ordinary rate), has increased. The average married couple with two children in 1978–79 paid 35·2 per cent of their income in tax: in 1989–90 the figure had increased to 37·6 per cent. The reduction of higher tax rates, however, from 83 per cent to 40 per cent in the 1988 budget has had a dramatically beneficial effect upon the bank balances of the higher paid.

10. Unemployment levels of 3 million plus have left scars which will perhaps never heal. The hundreds of thousands of young people who have never worked in their lives represent social and moral problems, which will stay with us for generations. Critics argue that the government's policies on education, training and retraining are wholly inadequate, especially when they are compared with those of our competitors. Unemployment in any case began to increase in spring 1990, as the economy hovered on the edge of recession.

11. The European Monetary System (EMS). Since 1988, Mrs Thatcher has followed the advice of Sir Alan Walters and opposed Britain's entry into the EMS, a system which stabilises exchange rates for European currencies. He believes the British economy will best flourish if the pound is allowed to float in accordance with market conditions. Chancellor Nigel Lawson favoured an early entry and disagreements with Mrs Thatcher caused his resignation in October 1989. His successor, John Major, also favours an early entry as the best means of keeping inflation under control. Critics say that this semi-public row over entry into the EMS had adversely affected British financial interests in the late 1980s.

How one judges Mrs Thatcher's stewardship of the economy depends upon the perspective adopted and developments which are still under way. Since the punishing 1979−81 recession, the economy showed such apparent dynamism in the late 1980s that no less a person than the Japanese ambassador to Britain was moved to describe it as 'an economic miracle'. Productivity, investment and inflation figures tended to reinforce this view, but critics argue that much of this prosperity did not reflect basic improvements in the economy, but a credit boom caused by injudiciously low interest rates. Certainly, the consequences of overheating in the economy blighted Mrs Thatcher's third administration and poses serious questions as she prepares for her fourth general election contest.

Further reading

Peter Curwen (ed.), *Understanding the UK Economy*, Macmillan, 1990.

R. Dornbusch and R. Layard, *The Performance of the British Economy*, Oxford University Press, 1987.

John Eatwell, *Whatever Happened to Britain?* BBC, 1982.

Milton Friedman, *Free to Choose*, Penguin, 1980.

Andrew Gamble, *Britain in Decline*, Macmillan, 1985.

William Keegan and R. Pennant Rea, *Who runs the Economy?*, Temple Smith, 1979.

A. Walters, *Britain's Economic Renaissance*, Oxford University Press, 1987.

Martin J. Wiener, *English Culture and the Decline of the Industrial Spirit 1850–1980*, Cambridge University Press, 1981.

Questions

1. Is central government planning for the economy essential or inimical to economic prosperity?

2. 'Britain's economy is in decline because the British workman is the laziest in the world.' Criticise this view.

3. 'Britain will have to accept high levels of unemployment for the indefinite future.' Discuss.

17

PRESSURE GROUPS

The theory which underpins our government is that of representative democracy. At least once every five years voters elect their representatives to the House of Commons. The majority party forms the government and proceeds to carry out its programme with the help of the civil service and the regular parliamentary endorsement which its majority provides. At the next election voters can decide whether or not the ruling party deserves another term of office. The diagram below illustrates the theory.

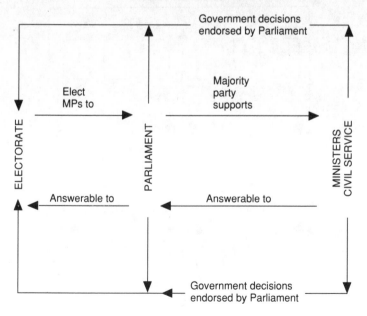

This is a very simplified view, of course. In reality voters never express a genuine collective wish, and even those who have voted for the party in power will disagree with aspects of government policy. Many will use their membership of pressure groups − over half the population belong to one kind of pressure group or another − to influence, counteract or reverse government policy in certain cases. Similarly, governments do not faithfully carry out their programmes in a vacuum. At every stage they consult and negotiate with these organised groups, amending, transforming or even abandoning their policies where necessary.

What happens at elections sets the general context for policy decisions − by selecting the party which forms the government. Remember, too, that policies are usually formed in opposition only in outline. The determination of specific policies in government emerges from a complex process involving, at its heart, consultation between Ministers, civil servants and representatives of those interests likely to be affected. The latter are often pressure-group

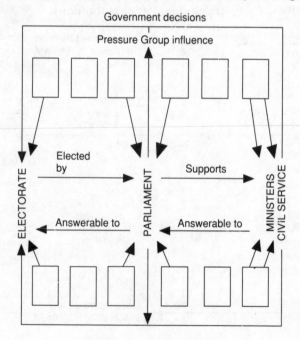

leaders, who seek to strengthen their hand in dealing with Ministers and civil servants by influencing Parliament, other pressure groups, the media and public opinion. A classic study of pressure groups concludes that 'Their day-to-day activities pervade every sphere of domestic policy, every day, every way, in every nook and cranny of government' (Finer, p. 17). The second diagram shows how the theory is affected in practice by the permeation of pressure-group influence.

Representative democracy, which under the present voting system is based upon geographical areas, is therefore supplemented in practice by what can be seen as *functional* or *group* representation.

Some scholars, S. E. Finer and S. H. Beer included, have argued that such 'informal' representation is now more important than the 'formal' parliamentary system. Certainly people are more prepared to join and be active in groups which defend or advance their various interests than political parties which organise electoral representation. Some see the two systems as complementary, but others fear that pressure groups 'short-circuit' the democratic chain of representation and accountability. This question is returned to in the final section.

Development of pressure groups

Government has always had to deal with groups in society, but in the last two centuries they have organised themselves more effectively as society has become more complex and government intervenes in more areas of life. The anti-slavery movement and the Anti-Corn Law League were two early examples. Many philanthropic societies grew up in the nineteenth century, and government came to support, subsidise or even take over their roles altogether.

The nineteenth century also saw the formation of the major economic groups concerned with industrial production. Trade unions increased in membership and coalesced to form bigger units, while business groups too formed federations in order to negotiate more effectively with the unions and the government, itself an increasingly important economic interest. This process was catalysed by two world wars and Labour's 1945–50 nationalisation measures.

G

Types of pressure group

Pressure groups can be described as organised groups which seek to influence government policies. This definition is a useful catch-all for all the extra-governmental influences upon policy, but it puts a youth club that writes to its local MP on the same level as the TUC seeking to influence economic policy. When over half the population belong to groups which at some time or other try to influence government policy is hardly surprising that most definitions are unsatisfactory.

Useful distinctions can be made between:

1. Economic (or interest) groups

(a) *Trade unions*, representing workers, seek to improve their members' pay and conditions of employment, and to influence public and government thinking on a whole range of social and economic issues. Their central or 'peak' organisation is the Trades Union Congress (TUC).

(b) *Business organisations* are interested in maintaining the social and political conditions that favour their activites. Their peak organisation is the Confederation of British Industry (CBI). Increasingly important are the multinational companies. These are large international businesses with varied interests which use enormous investment power and the ability to switch operations to other countries (where conditions might be more favourable) to influence government decisions.

(c) *Professional associations* that represent and defend the interests of people with advanced training and qualifications, e.g. the British Medical Association, the National Union of Teachers. Increasingly these organisations are affiliating to the TUC.

2. Cause groups

(a) *Sectional groups* defend and promote the interests of specific social groups, e.g. Age Concern (old people), Shelter (the homeless or badly housed), the Child Poverty Action Group, the Automobile Association (motorists), and the typically British local voluntary associations which exist in great numbers.

(b) *Attitude groups* share common beliefs and objectives on a particular issue and seek change in the interests of society as a whole, e.g. the Howard League for Penal Reform, the

Electoral Reform Society, the National Council for Civil Liberties
(NCCL).

Such classifications can be misleading in that some pressure
groups have more than one of the above characteristics: for
example, inasmuch as they represent the interests of working-class
people, trade unions are also sectional groups; and the Politics
Association – closely connected with this book – is both a
professional organisation representing the interests of politics
teachers and an *attitude* group seeking to alert government and
society to the need for political education.

3. Values and pressure groups are closely related and provide
an interesting alternative form of classification. The more acceptable its objectives the more likely a pressure group is to achieve
them. Richard Rose (*Politics in England*, 1980, pp. 234–5)
identifies six possible relationships between group aims and cultural
norms briefly summarised and adapted as: (*a*) *harmony*, e.g. the
RSPCA; (*b*) *increasingly acceptable values*, e.g. the women's
rights movement; (*c*) *fluctuating acceptability*, e.g. trade unions;
(*d*) *indifference*, e.g. the anti-smoking movement before it was
backed by medical evidence; (*e*) *fading support*, e.g. the Lord's Day
Observance Society, and (*f*) *conflict with cultural values*.

Having no need to win acceptability, a group in harmony with
cultural norms may seek to identify its aims with the interests of
the country as a whole or, more typically, to concentrate upon
influencing administrative decisions; other groups will need to
spend time and resources fighting for acceptability.

Insider and outsider groups

Wyn Grant (1989 and 1990) uses a somewhat similar typology based
upon the degree of intimacy pressure groups have with the policy-
making process. He identifies three kinds of insider groups, all of
which are constrained to some extent by the 'rules of the game':
prisoner groups dependent upon government support (e.g. those
Third World charities financed mainly by government); *low-profile*
or *high-profile* groups (e.g. the CBI used to be a discreet, behind-
the-scenes group, but then chose to court the media and acquire a
higher profile). *Outsider groups* are less constrained; once again
there are three. *Potential insider* groups will strive to establish

credibility through media campaigns, meetings with ministers and civil servants. *Outsider groups* by necessity lack the political skills to become insiders; for example, they will tend to couch their demands in extravagant or strident language, instead of the sophisticated, esoteric codes of the Whitehall bureaucracy. *Ideological outsider groups* deliberately place themselves beyond the pale of Whitehall because they wish to challenge its values and authority. Grant illustrates his typology with the example of animal welfare groups, which range from the respectable, 'insider' RSPCA, to the outsider, Animal Liberation groups, using threats and violence to pursue their ends.

Pressure-group personnel

Cause groups usually have only a small permanent staff and rely upon voluntary help which is often middle or upper-class in origin. Government sometimes channels funds into cause groups which it regards as particularly important – e.g. MIND receives one-fifth of its income from central government – or helps establish them where they are thought to be necessary, e.g. in the field of race relations. Trade unions and professional and business associations have large staffs, and the TUC and CBI employ several hundred people who shadow the work of government departments. Over the years the large pressure groups and government bureaucracies have become increasingly similar in recruitment and mode of operation, and pressure-group personnel are often drawn into government employ. Nowadays they are often career professionals rather than activists, but this is not so true of pressure-group leaders, who tend to be committed people who often move over into mainstream politics, e.g. in the 1970s John Davies from CBI to Conservative Cabinet, David Ennals from MIND to Labour Cabinet, and Frank Field from CPAG to Labour MP.

Relations with government

These are usually cordial and co-operative: each can give what the other wants.

Pressure groups want to protect and advance the interests of their members through: access to the decision-making process;

the recognised right to be consulted; contacts with Ministers and civil servants; real influence on policy formulation.

Governments rely heavily upon pressure groups for information and advice; civil servants, after all, are not experts in all the matters they must advise Ministers upon. They also hope that, in exchange for a say in policy-making (i.e. becoming 'insider' groups), pressure groups will: support measures passed; co-operate in their implementation; accept the authority of government; respect the confidentiality of discussions and behave in a 'responsible' fashion.

Hidden from public view, these transactions take place all the time. Indeed, without them government would be impossible. With government controlling nearly half of all economic activity it is inevitable that it should work closely with the economic pressure groups: they are virtually interdependent. Occasionally, however, they cannot agree and conflict ensues. It may be because government policy has changed radically, as in 1945 when the British Medical Association challenged Labour's plans to nationalise the health service or as in 1971, when Mr Heath tried to bring trade unions within the framework of his Industrial Relations Act. On such occasions both government and pressure groups are forced back upon the power they can command.

Government naturally has the greater power. It controls the vast economic resources of the State and the decision-making process, can freeze out a group from the process if it chooses, has the authority of law and in the last resort commands the forces of law and order.

Pressure groups do not have such monolithic power but they can bargain, threaten or retaliate in a variety of ways, as follows.

Methods

1. Violence and illegality. Hijackers and terrorists have shown how effective these techniques can be, albeit at high risk to themselves. Few groups would consider such extreme measures, but some do occasionally break the law to draw attention to their cases. Particularly active from the mid-1980s onwards have been various Animal Liberation groups, which have frequently broken the law to direct attention to the use of live animals in scientific experiments, the killing of animals for furs, and so forth. In June

1990 a bomb under the car of a scientific researcher exploded, badly injuring a one-year-old in Bristol.

2. Denial of function. As most cause groups seek to publicise ideas or serve the interests of social groups, this is not a technique they can use: it is the preserve of economic groups. Business concerns can lock out their workers, or direct investment elsewhere; multinationals can, and often do, threaten to move their activities to other, more agreeable countries. Trade unions, of course, can withdraw their labour through strike action.

3. Publicity-seeking techniques are used by all pressure groups and include demonstrations, marches, advertising, articles, books, specialist reports, broadcasts and so forth: a glance at the papers any day will reveal how successful their efforts have been. The more unusual the technique the more likely the media are to be interested; women camping outside the cruise missile site at Greenham Common in the 80s attracted considerable media coverage.

4. Political parties. Most cause groups try to pitch their message above the party political debate, but some seek to influence one party in particular. The Campaign for Nuclear Disarmament (CND), for example, has been able to command substantial support in the Labour Party and this was a key factor in the party's adoption of a non-nuclear defence policy for a time in the 80s.

5. Parliament. Many MPs automatically represent economic interests by virtue of being businessmen, trade unionists, doctors, lawyers or whatever, and can be relied upon to articulate and defend the interests of such groups. Additionally, certain pressure groups persuade MPs, and often pay them a retainer, to represent and defend their interests in Parliament. The practice is regarded as acceptable as long as MPs do not prejudice their voting freedom in the Commons – though some do have contractual agreements. Some MPs strongly criticise this practice as a form of 'buying' support. Also criticised is the increasing activity of professional lobbyists who seek to influence MPs on behalf of powerful economic interests.

6. Ministers and civil servants, substantially control the taking of executive decisions and the initiation of major legislation. Consultations with pressure groups take place mostly away from public view, most typically in the hundreds of joint advisory committees. This is the inner sanctum of influence to which most groups seek access.

Governability

As the economy has become more complex since the war its elements have become more interdependent. Small groups of key workers are consequently able to wield great power by threatening to disrupt the working of the economy. To be successful, government economic policy has to win general acceptance, but this is not easy. In the 1970s many urged the TUC and CBI to reach annual agreements on such subjects as wage levels – as in Sweden or West Germany – but these bodies are only loose coalitions: they cannot enter into agreements and be sure their members will keep to them.

Some commentators, like Professor Anthony King, have argued that the difficulties of reaching consensus between such wide ranges of antithetical, autonomous groups has made Britain harder to govern. Mrs Thatcher's answer was to disavow the consensus approach and assert the executive power of government. Her style, and to an extent the style of her government, has been to squeeze pressure groups towards the periphery of decision-making, to be less interested in listening and more concerned to act in accordance with what has already been decided as necessary.

Economic groups and political parties

The support of important economic groups has proved vital to political parties as a source of finance and membership.

1. Business and the Conservative Party. Whilst there is no formal link, businessmen are to be found at every level of Conservative Party organisation. Constitutency associations provide only a quarter of party finance: some 60 per cent derives from company donations – 80 per cent in election years. 'Front' organisations like British United Industrialists or Aims of Industry exist to channel donations from companies to the party coffers. However, in 1981 three-fifths of the top fifty industrial and commercial bodies did not give money for political purposes, and the amount from those that do is subject to the vicissitudes of the economy. The close congruence of values which obviates the need for formal connections does not prevent business from falling out with Conservative governments. The Director-General of the CBI once called for a 'bare knuckle' fight to make Mrs Thatcher change her deflationary policies, but the CBI normally takes a markedly pro-Conservative line on economic issues.

2. Trade unions and the Labour Party

(a) *Institutional links.* The Labour Party emerged out of collaboration between trade unions and socialist societies in 1900, so it is hardly surprising that the unions retain close institutional links. Some 10 million workers are trade unionists, half of whom belong to unions affiliated to the Labour Party, providing seven-eighths of its overall membership. The TUC is not officially attached to the party, but close personal and institutional contacts exist between the respective leaderships.

(b) *Finance.* Unless an affiliated trade union member 'contracts out' a regular contribution is made from his pay to a political fund which is used to support the Labour Party. Unions contribute about three-quarters of party funds in this way and substantially more in election years. In addition about 40 per cent of Labour MPs are directly sponsored by unions (who provide 80 per cent of election expenses). This does not guarantee that MPs will always support union policy in Parliament, but they usually do.

(c) *Voting power.* In accordance with their financial contributions trade unions dominate the annual conference through the system of block voting, which enables unions to cast votes according to the number of levy-paying members. Critics of this system point out that it often enables the leaders of large unions — three-fifths of members belong to the eleven largest, and a quarter to the TGWU and AUEW — effectively to determine decisions. They also dispute the numbers of levy-paying members which some unions claim.

Of the twenty-nine members of the party's National Executive Committee, trade union block votes annually elect eighteen at the party conference, and from January 1981 trade unions were give a 40 per cent say in the election of the party leader and deputy leader.

Neil Kinnock would like to reduce the power of block voting and replace it eventually by a 'one member, one vote' system. At the constituency party level, some changes have already been introduced and more initiatives will be debated in future conferences. Some commentators point out, however, that block votes have traditionally reinforced leadership policies and that Kinnock, too, has benefited in the past from such support.

(*d*) *Political interaction.* Trade union relations with the Labour Party have been an uneasy marriage, particularly when Labour has been in government and has attempted measures perceived as threatening union interests. In 1969 unions used their influence with Labour MPs to prevent legislation altering trade union freedom to take strike action. When Heath passed his own Industrial Relations Act in 1971 the unions refused to co-operate, and the miners' strike in January 1974 precipitated a general election which the Conservatives lost.

Labour won power as the party which could work with the unions: its 'social contract', worked out by the TUC–Labour Party Liaison Committee, was its blueprint for success. However, the unions, increasingly led by left-wingers, now appreciated the leverage which government fear of inflation had provided. Having flexed their muscles against Heath, their wage demands proved beyond the control of the Wilson government. When wage and price inflation soared to 30 per cent, the big unions led the move towards voluntary restraint. For two years it held, and inflation fell to 8 per cent, but when the unions refused to accept pay restraint after 1978 they embarked on a collision course with the Callaghan government which culminated in the 1978–79 'winter of discontent' during which industrial disputes paralysed the country. In the ensuing general election (May 1979) Labour's trade union connection was a liability, and Mrs Thatcher came to office with substantial support for her tough policy towards the unions.

Mrs Thatcher and the unions. In May 1979 Mrs Thatcher could point out that, despite the pro-Labour stance of union leaders, only half their members had voted Labour, and surveys supported her contention that a high proportion disagreed strongly with official Labour policy demands for more nationalisation and so forth. Certainly public support for the unions had been eroded by the traumas of the preceding winter, and the unions themselves were in no mood for an immediate fight.

Mrs Thatcher maintained the initiative by freezing trade unions out of top economic policy-making: she met TUC representatives only three times between May 1979 and October 1981. Len Murray, then General Secretary of the TUC, commented in a radio interview, 'The government doesn't see the point of trade unions. They see them as at best irrelevant and at worst a danger.' Unemployment at 3 ¼ million reduced the bargaining power of the unions: when employment is so precarious workers are reluctant to strike. Fear of unemployment consequently was a startlingly potent government weapon, reducing the TUC from a virtual partner in government under Labour to a pressure group on the periphery of power under the Conservatives. Having lost 3 million members since 1979, the unions face a situation in which less than half the work force is unionised. Fewer members are now coming forward as shop stewards: in manufacturing industry the 1986 figure was down 40 per cent on 1976.

Mrs Thatcher has also bound the trade unions within a new legal framework. Avoiding the precipitate approach of Mr Heath in the early 1970s, she initiated three pieces of legislation: the Employment Acts, 1980 and 1982, and the Trade Union Act, 1984. The main effect has been to end some of the traditional legal immunities which trade unions have enjoyed. More particularly they:

(a) Make trade unions legally responsible for actions by their members and officers who breach the law.

(b) Require unions to obtain a majority vote of members by secret ballot before industrial action can proceed. There were ninety-four such ballots in Britain in 1985, sixty-eight of which said 'yes' to strike action and twenty-five 'no'.

(c) Make secondary picketing and sympathy strikes illegal – the weapons used so tellingly by Arthur Scargill in the 1974 miners' strike.

(d) Require an 80 per cent favourable vote by employees before a closed shop can be established by agreement with an employer.

(e) Require union executives and officers who have a vote on their national executive to be elected by secret ballot at least once every five years.

(f) Require unions to ballot their members every ten years (from 1986) over the maintenance of a political fund.

Some of this legislation was tested during the astonishingly bitter year-long miners' strike of 1984–85. In 1981 Mrs Thatcher had avoided a clash with the miners, but in 1984, with plentiful reserves of coal, an election victory behind her, and new legislation, she took on Arthur Scargill. The police were well prepared for violence on the picket lines, and the sequestration by the courts of the NUM's assets helped eventually to bring the union to its knees. Any doubts that the power the unions enjoyed in the 1970s had been finally shattered were removed. When Rupert Murdoch set up his new printworks at Wapping in 1986, in defiance of the printing unions, the electricians' union breached traditional solidarity and allowed its members to take up the new jobs offered. The TUC seemed powerless to heal these divisions in its own ranks. Strike action, moreover, has declined dramatically. Between May 1985 and May 1986 only 2·4 million working days were lost, compared with an annual average of 11·1 million for 1975–84.

Weakened, poorly led and divided, the position of the unions seems distinctly unfavourable in the early 1990s. However, they may draw encouragement from the almost total success of ballots held on the maintainance of political funds.

Any hopes that trade unionists may have harboured about Labour restoring their traditional, favoured and protected position must have been dashed by the May 1990 policy document.

In 1974 Labour's special relationship with the unions helped it to come to power, but in 1979 this relationship was transformed into a severe liability. Kinnock is concerned to dispel any notion that his party is in thrall to the unions. The old Labour axiom that the law should be kept out of industrial relations has been abandoned: 'This issue today is not "law or no law", but "fair or unfair law".' To this end, Labour proposes a separate, industrial relations court with power of partial sequestration of union funds. Mass picketing would be banned and secondary action restricted to those with a 'direct occupational or professional interest' in the primary dispute.

Pressure groups and democracy

It can be argued that pressure groups complement the process of government by providing:

1. Detailed information on specific areas of economic and social activity without which good government would be impossible.

2. Continuity of communication and consultation between government and public between elections.

3. Defence for minority interests, particularly those connected with parties not in government.

4. Increased participation in the political process by people not necessarily active in political parties.

5. A counter to the monopoly of the political process in Parliament by political parties. Cause groups raise items for discussion which fall outside party manifestos, and economic groups by-pass much potential party conflict by dealing direct with Ministers and civil servants.

6. Dispersal of power downwards from the centralised legislative and executive institutions and in the process providing checks upon their power.

Against this it can be argued:

1. Pressure groups are often unrepresentative and only rarely reflect the broad mass of their membership. Union leaders are often elected by small activist minorities, though we should note that business organisations and other pressure groups often have appointed officers. Neither is accountable to the public as a whole, despite the fact that their influence on policy is considerable.

2. A corporate state? Pressure groups have reduced the power of Parliament by working so closely with Ministers and civil servants. By the time Parliament sees legislation it is all but decided, and only a small minority of Bills are substantially amended on the way to the Queen's signature. Some commentators have discerned the rise of a 'corporate state' in which decisions are shaped and even made by Ministers and officials who are not elected by the public (see Moran, pp. 144–9).

*3. **Pressure groups do not represent society equally**. For example, they favour the strong groups in society – key industrial workers, educated professionals, the business elite – and they favour producer groups rather than consumer interests. Weaker groups like immigrants, old-age pensioners, children or the unemployed have low bargaining strength, and are often poorly organised.

*4. **They often work in secret**. Their consultations with top decision-makers take place behind closed doors, hidden from public scrutiny. S. E. Finer rather dramatically ends his classic study of pressure groups with a plea for 'More light!'

Concluding comment

The nature of pressure-group politics has demonstrated considerable change over the last twenty years: business interests are concentrated into fewer and fewer hands; the traditionally powerful pressure groups – especially the unions – have found their access to decision-making less easy and less effective. On the other hand, there has been a startling increase in nation-wide popular movements, many of them using opinion-influencing techniques to good effect.

This has been particularly true of environmental groups. Between 1971 and 1988, membership grew from 1,000 to 65,000 in Friends of the Earth: 278,000 to 1,634,000 in the National Trust and 98,000 to 540,000 in the Royal Society for the Protection of Birds. Band Aid, Live Aid and, in 1990, the Mandela Concert, have shown the power of the media and popular music to change people's minds and win their support. The anti-apartheid movement, moreover, has chalked up many successes in the last decade, notably the withdrawal of Barclays Bank from South Africa in 1986.

The professional campaigner Des Wilson has been a potent influence in the development of citizen power. Despite Mrs Thatcher's assertion of executive initiative and the decline of trade-union power, pressure-group politics at the national and local level seem to be as vigorous as ever.

Further reading

S. H. Beer, *Britain Against Itself*, Faber, 1982.

A. Cawson, *Corporation and Welfare: Social Policy and State Intervention in Britain*, Heinemann, 1982.

S. E. Finer, *Anonymous Empire*, Pall Mall Press, 1966.

W. Grant, *Pressure Groups, Politics and Democracy in Britain*, Philip Allan, 1989.

— 'Insider and Outsider Pressure Groups', *Social Studies Review*, January 1990.

W. Grant and D. Marsh, *The Confederation of British Industry*, Hodder & Stoughton, 1977.

Anthony King, *Why is Britain Becoming Harder to Govern?*, BBC, 1976.

G. Lee, 'The peace movement' in Bill Jones (ed.), *Political Issues in Britain Today*, Manchester University Press, 3rd edn, 1989.

J. McIlroy, 'Trade unions and the law', in Bill Jones (ed.), *Political Issues in Britain Today*, Manchester University Press, 3rd edn 1989.

M. Moran, *Politics and Society in Britain: an Introduction*, Macmillan, 1989, pp. 121–50.

Richard Rose, *Politics in England – Persistence and Change*, Faber, 1985.

Questions

1. Are pressure groups a necessary evil in democratic society?

2. You are secretary of a local action group which wants to prevent the demolition of your historic town hall. How do you organise your campaign?

3. Should professional lobbyists be allowed to operate in the corridors of Westminster and Whitehall?

18

IS LOCAL GOVERNMENT NECESSARY?

It is easy to gather the impression from frequently voiced criticisms that local government is virtually unnecessary. The cases for and against are considered below, together with some recent changes in local government finance.

The theoretical justification

is similar to the case for any representative government. Elected councillors ensure that government is carried out in the interests of those who ultimately control it: the community as a whole. If representatives are judged to have failed, then they can be replaced by the electorate at local elections. Within the broad guidelines set by central government, local government provides the opportunities for:

1. Participation by local people in the making of decisions which affect them and for their *civic education*.

2. Representation of local opinion and the accountability of local government officers to it.

3. Greater efficiency through popular control and the adaptation of national policies to local conditions.

4. The autonomy of local councils from central control.

Reform of local government

In 1974 an ancient patchwork system of 1,400 local authorities, varying enormously in size and function, was replaced in England and Wales by a two-tier system: fifty-four county councils and 402 constituent district councils. Six new metropolitan counties were created in heavily built-up areas in the north and the West Midlands. Dissatisfaction with the earlier system had been widespread, and the reforms were presaged and strongly influenced by the report of the Redcliffe-Maud Commission, 1966–69. Judgements on the new system, however, have been divided, and some critics argue that practice still deviates alarmingly from theory.

Below arguments for and against local government are considered in an attempt to answer the question posed in the title of this chapter. Some of the critical arguments, of course, could equally be used, and frequently are, to urge a strengthening of local government rather than its abolition.

Participation

1. Against

(a) By *reducing* the number of authorities, and hence councillors, the new system has reduced participation and accessibility.

(b) *Electoral turnout* in local elections averages about 40 per cent – compared with about 75 per cent at general elections – and 40 per cent of local government seats are uncontested. Surveys show that only about 15 per cent of voters ever contact their local councillors; slightly more people contact officials direct.

(c) *Ignorance* of local government is widespread. A survey by this writer in 1974 revealed that out of 100 people intereviewed in an inner-city ward of Manchester only one person knew the names of all three councillors, and he was himself an excouncillor! In July 1981 Michael Heseltine asked an unemployed Liverpool youth whether he had consulted his local councillor; the youth replied, 'What's a councillor?'

(d) *Reorganisation* has confused what understanding of the system already existed, and the larger areas have made town halls even more remote and anonymously bureaucratic. Neighbourhood councils, the bodies which the government hoped would involve people at grass-roots level, have, despite some successes, generally failed to gain support and acceptance.

(e) As councils have become increasingly *dominated by central government* people have accorded local government less attention.

(*f*) Despite the recommendations of the Skeffington (1968) and Dobry (1975) reports on increasing public participation in planning, many local authorities prefer *secrecy* in decision-making and regard public participation as merely a public relations exercise (see Minogue, pp. 184–202).

(*g*) *Pressure groups* in Britain are not well developed at the local level, at least by comparison with the USA, often preferring to work through headquarters rather than liaise direct with councils.

2. For

(*a*) The new system is *more logical* and easier to understand than its predecessor: local government units are now roughly similar in size, and the distribution of functions is the same country-wide.

(*b*) It may be a lower figure than that for general elections but a large number of *people do vote* in local elections, and a substantial number are very active; after all, it is the local party activists who select parliamentary candidates and organise general election campaigns. Councillors themselves become passionately involved in local issues, which also offer a valuable training ground for those who may go on to make their mark at national level.

(*c*) *Pressure groups* may not be as powerful as in the USA but thousands, particularly voluntary organisations with a social purpose, constantly engage in lobbying locally to win resources and advance their causes.

(*d*) A *new emphasis* on local participation is evident in certain party policies. The Liberals and Social Democrats made decentralisation and local democracy a major plank of their political programmes in the 80s. They argued that low levels of knowledge and participation are arguments for reinvigoration rather than further contraction or abolition.

Representation

1. Against

(*a*) Councillors are *unrepresentative* of the public, being dominated by middle-class, middle-aged men: only 13 per cent of local councillors are female (see Stanyer, pp. 95–116).

(*b*) Councillors are of *poor quality*, it is often maintained, too often inflated by self-importance and awareness of their status. Moreover, too many seek office for their own private interests rather than those of the community, e.g. the business contacts that can be made or the planning and financial power that can be wielded. Evidence of corruption at the local level, e.g. the extensive Poulson network in the early 1970s, suggests that desire for personal gain all too frequently tempts councillors into illegal activities.

(*c*) The *increasing domination* of local politics by political parties has diminished representation in that:

(i) Local councillors can no longer exercise their independent judgement on issues that have to follow the party line.

(ii) 'Non-party' men of goodwill in local communities have been deterred from involvement.

(iii) National political issues like education or social policy tend to squeeze out the truly local ones.

(iv) Splits in national parties tend to be mirrored at the local level, e.g. after 1979 Manchester councillors split into bitterly opposed *moderate* and *leftist* factions.

(v) Local elections have become mere occasions for registering dissatisfaction with the governing majority party. When their party wins a general election party activists must allow themselves an inward groan as they contemplate their virtually inevitable losses in mid-term local elections. In June 1986 the Widdicombe report judged this permeation of politics to be a 'malign influence' on local government and urged party balance on committees, a register of interests for councillors and no political affiliations for senior officers.

(*d*) *The establishment of local Ombudsmen* in 1974 to receive complaints about maladministration suggests that councillors are not properly doing their job of redressing public dissatisfactions and grievances.

2. For

(*a*) *No council* can be a truly representative sample of the public: mature, educated people are bound to be overrepresented and maybe this is no bad thing. Moreover local councils are generally less unrepresentative than the House of Commons, which contains, for example, only 6 per cent women.

(*b*) Everyone must make up their own mind on the motivations of councillors, but many are genuinely *public-spirited people* who devote much of their time and energy to the benefit of the community. A 1973 Maud Committee report and the 1976 Salmon report on *Standards of Conduct in Public Life* both revealed the incidence of fraud and corruption in local government to be very low. There seems little doubt that the majority of councillors are honest, and safeguards such as open committees, opposition parties, the press and the Ombudsmen ensure that this will remain so.

(*c*) *The development of parties in democratic systems* is almost inevitable and is indeed necessary for consistency of policy and stability of government. It is natural that local parties should be influenced by national policies, as many of them – education, housing, social services – are concerned with how local government should operate. On the other hand, studies reveal a wealth of essentially local issues which engage councillors from day to day and in election campaigns. Not all councils are dominated by parties, though some studies suggest, interestingly, that these councils are less democratic in their operation than those that are (Minogue, p. 106).

(*d*) On the *Ombudsmen*, some councillors argue that their 'failure' to deal adequately with local grievances was never established and that the utility of the new officers has yet to be proved.

Efficiency

1. Against

(*a*) *Since the war* local government has lost a wide range of functions to central government, e.g. hospitals, social security (or 'poor relief' as it used to be called), gas, electricity and water. Why, then, should this centralising logic not be applied to education, housing or social services? Such a development – it can be argued – would avoid duplication of effort, and ensure uniform standards throughout the country.

(*b*) *Reorganisation of local government* into bigger units has not led to staff savings; quite the opposite. In 1959 there were 1·6 million local government employees; in 1990 there were some

2 million. Few would argue that the country is now substantially better served by its local government.

(c) *Elected councillors are part-time amateurs* in the complex business of government. When their influence is not being skilfully bypassed by professional officers they can just as easily harm the public interest as advance it.

(d) *Certain local government functions* could be performed more efficiently by private companies, e.g. Southend Council contracted its refuse collection to a private company which increased efficiency, cut costs and raised workers' wages and (allegedly) their morale.

2. For

(a) Efficiency is not and should not be the sole yardstick of local government: it is also important that, even when they conflict with efficiency, people's needs should be met and their rights protected. For example, a decision to build a multi-storey car park for council employees in the middle of a park near the town hall might promote efficiency, but is it right to spoil a park and deny its use? Pushing the decision through without consultation will avoid delay, but is it right that objections are not heard and considered? Moreover, such 'efficient' procedures may be counter-productive in that they may generate a groundswell of opposition later, alienate public opinion and harm the co-operative relationship with the public upon which local government is, to an important degree, based.

(b) In certain cases accountability to local councillors might be salutary. Some argue that if Social Security officers were responsible to local councils the fear of councillors intervening on behalf of constituents would improve the quality of service provided.

(c) Larger units can provide more and better services than the previous small, uneconomic councils.

(d) Councillors are not impediments to good government. On the contrary, as Maud pointed out, 'The control of the expert by the amateur representing his fellow citizens is the key to the whole of our system of government ... The best professionals readily agree that they do their best work when they can rely on the informed criticism, stimulation, counsel and support of good councillors. Good professionals and good councillors need one another. Neither is likely to remain good for long without the other' (1969, para. 235).

(e) The changes recommended by the Bains report in the early 1970s, and widely implemented since, have served to streamline committee structure. Previously councillors had sought direct control of services through a large number of committees which frequently concerned themselves with the minutiae of day-to-day matters. Bains urged the gathering of functions together under a reduced number of committees and sub-committees with a powerful 'cabinet'-like committee – commonly called 'Policy and Resources' – to co-ordinate the work of the council and concentrate on policy. Bains also urged the 'corporate planning approach', which has been widely accepted; it emphasises clarity of purpose, co-ordination of departments and future policy.

(f) Privatisation may improve efficiency in certain areas but it is inappropriate in others, e.g. could private companies provide cheaper and more efficient social workers (if indeed one could measure their efficiency?) Moreover the introduction of the profit motive conflicts with the whole spirit and purpose of local government as it has developed in the UK.

Autonomy

1. Against

(a) Strict legal control is exerted by Parliament. The 1972 Local Government Act established a framework of legal powers, and other Acts impose similar constraints, some very specific. Local councils, therefore, have no real autonomy in that they are legally subject to Westminster. They can only do what Parliament says, and have no right to initiate action not so sanctioned, however, sensible.

(b) Extensive judicial control is exerted by the courts. If councils do anything which exceeds the authority granted by parliamentary Act, or its equivalent (e.g. provisional order or delegated legislation), they can be judged to be acting *ultra vires*, 'beyond the law'. If expenditure has been incurred, then the government accountant who annually inspects local government spending, the District Auditor, can 'surcharge' the people responsible. The Maud Commission felt this form of central control deterred enterprise and initiative. Similarly, if a council fails to perform its legal duties a court can order it to do so with an order of *mandamus*.

(c) Substantial administrative control is exercised by central departments via detailed directions and regulations. Close supervision and inspection are exercised over certain services such as the police, the fire service, education and children's services. Further influence and informal control are exerted by regular circulars from central government which advise and urge desired courses of action. Personal contacts with senior servants and exhortatory statements by Ministers complete this dense network of formal and informal administrative controls.

(d) Financial control by central government is the most important form of control, as it underpins the three mentioned above. Central government provides over half the funds required by local authorities and uses them to ensure compliance, some say subservience (see below).

(e) *Attempts at reform have been fruitless.* The larger units created by reorganisation have not succeeded in asserting local government against the encroachments of the centre, which since 1974 have even gathered pace. In the late 70s devolution of power from Westminster to regional Assemblies was seen as an antidote for administrative delays due to centralised control and a possible device for making regionally based central government functions, like social security and employment, accountable to locally elected representatives. However, no one could agree on the form such devolutions should take; the proposals ended in farce and disaster for the Callaghan government and helped to bring it down.

2. For   Supporting arguments accept that some measure of central control is necessary to maintain uniform standards and for the management of the economy as a whole (local government spending, after all, is some 15 per cent of GNP), whilst stressing the freedom of action which councils enjoy.

(a) Legal control is not rigidly applied. Section 110 of the Local Government Act, 1972, gives some latitude in that councils can do anything 'which is calculated to facilitate or is conducive or incidental to the discharge of any of their functions' even if no statutory power authorises it. Moreover legislation distinguishes between duties − functions which authorities must perform to a given standard, like school education − and discretionary powers, like adult education, which leave wide scope for initiative to individual councils. In 1979 300 central controls over local government were abolished.

(b) Once minimum standards are achieved, central government is happy to allow local authorities to set a standard of service which they think appropriate for local conditions.

(c) There is a wide and important area, occupied by local councils, between forming policy in Whitehall and applying it in particular local circumstances. The application of national policies poses all kinds of questions and options upon which councils can take decisions. Further, central departments vary considerably in the degree of control they apply even over the services which councils have a duty to perform. Ministers of Education, moreover, have been known to complain that they have no real executive power; that their role is essentially one of persuading local authorities to accept and apply central policy.

(d) The ability of councils to set local poll tax rates (subject to some central control) gives them an independent source of finance (see below).

(e) Local authorities can exert substantial influence on party organisations and central government via the three powerful local authority Associations, of Metropolitan, County and District Authorities. These bodies liaise closely with Whitehall departments and act as permanent pressure groups for local government interests. Government needs the co-operation and advice of local government and does not lightly ignore its representations.

Assessment

Considered together, the complex network of legal, judicial, administrative and financial controls seem to offer a formidable constraint on local freedom of action and initiative. Local government cannot be said properly to exist if it is merely doing the bidding of Westminster and Whitehall. Those who argue thus have a powerful case, particularly when it is considered that local government has lost many functions since the war, had a less than ideal two-tier structure imposed upon it by way of reform, and has been disappointed over the saga of devolution. If local government is merely the agent, the servant of central government, then why not dispense with the fiction altogether?

The answer is that local government is a vital democratic element in our government. In practice it enjoys considerable lattitude. Central government for the most part has no wish to dominate local councils, merely to ensure their efficiency; control is usually applied with understanding and sensitivity. In a large number of areas the relationship is one of genuine partnership and mutual assistance. People should be involved in decisions which affect them and have the power to influence and alter, if not reverse them.

Joseph Chamberlain, the great nineteenth-century prophet of local government (and later a Conservative Cabinet member), put it neatly as long ago as 1874: 'I have an abiding faith in municipal institutions, an abiding sense of the value and importance of local government ... our corporation [Birmingham] represents the full authority of the people. Through them, you obtain the full and direct expression of the popular will.'

Central control may seem seductively efficient but in the long run it would more than likely prove counter-productive. Government cannot work without the consent and co-operation of the governed. If the balance has been shifting towards the centre since the war, then – as Maud (1968), Layfield (1976) and a wide body of councillors and officers argue – it should be corrected. The problem is that, in the view of her critics, Mrs Thatcher has transformed a shift into a veritable stampede.

Mrs Thatcher and local government

Mrs Thatcher has been unwilling to grant local government greater freedom of action if the result is more latitude for Labour councillors. She maintains that certain socialist-led councils tend to be profligate, inefficient and not especially popular. A number of measures have resulted.

1. Abolition of the metropolitan county councils and the GLC. By 1981 Labour had won control of all six metropolitan counties and the GLC. Ken Livingstone, leader of the GLC, used the national prominence of his post to criticise the government. Attempts by Ministers and the right-wing press to denigrate him backfired; he became a popular national figure. In 1983 a Cabinet committee recommended abolition of this tier of government and a commitment to this effect appeared in the Conservative's election manifesto. A bitter three-year fight ensued to turn the undertaking into reality.

In support of abolition the government argued that the main functions of the metropolitan counties – police, public transport and the fire service were: not important enough to need elected councils; overlapped confusingly with district councils; and cost disproportionately more than other local government services.

Opponents of abolition argued it was: undemocratic and inconsistent (Conservatives, after all, had set them up in 1972); contrary to the popular will as expressed in opinion polls; unlikely to save money; and likely to create a bureaucratic nightmare of joint boards running city-wide services.

Despite the opposition of influential Tories and one major reverse in the Lords (see Chapter 11) the GLC and the other counties disappeared in April 1986. The Inner London Education Authority survived the process as a new, separately elected body, but it too bit the dust four years later. Despite all the apocalyptic warnings, the abolitions, especially outside London, have had remarkably few repercussions.

2. City technology colleges. Conservative unhappiness with low-achieving Labour-controlled schools in the inner cities had been well known for some time, but the Education Secretary's announcement of twenty new city technology colleges (CTCS) at the Conservative Party conference in 1986 nevertheless came as a surprise. The colleges are controlled centrally, not locally, and have selective rather than general entry, with emphasis on science and technology to aid the national economy. Private finance for CTCs, however, are of the conditions of their establishment, has been hard to come by.

3. Local government finance

(*a*) *Changes in the rates, 1979–87.* Whilst at Environment, Michael Heseltine changed the system of funding local government in an attempt to achieve expenditure cuts and exert stricter financial control. Under the old system *revenue account* income (for day-to-day running expenses) was derived from rates on local property, income from certain services and grants from government amounting to about 60 per cent of total spending. The largest of these was the Rate Support Grant, calculated on the basis of a *subsidy to domestic ratepayers*, a *resource element* to compensate areas of the country with low rateable values, and a *needs element* based upon social need, using past spending patterns as criteria. In theory there was no limit to how much a local authority could spend, and this open-ended remit conflicted with government determination to rein in public expenditure and curb inflation.

The Local Government Planning and Land Act, 1980, replaced the RSG with a block-grant formula − Grant Related Expenditure based not upon past spending but upon a Whitehall estimate of how much local authorities needed to provide services at a uniform national level. Civil servants calculated average spending on particular services and allocated each authority a sum which it 'should' spend. The idea was to enable Ministers to control the overall level of grant and distribute it in a way that hit the 'overspenders'. Hesletine believed they were politically motivated, i.e. Labour-controlled.

Naturally, councils denied grant which they had formerly received could raise extra finance by levying higher rates, but the new system allowed only a 10 per cent excess over the 'correct' figure; if they exceeded it they would be penalised by a corresponding reduction in grant.

The *Rates Act*, moreover, in 1983 enabled the government to control the expenditure of 'extravagant' authorities and provided a reserve power to control all local authority expenditure. Of the eighteen councils in 1984 selected for *rate-capping*, the sixteen Labour-controlled councils agreed not to comply. Several refused to reduce expenditure and ran a deficit, but by the end of 1985 only the Militant-led Liverpool Council had refused to accept the new system. In 1984 a deal with Patrick Jenkin enabled the city to survive, but in 1985 its leaders were forced to borrow from Swiss banks to make ends meet. By this time Derek Hatton and his colleagues had exhausted their credibility in the Labour Party and its NEC moved in 1986 to expel them.

Background to the poll tax

By 1988/89 the percentage of local government finance provided by central government had fallen to 48 per cent compared with 60 per cent in 1979. Local government spending, however, had continued to rise through creative accounting of many and ingenious kinds − some councils sold off property and then leased it back − and sustained increases in the rates. The 1985 revaluation of rates in Scotland had already provoked protests from badly hit Conservative property owners, which helped reinforce Mrs Thatcher's resolve to replace the rates with root and branch reform.

Conservative critics of the system focused upon its low degree of popular accountability. Only half of the electorate paid rates and one-third of those received rebates. That meant that in most places a majority of people did not bear the full burden of the rates and were not too worried if their elected representatives levied high rates to pay for services. As Nicholas Ridley, the Environment Secretary, noted: three out of four people in local elections vote to 'spend other people's money'. As business rates provided more than half of locally raised revenue, Conservatives also argued that councils which set a high rate unfairly penalised the business community, thereby deterring the creation of wealth and employment. In their favour, however, rates were widely understood, cheap to collect, difficult to evade and were levied roughly in accordance with ability to pay (people in large properties paid more, but usually earned more, and the lower paid were either exempt or qualified for rebates).

The 1981 White Paper *Alternatives to Domestic Rates* found against the rates, but also opposed the introduction of local income, sales or payroll taxes and specifically opposed a per capita charge, or 'poll tax'. By 1986, however, the atmosphere had changed. The 'poll tax' concept was exhumed, dusted down and presented anew. The Conservatives' 1987 manifesto declared the rates would go.

The extended debates over the resultant Local Government Finance Bill resembled the trench warfare of the First World War. At times it seemed as if no one in the Conservative party, from backbenchers to senior Cabinet Ministers, really supported the measure except for Mrs Thatcher herself. Rebellions were frequent (some of them involving Thatcher loyalists like Dr Rhodes Boyson), both in the Commons and the Lords, but the bill finally became law in July 1988. Subsequent events proved that Conservative reluctance to support the measure was justified.

The Act simplified the block grant system into a centrally-determined revenue support grant which could be adjusted during a transitional period (1990–94) to mitigate the effects upon the new *business rate* and *community charge* or *poll tax*: the name Mrs Thatcher does not like (though she used it once by mistake in PM's Questions) but which the public prefers.

The uniform business rate

The principle of taxing business properties was maintained (agricultural land, churches and charities exempted), together with the practice of local collection. But the rate of tax is now set nationally, gathered into two pools for England and Wales, and disbursed to local authorities from the centre in accordance with population densities. The new tax, which came into being in April 1990, has been unpopular with councillors and businessmen alike. City-centre businesses, especially in the South have been seriously affected and some will be non-viable once transitional, protective arrangements have expired. Now that the tax is national:

(a) Chambers of Commerce and other bodies will no longer be able to negotiate with local authorities over the levels to be set and the extent and quality of services to be provided.

(b) Another substantial slice of local government finance has been drawn into the centre.

The community charge/poll tax

This comprises three elements:

(a) The *personal* flat rate charge upon all adults over eighteen, excluding the homeless, mental patients, prisoners and certain other categories. Rebates of up to 80 per cent are available for those on low incomes; students pay 20 per cent; and receipients of Income Support also receive assistance with their 20 per cent liability.

(b) The *standard* charge is levied upon second homes or empty properties.

(c) The *collective* charge is paid by hoteliers, hostel managers and landlords on numbers of guests resident.

Criticisms of poll tax have concentrated on its:

1. Unfairness. A roadsweeper living in a terraced council house could pay as much poll tax as the Duke of Westminster, the richest man in Britain. Some analysts calculate that twice as many people will pay more as a result of the tax than those who pay less, but the tax is widely perceived as unfair even by those who benefit from it − the Duke of Westminster, incidentally, included.

2. Cost. In April 1990 the Institute of Fiscal Studies calculated that the average cost of collecting rates in 1989–90 was £560,000 per local authority; the estimated costs of collecting the poll tax, however, was calculated at £1·3 million. Not only will they have to send bills to twice as many people, but local authorities face particular problems in collecting the *standard* and *collective* charges. The Institute of Revenues Rating and Valuation calculated in May 1990 that the cost of collecting poll tax from the 5 million poorest people in the country would actually exceed the revenue generated.

3. Ease of evasion. Because property is highly visible and static, rates were difficult to evade. Poll tax poses problems in that the individuals it is based upon can avoid registration or keep on moving from one district to another. Two months after the introduction of the tax, the *Independent on Sunday* (6 June 1990) revealed that one adult in eight was refusing to pay, most of them on grounds of principle rather than hardship.

4. Lack of accountability. The central idea of the poll tax was to make councils more accountable. If all voters had to pay some element of taxation they would, so the argument runs, use their votes more discriminatingly at election times. They might vote in parties proposing high poll tax levels or, as the government hoped, would vote to keep taxes down. Either way, the voter would decide.

In the spring of 1990, government computers calculated the 'standard spending assessment' (SSA) or the poll tax figure required to meet Whitehall's calculation of local authority needs. In the event, the majority of councils, many of them Conservative, exceeded their SSAs by up to £100 or more. But instead of leaving decisions to the voters, the government proposed to use its capping powers on twenty-one selected councils – all of them Labour. Critics claimed that the criteria of selection had been chosen deliberately to indict Labour councils.

Other critics, often Conservative, objected to the 'safety net' arrangements, whereby those councils benefiting from the new system should contribute towards those which did not. This meant that some councils which had tried hard to set a low tax were prevented from presenting it as such.

5. *Centralising tendencies*. Ostensibly, the 1988 financial reforms were designed to make local government more democratic, but paradoxically they took authority away from councils, took accountability away from the voters and gave yet more power to Westminster.

6. *Complexity*. The poll tax was supposed to be simple and easy to understand. Like many ill thought-out ideas, however, its simplicity was lost when it became submerged in the plethora of amendments and alterations attending its implementation.

The poll tax and public opinion

Polls showed that majority opinion hardened against the poll tax after the 1987 election; by March 1990 it was perceived as the most important political issue and riots took place in various big cities in protest against its imminent introduction. On 23 March, poll tax was the major issue on the Mid-Staffs By-Election. Labour's Mrs Sylvia Heal overturned a 14,654 Conservative majority to win by 9,449 votes. In early April, an anti-poll tax demonstration in the West End of London turned, according to *The Economist* (7 April 1990), 'into the worst assault on police and property for more than 100 years'. Small wonder commentators drew parallels between the Peasants' Revolt in 1381, occasioned by the last attempt to impose a poll tax on British people.

The local elections on 3 May 1990 became something of a plebiscite on the new tax. Labour won hundreds of seats and polled 42 per cent of the votes to the Conservaties' 31 per cent. However, there were some gleams of comfort for the Tories; they polled best in Conservative authorities setting a low tax and in Labour authorities setting a high tax. Voters, it appeared, responded to poll tax levels to a degree, but for the most part, they appeared to blame the government for higher local taxes rather than local councils, as the government had hoped. In London, however, the two Conservative flagship councils of Westminster and Wandsworth, which had set very low poll tax rates, were resoundingly returned with increased majorities. Party Chairman, Kenneth Baker, claimed the prinicple of the tax had been vindicated by these spectacular successes, but critics dismissed them as fig leaf victories, won only through politically inspired government subsidies which kept tax levels artificially low.

Improving the poll tax

In May 1990 Michael Heseltine offered a package of proposals to make the poll tax more acceptable, including the idea of banding payments in accordance with ability to pay. This proposal, however, had been embodied in a much debated amendment by Michael Mates, MP in 1988 and eventually defeated by just twenty-five votes. Heseltine was opposed to the obvious expedient of feeding central government funds into local government in order to keep tax levels down. This however is what the government decided to do in July 1990 when Mr Patten announced £3 billion would be spent for this purpose.

Labour exploited Conservative discomfort to the hilt, but would not elaborate too much on its own alternatives to the poll tax, apart from saying that it would be a reformed version of the old rates system. Labour also proposed to return the business rate to local control.

From a simple, well-intentioned idea, Mrs Thatcher's Third Administration managed through lack of foresight and political mismanagement, aided and abetted by Tory MPs who suppressed their doubts, to create a monster which devoured the government's credibility in 1989–90. The protracted debate on the poll tax also drew unflattering attention to Britain's ailing local government system. Whilst decisions have been progressively decentralised in other European countries, Britain has been reacting to problems by prescribing successive doses of centralisation. In retrospect, the 1972 restructuring has been found wanting and a number of new possible reforms have established themselves on the agenda for serious discussion.

Reform of local government

These proposals include:

1. Transfer of education funding to central government. This would remove a vital function from the vicissitudes of local politics, but would be a further centralising measure and would merely transfer a burden on to central taxation.

2. *Unitary authorities*. This would end the confusing two-tier system of accountability. Under this proposal one council would have accross-the-board responsibility for local government functions throughout its area.

3. *Directly elected, paid chief executives or 'mayors'*. This idea, based on American experience, is much favoured by Mr Heseltine. He wants someone 'in command in order to bring local spending under control' and provide clearly accountable leadership.

4. *Annual elections* with one-third of councillors standing for re-election in *all* councils rather than just district councils as at present.

5. *Devolution and regional government*. Since devolution brought down the Callaghan government in 1979, this proposal has languished, but calls for more autonomy in Scotland and Wales have recently gathered force and Britain's increasingly close contacts with the European Community have revealed how anomalous Britain's lack of a regional structure is compared with our European partners.

Chris Patten, the Conservative Environment Secretary in 1990, has sensibly ruled out any possibility of local government reform until after the next election. Labour, however, have set out their stall in the form of: a Scottish Legislative Assembly and an elected Welsh Chamber with limited powers; ten regional districts with powers devolved from Whitehall; annual elections and unitary authorities.

Further reading

Richard Bailey and Richard Stokes, *Local Government Rules OK*, 1990.

M. A. Baines, *The New Local Authorities: Management and Structure*, HMSO, 1972.

Howard Elcock, *Local Government*, Methuen, 1982.

Sylvia Horton, *The Local Government Finance Act, 1988: The End of the Rates*, *Talking politics*, Summer 1989.

F. Layfield, *Local Government Finance*, HMSO, 1976.

G. Lee, 'Town Hall Versus Whitehall', in Bill Jones (ed.), *Political Issues in Britain Today*, Manchester University Press, 3rd edn 1989.

Martin Minogue, 'Comments on contemporary British Government', *Local Government in Britain*, Vol. 2, Cambridge University Press, 1977.

Redcliffe Maud Report, HMSO, 1969.

J. Stanyer, *Understanding Local Government*, Martin Robertson, 1980.

Gerry Stoker, *The Politics of Local Government*, Macmillan, 1989.

Questions

1. Do you think that most government should be local?

2. 'For the most part, elected councillors are merely puppets of full-time local government officers.' Is this fair comment?

3. Consider the arguments for and against the abolition of metropolitan county councils.

19

POLITICAL CONCEPTS

This chapter asks what is meant by a 'concept', and by the term 'politics', and examines a number of key political concepts.

What is politics?

'Politics' is one of those words which describe an activity, as well as the study of that activity, so it is important to be clear about the sense which is being employed. What activity does 'politics' describe? Let's begin with what 'politicians' do. A number of functions immediately spring to mind:

1. They direct or help direct our system of government.
2. They help formulate laws.
3. They are responsible for the defence of the country and for law and order.
4. They try to resolve disputes between different groups in society.
5. They take decisions upon how resources should be distributed.

The list could be much longer, of course, but the message seems to come through that politics is concerned with government, institutions and processes. But is this all that politics means? Consider the following news items:

1. American President is criticised by Congress
2. Shelter demands more financial aid for homeless
3. Car workers threaten strike action for more pay
4. Soap-opera star sacked after dispute with producer

Which are political? Clearly the first is highly political: the American government's chief decision-maker is being criticised by that nation's legislature. The second is not so obviously political but relates to a call by a pressure group − a body seeking to influence government policy – to increase the resources society makes available to the homeless. The third is even more remote from government but is surely political to some extent. All strikes in major industries have implications for employment, inflation, exports – and isn't there a broader sense in which we talk of 'the politics of the car industry' or the 'politics of the shop floor'? The fourth item appears to have nothing to do with politics at all – yet think about it. Do we not talk of the 'politics of the staff room', 'the politics of small groups', even the 'politics of the family'?

There would appear to be a sense of the word 'political' in topics as diverse as congressional attacks upon the US President and disagreements within the cast of *EastEnders*! What is this sense?

The common thread is conflict. In its most general sense – politics with a small p, if you like – politics is about conflicts and their resolution. That is to say, politics is concerned with the conflict of interest between individuals and groups, and with the processes whereby such conflicts are resolved. 'Interests', the object of the conflict, are the things people care about and are prepared to struggle over, e.g. money, power, status, privilege, dignity, honour. At the personal or 'micro' level the means of resolving conflict can take the form of tact, diplomacy, compromise.

Politics also has a specific sense – politics with a big P – relating to the national, or 'macro', level. This sense is more complicated but at heart still relates to the way society manages conflicts of interest. The devices it uses are elections, laws, government, regulations or organisations, public debate, demonstrations, and so forth. Typical conflicts at the national level revolve around:

(*a*) The distribution of wealth, status and power.

(*b*) Debates about the most desirable forms of social and economic organisation.

(*c*) Discussions about the values or moral rules which should govern public decision-making.

Harold Lasswell summed up politics as being about 'who gets what, when and how'. This is a neat summary. Less pithily one might say that politics in its broad sense relates to conflicts and their resolution, and in its specific sense to the national dimension of such conflicts and to the governmental processes designed to manage or resolve them.

What is a concept?

Let us stop for a moment and ask precisely what we have been doing. We have been discussing what it is people generally mean when they use the word 'politics'. Consideration of the various ways in which the word could be used revealed that it pertained to more than mere governemnt and had both a general and a specific meaning. Eventually an essential core of meaning was isolated and offered as a general definition. Most words have this central core of meaning. For example, take the concept of an object near by – a chair. What are the essential characteristics of a chair?

Answering the question is not as easy as it might at first appear. We can all recognise a chair but can we define its features in advance, so that someone who had never seen a chair before could recognise one? Clearly the idea or *concept* of a chair embodies a horizontal platform designed for seating oen person. Should it have a backrest? Yes, otherwise it would be a stool. Should it have legs? Well, usually it will have four, but some designs, dispense with legs: maybe it is better to talk of a chair as being raised above floor level by some form of support. So we end up with three basic elements which go to make up a chair. If an object lacks any of them – a backrest, a horizontal platform for one person and some degree of support from the floor – it is unlikely we would call it a chair. But we must always be aware that inventive designers are constantly challenging our ideas; maybe the concept of a chair in future will be less specific and allow for more variation.

This kind of argument is not always merely semantic. An ecclesiastical dispute arose in 1986 over an altar carved by Henry Moore for a church in London. The 'altar' was a circular marble block some 3 ft high, weighing 8½ tons. Unfortunately the official definition of an altar, dating back to 1845, was that it should be 'a raised surface incorporating legs or a central pillar at which people might sit'. As a result permission for the installation of the carving was withheld, but the decision was hotly contested by those with a different concept of what an altar could or should be.

The conclusions to be drawn by this brief foray into the philosophy of language should be fairly obvious. Words provide frameworks for interpreting the world. Everyday concepts like 'chair', 'table', 'cup', etc., enable us to recognise and use such objects to our advantage. More abstract concepts help us to organise the world, again to our own advantage; the concept of 'number', for example, enables us to count, record and assess quantity. In academic disciplines special concepts have been developed which help us to understand the subject matter. Some (e.g. 'power' and 'authority' in the case of political science) are in general currency but are often used carelessly or wrongly outside the discipline. Sometimes new concepts have been developed within a discipline to help understand its more refined areas (e.g. 'partisan dealignment', 'government overload').

As we have seen from our discussion of the concept of politics itself, part of the debate within a discipline will focus on the precise meaning of its central terms or concepts: what elements precisely do they or should they comprise? To become familiar with politics, therefore – or any academic discipline – we need to be aware of the concepts we employ and alive to their strengths and weaknesses. We must regard them rather like a camera lens which has to be focused so that the picture of the world we receive is sharp and accurate. What follows is an attempt to explain some of the most familiar and much used concepts in political science and in so doing enhance their own explanatory value for embryonic political scientists.

Power and authority

These two key concepts are perhaps best explained by comparing their meanings. Consider the two following events.

(*a*) A man with a gun orders you to accompany him. You comply.

(*b*) A policeman orders you to accompany him. You comply.

The outcome is the same but the nature of your *relationship* with the person giving the orders is vastly different. In event (*a*) the gunman was able to get his way through your fear of what would happen if you didn't. In event (*b*) you obeyed the policeman, almost certainly, because you accepted his right to order you. *Power* is the ability to command: to get others to obey, even if they are reluctant. *Authority* is achieved when other people accept your *right* to tell them what to do.

The similarities and differences between the two concepts are illustrated by the responses to these three questions:

1. How do people exercise power over others? Most commonly by the threat of unpleasant consequences, e.g. physical or economic, but also through the offer of rewards. It is a crude relationship, which is frequently found in everyday life and in everyday politics. One point needs to be stressed: in event (*a*) you would only obey the gunman if you thought the gun was real and he seemed likely to use it. His power is a function of the credibility of his threat. The same goes for the power which government can exercise, e.g. if the credibility of its law enforcement agencies is low its ability to maintain law and order may be reduced.

2. How do people come to have authority over others? There are a number of ways. They include:

(*a*) Special expertise, e.g. doctors.

(*b*) Natural leadership or 'charisma', difficult to define but not to recognise.

(*c*) Democratic decisions, e.g. those reached by elected representatives.

(*d*) Appointment by acknowledged authorities, e.g. policeman are appointed ultimately by the State, which is controlled by elected representatives in Parliament.

Political 'authority' in a democratic country is not consciously granted by its people to a government at a particular time (as some of the early 'social contract' theories seemed to imply) but develops gradually over the years; it is partly inherited by the national culture and partly reinforced through regular events like elections.

3. Are political power and authority necessarily related? No, it is possible to have political power without authority and authority without political power. But in practice the two are often closely associated. Democratic government, for example, combines the authority with which popular support invests it together with the power of the police and, ultimately, the armed forces. To return to event (*b*): if you refused to accept the policeman's authority he could ultimately − if you had broken the law − force you to, even if his colleagues had to assist him. Similarly, if a particular group of people refuse to accept the authority of government the force at the disposal of government can be used to make them. However, even though its strength may in the last resort rest upon organised force, no democratic government wishes to exercise it more than it has to. Government by popular consent is easier and more stable.

This short discussion has revealed that:

(a) Political concepts are the tools of the political scientist's trade.

(b) Such concepts are often used carelessly and inaccurately by non-political scientists. It is better to be absolutely clear about the terms you use and the way in which you use them.

(c) By thinking about these key concepts we gain important insight into the subject itself. *Conceptual analysis* of this kind almost provides an alternative way into the subject matter of the discipline. This chapter is too short to compare and contrast other key concepts, so short definitions will have to suffice. But to make the exercise more useful they are organised into four categories.

The political process

A number of concepts help us to understand the way in which the political process takes place. Central are the concepts of power and authority already considered. But also important are:

1. Influence. This concept is much used but is quite hard to pin down. It describes a weak form of power and authority: it is the ability to dispose people favourably – normally without the use of threats – towards behaving in a particular way.

2. Force. As already mentioned, governments rely upon popular acceptance to conduct political business on a day-to-day basis, but they can all fall back on force should their authority prove insufficient. In Britain the State rarely uses force but in times of civil strife, for example the 1984–85 miners' strike – its existence and extent are revealed.

3. Pressure is the means by which people seek to influence government across the whole spectrum of political activity. It could entail strike action, demonstrations, use of the media, private meetings and so forth.

4. Consent. The general acceptance of a government's right to command obedience provides its authority, or 'legitimacy', to use a closely related term. But be aware of the distinction between *explicit* and *tacit* consent. Explicit consent is thought to be provided by electoral victories: parties claim a mandate to implement their programme based upon their success. However, can Mrs Thatcher's 42·5 per cent of votes cast in 1987 have been said to represent such a form of consent – and what about the *majority* who did not vote for her? Opinion poll findings are cited as evidence of consent but they are often unreliable and in any case reflect rapidly changing views. Tacit consent is often claimed by governments when no significant opposition is voiced to a particular policy. If such 'consent' is based not upon understanding but upon ignorance or indifference, can it be said to be genuine?

Another body of concepts are associated with forms of:

Political organisation

1. The State. What constitutes a state has long been the subject of profound philosophical and legal debate. What seems reasonably clear is that a state is a geographic and institutional entity widely recognised as such. Its other characteristics are less certain, but according to one popular view its government must have *sovereign* power: it must have monopoly control over the legitimate use of force within its borders.

2. Constitution. Politically, constitutions comprise the rules by which government is conducted. Most countries have a written constitution and special legislative procedures are necessary if it is to be changed. Britain is unusual in having no formal written constitution but a collection of laws and conventions (traditional ways of doing things). No special procedures exist for changing our constitutional arrangements: a majority vote in the House of Commons is basically all that is required, allowing, of course, for the Lords' delaying powers and the need for the Royal Assent (see Chapter 6).

3. Bureaucracy. This term is often used to describe the civil servants who carry out the commands of government. Weber maintained that as governments try to control increasingly complex societies the power of bureaucracies inevitably grows, whatever the colour or system of government. He believed, possibly with justice, that the expertise of bureaucracies would create a new kind of distant and increasingly centralised authority.

4. Representation is the idea that the interests of the many can and should be taken care of by people chosen – usually by election – to act on their behalf. An MP's relationship with his constituency on the one hand and Parliament on the other is the focus of a great deal of debate and attention from political scientists. Burke, for example, drew a classic distinction between a representative and a delegate: 'a delegate merely mirrors and records the views of his constituents, whereas a representative is elected to judge according to his own conscience'. Members of Parliament, asserted Burke, should be representatives rather than delegates. This view is maintained by most MPs.

Values

Another set of concepts are associated with values: things which are believed to be desirable and ought to characterise the means and the ends of political activity.

1. Justice is what people feel to be fair and reasonable. This judgement will vary enormously according to individual values, but in practice there is substantial agreement when justice has not been done. Aristotle made the important distinction that justice is not necessarily what is in the interests of the powerful; might does not make right, so it is conceivable that laws may not accord with commonly shared views of what is right. If this dichotomy is too wide and too frequent, and if the legal system is not seen to be equally fair towards all groups, society may judge the government itself to be unjust, and instability will result.

2. Natural rights are usually defined as the basic requirements of a tolerable way of life – 'life, liberty and the pursuit of happiness', said Jefferson, but others have their own formulations. These rights are held to be fundamental and superior to purely legal rights, which can be influenced by governments.

3. Individualism is the emphasis upon each person's uniqueness and the idea that the purpose of political activity is to constrain the individual as little as possible and provide the conditions in which he can achieve personal fulfilment and happiness.

4. Liberty, or freedom, has two senses: freedom from oppressive controls; and freedom to pursue one's choices. It has long been a principle of English law that citizens can do as they please provided no law says they cannot. But J.S. Mill's idea, that individual freedom should not encroach unjustifiably upon the freedom of others, is widely accepted. Precisely when such encroachment becomes unjustifiable, of course, is a constant source of debate.

5. Collectivism is the antithesis of individualism in that it asserts the rights of a group of people above those of the individual, and the obligations of individuals towards them.

6. Equality is a complex concept and the word is frequently misused. It has at least three main senses:

(*a*) Equality of treatment before the law.
(*b*) Equality of opportunity, especially career opportunity.
(*c*) Equality of result, i.e. people have a right to a more equal − or a less unequal − share of economic, social and political resources.

Politicians argue about the extent to which people are born with equal capacities and the extent to which the potential for personal development can be influenced by social and economic background.

Analytical

Political scientists have created hundreds of conceptual frameworks which, to a greater or lesser extent, help us understand political reality. Some are very specialised and, depending upon the degree to which they have become accepted, occasionally obscure. Here only three of the main analytical concepts can be mentioned.

1. The political spectrum: left, right and centre. Terms like 'left', 'right' and 'centre' are regularly used to distinguish and analyse political arguments, policies and so forth. The idea óriginated from the Estates General in France after 1789, in which the nobility sat on the king's right and the representatives of the popular political movements on his left. The right of the spectrum is usually associated with tradition, individualism, liberty and free enterprise, while the left asserts change, equality, collectivism and the common ownership of resources. *Conservatism* is associated with ideas towards the right of the spectrum and *socialism* with those on the left. There are a variety of positions inbetween these two poles, most importantly liberalism and social democracy.

The dichotomy between left and right can be seen as a gross oversimplification. Many people subscribe to right-wing ideas on some issues and left-wing ones one others; to place them on the left–right continuum is to offer a crude synthesis indeed. H. J. Eysenck suggests that a 'tough' and 'tender' spectrum should be added to the inadequate but widely accepted left–right axis. It would enable political means or methods to be separated from ends or objectives, as the diagram illustrates. According to this two-dimensional approach, 'tough' authoritarian right-wingers would occupy positions in the top right-hand quarter; tough left-wingers in the top left; 'tender' or democratic right-wingers the bottom right and tender lefties the bottom left.

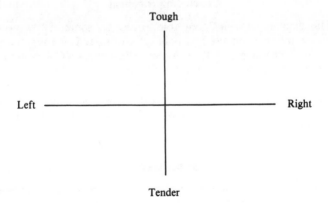

2. *Class*. This term is used to distinguish between groups of people who differ in wealth, power, status and privilege — hence upper, middle and lower classes are commonly distinguished. Marx argued that social classes were created and changed in accordance with the economic means of production at any particular time. He argued that classes are constantly engaged in bitter conflict, that morally superior social orders result from such conflict and that ultimately a classless society will emerge when the conflict between the property-owning middle classes and the exploited wage-earning working classes reaches its climax. Class is therefore a concept which is used in a neutral analytical sense but can also have strong political and value-laden overtones.

3. *Elite*. In its general sense an elite consists of those in charge of a particular activity, but in its more specific political sense it refers to those who control the institutions and processes of government. G. L. Guttsman calculated that the people who controlled the United Kingdom's system of government numbered just over 11,000 (Members of Parliament, civil servants, industrial leaders, etc.) and were in effect a 'self-perpetuating' ruling class irrespective of which party was in power.

Concluding comment

This chapter has only been able to identify some of the most important concepts used by political scientists. There are many more which students will encounter and assimilate. Concepts are the means whereby we learn more efficently and are able to explore new aspects of the subject. To be aware of concepts and the way we use them guards against misuse and sharpens our ability to make greater sense of the many-faceted world of politicians and political activity.

Further reading

Bernard Crick, *In Defence of Politics*, Penguin, 1982. See also his 'Basic concepts of political education', in Crick and Porter, *Political Education and Political Literacy*, Longman, 1978.

Michael Laver, *Invitation to Politics*, Martin Robertson, 1983.

Adrian Leftwich, *What is Politics?* Blackwell, 1984.

A. Renwick and I. Swinburn, *Basic Political Concepts*, Hutchinson, 1980.
David Robertson, *The Penguin Dictionary of Politics*, Penguin, 1985.
Roger Scruton, *A Dictionary of Political Thought*, Pan, 1983.

Questions

Describe and explain the concepts of (1) pluralism, (2) hegemony, (3) feminism, (4) alienation, (5) charisma, (6) false consciousness, (7) privatisation, (8) separation of powers.

INDEX